STORIES LEFT IN STONE

STORIES LEFT IN STONE

Trails and Traces
in Cáceres, Spain

TROY NAHUMKO

UNIVERSITY *of* ALBERTA PRESS

Published by

University of Alberta Press
1-16 Rutherford Library South
11204 89 Avenue NW
Edmonton, Alberta, Canada T6G 2J4
amiskwaciwâskahikan | Treaty 6 |
Métis Territory
ualbertapress.ca | uapress@ualberta.ca

LIBRARY AND ARCHIVES CANADA
CATALOGUING IN PUBLICATION

Title: Stories left in stone : trails and traces in
    Cáceres, Spain / Troy Nahumko.
Names: Nahumko, Troy, author.
Series: Wayfarer (Edmonton, Alta.)
Description: Series statement: Wayfarer
Identifiers: Canadiana (print) 20240327187 |
    Canadiana (ebook) 20240327209 |
    ISBN 9781772127744 (softcover) |
    ISBN 9781772127836 (EPUB) |
    ISBN 9781772127843 (PDF)
Subjects: LCSH: Cáceres (Spain)—Description
    and travel. | LCSH: Cáceres (Spain)—Social
    life and customs—21st century. | LCSH: Art,
    Ancient—Spain—Cáceres. | LCSH: Art and
    society—Spain—Cáceres. | LCSH: Cáceres
    (Spain)—Antiquities. | LCSH: Cáceres
    (Spain)—History. | LCSH: Travelers'
    writings, Canadian—Spain—Cáceres.
Classification: LCC DP402.C15 N34 2024 |
    DDC 914.6/28—dc23

First edition, first printing, 2024.
First printed and bound in Canada by Houghton
Boston Printers, Saskatoon, Saskatchewan.
Copyediting and proofreading by
Kirsten Craven.
Maps by Anka Nahumko.
Drawings by Fátima Gibello.

University of Alberta Press gratefully
acknowledges the support received for its
publishing program from the Government of
Canada, the Canada Council for the Arts, and
the Government of Alberta through the Alberta
Media Fund.

Frontispiece: *View down the Adarve Santa Ana
(parapet) towards Palacio de Moctezuma.*

For my Canacereña girls, whose stories begin behind these stones and who will leave their mark on them as well.

What you leave behind is not what is engraved in stone monuments, but what is woven into the lives of others.
    —Pericles as quoted by Thucydides, *History of the Peloponnesian War*

CONTENTS

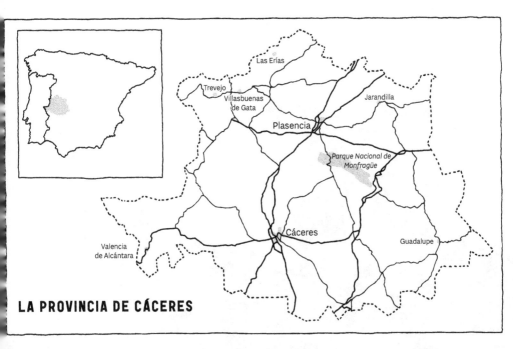

LA PROVINCIA DE CÁCERES

Las Erías

Trevejo

Villasbuenas
de Gata

Jarandilla

Plasencia

Parque Nacional de
Monfragüe

Valencia
de Alcántara

Cáceres

Guadalupe

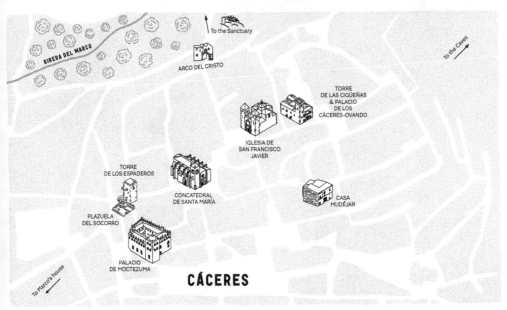

RIBERA DEL MARCO

To the Sanctuary

ARCO DEL CRISTO

To the Caves

TORRE
DE LAS CIGÜEÑAS
& PALACIO
DE LOS
CÁCERES-OVANDO

IGLESIA DE
SAN FRANCISCO
JAVIER

TORRE
DE LOS ESPADEROS

CONCATEDRAL
DE SANTA MARÍA

CASA
MUDÉJAR

PLAZUELA
DEL SOCORRO

PALACIO
DE MOCTEZUMA

To Marco's house

CÁCERES

Entrance to the Cave of Maltravieso in Cáceres, Spain.

GUIDING HANDS

1

AFTER ALMOST HALF A CENTURY, I can still remember how smooth it was as I traced my finger along my lifeline that was set in what seemed like polished stone. It was a simple art project at Laurier Heights Elementary School in Edmonton, Alberta, Canada. Madame Carole had us cast our handprints in cement in aluminum trays, and we then scratched our names and the date in the hardening mold, but to me it seemed so much more. I stretched my fingers as wide as possible to make my five-year-old hand seem that much bigger, that much more important. I had learned to write my name by then, but leaving a mark like this seemed to be more lasting, more permanent than scratching my initials in the bark of a tree, my desk, or worse, my mother's favourite table. I kept it for years, perhaps the only art project that didn't eventually end up in the bin after the initial excitement of creation wore off. Not only did I keep it, but, like a palm reader, I would go back to it again and again and trace the lines that stood out so clearly. All the while reflecting on the changes I had undergone when I saw that my growing hand no longer fit the mold. It's almost instinctual. Walk past some wet cement and you have to fight the urge to leave a mark, your mark. You have to resist a deep-down desire to leave some sort of record that you were there, were important in some way, and that you had something to say beyond an angry tweet fired off into the digital morass.

It's precisely that voice I was searching for as I lay on my back in fine red dust under five or six metres of living rock in pitch darkness. My breathing was irregular and I struggled to control it. The only sound I could hear was the rasp of my own breath through the FFP2 mask fogging up my glasses and making it even harder to see. The temperature of the cave was a near constant and, while I wasn't necessarily hot, sweat dripped down into my eyes as my mind kept coming back to the idea that the nearest chance of fresh air was more than one hundred metres away through a narrow, twisting tunnel. Here I was, dressed in a full PPE biohazard suit, as though I were a front-line soldier against the coronavirus, staring up into the sensual folds of the cave's ceiling. The only light to pierce the absolute black shone out from the lamp on my hard hat. There I lay, trying to decipher what that handprint above me, left more than sixty thousand years ago, was trying to tell me.

A few days before, a friend of mine, Carlos Blay, had let me know there would be a few slots available on the limited tours they were giving to see the prehistoric artwork in the Cave of Maltravieso in Cáceres, Spain. Carlos, an art historian who has been working for the regional government for the past sixteen years, had volunteered to guide groups through the caves and was working that week at the centre and would be one of the two guides on the tour. We had talked about this before, and he knew this was something I had always wanted to see. He also warned me not to be lazy. That these visits were temporary, and this might be one of the last chances to see the artwork before the cave was closed up tight once again. Little did he know how right he would turn out to be. The cave was last closed to researchers and limited visitors back in 1999 due to the worrying, rapid deterioration of the cave's artwork. Before the pandemic struck, and the cave was sealed off once again, it had only been reopened for about ten months for a trial period to study the effect that small, limited visits would have on the extremely delicate cave art. It was clear the cave paintings had suffered more since their rediscovery than they had in the previous sixty-odd millennia they had been there. Carlos told me I just needed to log on to the town hall's website first thing the next morning and hope I was among the first four people to sign up. I heeded his advice, did as was told, and immediately got the confirmation email. I was going to be one of the lucky four.

The cave itself first came to the attention of the widespread public back in 1951 as workers were blasting away at the rich deposits of limestone in the area. Inside, human bones, ceramics, rudimentary tools, and animal remains were found. Although, it wasn't until 1956 that, according to the official story, Carlos Callejo Serrano, a self-taught local scholar, telegraph technician by training, and curator of the Museum of Cáceres, discovered the negative handprints and other motifs stencilled on the walls of the cave. The real story, however, as Carlos would later tell me, had a different, less academic twist. "It was a certain Joaquín, the young son of the quarry guard, who actually saw them first. For almost five years, from 1951 to 1956, Carlos Callejo had been exploring the cave to inspect it in detail, to make the first plans. But it was a ten-year-old boy's sense of wonder and curiosity that first brought the hands to light. I imagine that adults only see what we are looking for and that Carlos Callejo was focused on looking for remains on the ground. Especially if you consider that at the time it was totally inconceivable that paleolithic rock art could exist in these latitudes."

He went on to say that a find like this had happened before in Spain: "There was something similar with the famous discovery of the Altamira bison, the so-called paleolithic Sistine Chapel in the north of Spain. It wasn't really Marcelino Sanz de Sautuola who discovered them but in fact his eight-year-old daughter who told him one day, 'Look, papa, oxen!' This discovery took place four years after they first entered the caves and had begun explorations. The coincidences do not end there. Both had to face widespread, profound skepticism from the scientific community regarding the extraordinary nature of their respective discoveries. They were even accused of being forgers."

The extraordinary thing is that the prints and motifs were here at all. I knew that several sites had been discovered clustered in this area and asked Carlos if there were more in the region. "At the moment, Maltravieso is the only paleolithic pictorial manifestation in the region," he answered. "There are some engravings in nearby places like Cheles, Castañar de

Ibor, and Garlitos but no paintings. Due to the geological composition of Extremadura, there are very few karstic caves, which are the main canvas for paleolithic rock art. So the possibilities are few in comparison with other areas of the Iberian Peninsula such as the Cantabrian coast or the Baetic System." Here Carlos stopped and began drawing circles in the air. "If you look at a map of what has been discovered so far, Maltravieso is almost an oasis, very far from other points. This reinforced the incredulity of the scientific community when Callejo brought them to light. Imagine when it was discovered, until not long ago, talking about paleolithic art was literally synonymous with Franco-Cantabrian art way up to the north and there was nothing to the south nor in the west where we are." He continued, "On the other hand, Extremadura is renowned for being one of the richest areas in schematic rock art in the world, which is chrono-logically later, between the Epipaleolithic and the Iron Age. That is sometime between nine thousand years ago and the Romanization of the peninsula. Whether in the form of paintings or engravings, there are hundreds of sites throughout the geography of the region. In nearby Monfragüe alone, for example, there are about two hundred places with schematic cave paintings." Here he stopped for a moment and began to reminisce. "I was lucky enough to discover and document most of them when I was a student at university. When we're done here, I promise to take you out there to show you one day." Many of these sites are now included in the Council of Europe's Prehistoric Rock Art Trails that unite more than two hundred sites open to the public in countries like Azerbaijan, France, Georgia, Italy, Norway, Portugal, Sweden, and here in Spain.

Back in Maltravieso, blasting had continued throughout the inter-vening years and unfortunately quite a bit had been lost in the rubble by the time the paintings were discovered. In the intervening years, what was the largest gallery in the entire cave was also lost. Indeed, the "Discovery Room," which was more than thirty metres long by six metres wide and four or five metres high, disappeared. When we look back on losses like this, from the perspective of today, it seems almost criminal that something like this could be allowed to happen, but Carlos was able to offer a different perspective. "You have to remember that, on the one hand, what was found on the surface of the soil was a jumble of bone, ceramic fragments, and Neolithic remains that were not considered to be a very transcendent find, nothing out the ordinary and certainly not extraordinary." He shrugged his shoulders. "As far as we know, the walls and ceilings were not excavated, nor inspected, so they didn't even realize what was there. It's estimated that 90 per cent of the findings were either lost in the limestone and garbage dumps or looted along the way." He then lamented, "Only about 10 per cent of what was there is still preserved in the municipal museum here in Cáceres." To emphasize his point, he added, "An anecdote that reflects the level of unconsciousness regarding the value of the find was that at first the authorities' intention was to call a judge to formalize the removal of the human bones, to take them to a common grave in the cemetery.

"At that time archeology was more like a treasure hunt, more reckless than Indiana Jones. Treasure hunters were only out for the most striking artifacts. With today's science, any vestige, even a grain of pollen, is just as valuable to us as a sarcophagus to really understand a site." Carlos then laughed. "Think about it, Cáceres is mostly unknown and lost now. At that time, it was basically the equivalent of the Wild West! It was a small provincial town without a university, with only one secondary school, and completely alien to scientific circles. What is perhaps less understandable is that, even today, knowing what we now know about Maltravieso and El Calerizo, caution when touching the ground and the subsoil is still not as rigorous as it should be. But, hey, that's another story, and I'm sure the future will judge us harshly too."

The day of the tour, I walked down the Avenida de Cervantes towards the cave that lies on what used to be the fringes of the modern city. High-rise, somewhat tattered high-density housing flanks the broad avenue leading south towards the cave and then out of town. The tower blocks come to an abrupt halt near the edge of the cave, leaving the limestone-rich karst area that leads away towards the aquifer and meagre stream that springs from it relatively undisturbed. This aquifer is the only permanent source of water within reach and has been the giver of life and enabler of settlements over the centuries in this anomalous riverless city. Beyond this point were only occasional outbreaks of townhouses in various stages of development, supermarkets, a couple of gas stations, and bunches of quasi-legal industrial warehouses. The typical sprawl of failed urban planning that can be seen from here to Moscow. Carlos had told me before about his own family's relationship with the cave: "When my father was a teenager, he was fond of rock climbing, and he entered not only Maltravieso but also the other caves in the area that today have disappeared. This is because they were either excavated or filled with rubble." He gestured with his hands towards the road and said, "The monsters you passed on your way here were built on top of them. The Maltravieso cave is in fact just a little hole inside an immense Gruyère cheese of about 14 km² that we continue to eat up with very little urban control and regulation."

As I neared the caves, I passed by two secondary schools opposite each other. Two of the many more that have been built since the cave's discovery. Generations of graffiti cover every inch of the walls outside the schools, echoing the concurrent need of the past and the present to be heard. The meaning of the messages scrawled everywhere seemed to be equally oblique and obscure. Dispatches to be deciphered by those who understood and shared the code. The rest of us can only guess what they were communicating to each other and the rest of the world.

The interpretation centre was opened around the time when the cave itself was closed to the public and is located in one of those public spaces and squares that you seem to find all over the country. Places that are inaugurated with pomp, spectacle, and European Union (EU) funding only to be promptly forgotten or cast aside due to upkeep funds being sucked dry or a change in the administration's priorities. The abandoned installations are often left to their own devices and crumble under the merciless sun. The ever-present plaque praising the "*excelentísimo*" or "*ilustrísimo*" politician who had had the daring to have the square built with public money had, somewhat ironically, bleached away with the years, leaving the regent's magnanimity indecipherable. From the looks of the entrance and the half-finished-looking columns that led to the cave, the park had suffered through more than its share of Spanish summers. Tiles that had once hidden the rising damp had fallen off from the benches and the graffiti from the nearby schools had begun to creep across most of the available surfaces. Yet the grass and trees were well kept and the shock of green would be welcome respite under a mean Spanish summer sun. The esplanade, however, that led towards dried-up, cracked ponds that seemed to be perennially empty was devoid of shade. The only life to be seen were two tired-looking palm trees overlooking the place that held what some have said to be the world's very first representations of art.

The attempt to harbour the site was at least well intentioned, as something had to be done to protect this legacy. Carlos shared what he had learned about attempts to secure the site: "Since the discovery of the paintings in 1956, attempts have been made to control access to it with more or perhaps less success. Carlos Callejo's children told us how they would accompany their father almost every weekend and would often find that the padlock that sealed the cave had been snapped off. Mr. Callejo replaced each and every one with money from his own pocket, but it kept on happening. This part of the city bore the thrust of the urban expansion boom from the '50s to the '80s, building up the high-density, humble neighbourhoods you saw as you walked here. Neighbourhoods that still bear a certain stigma of humbleness even today."

The interpretation centre itself was another story. A welcome one in a region that can, at times, get its priorities confused. Even if it is off the tourist trail that the vast majority of visitors to the city follow, it is well equipped and well maintained. The centre might end up reflecting its surroundings in a few years, but for now, while modest, it definitely suits its purpose. The current local administration is looking to secure funding from the EU to build a centre fit for such an important site, complete with a replica of the cave, but for now these are only plans. Carlos would later tell me it had a different life before. "There used to be a neighbourhood bar where the interpretation centre sits today. Anyone from Cáceres from my parents' generation has either entered the cave or knows stories of people who have. In theory there was a guard, but with a little tip he would give you the key and off you went." He shook his head and went on. "This was the general trend until the end of the '80s, one of a complete lack of control. One example of this is that during the excavations at the beginning of this century a motorized scooter, like a Vespa, was removed from the deepest room. Not only that, up to seventy rubber shoe soles that had been used as torches were also found. Just imagine the black soot of burned rubber that had covered the walls."

Inside the centre, the panels and videos are very informative and there is even a somewhat spurious replica of a portion of the cave for visitors to experience. Something that must surely be a hit when disappointed school groups come through wanting to see the real thing, then realize they can't.

The lucky ones who had registered for the tour all arrived on time that day and Carlos and his colleague, Elena, met us at the door, immediately making us feel welcome. Rather than being dressed up in official park ranger-style uniforms, both were dressed for the street and this reassured me that I had come properly attired. Foreigners often get unwritten dress codes wrong in Spain, so it's always nice to, if not be exactly right, not be completely wrong. I had known Carlos for years and was glad to see he was as easy-going and relaxed at work as he was in his private life. Quick to laugh and smile, he quickly dispelled any nerves that we, or at least I, might have had about venturing into the depths of the cave. His engaging manner and seeming informality made everyone trust him and get ready for what lay ahead. He had more or less told me what to expect, but knowing Carlos and his zeal for adventure, I had wondered if I wasn't getting myself into something a little more intense than a walk in the park, albeit one underground. I had been wild mushroom hunting with Carlos before, and while being only a bit younger than me, he was able to hop stone walls with quite a bit more ease and grace.

Decked out in our PPE gear, we walked out towards the gated cave entrance like an inexperienced emergency team about to enter a disaster zone. Teens from the nearby secondary schools were sheltering in the shade provided by the outcrop of the cave, smoking cigarettes and eating snacks, all the while glued to their phones. Cigarette butts, chip bags, and empty Coke bottles were littered across the ground, foreshadowing the bones and remains we would soon come across in the cave. Our extraterrestrial appearance didn't faze the kids as we awkwardly lumbered past them. They might have been snickering at how we looked, but they wouldn't even give us the benefit of a laugh or an off comment. This was literally just days before Spain would go into complete lockdown due to the COVID-19 pandemic, when masks would become the norm on the streets and near constant images of frontline workers would occupy our screens. Even still, our odd appearance didn't register with them or even merit lifting their eyes from their WhatsApp chats. We were simply middle-aged ghosts in white and they were on their break. The nearer we got to the cave, I found it difficult to orient myself due to my fogged-up glasses. This markedly worsened as our guides unlocked the thick metal door and we closed ourselves into hermetic darkness.

The mouth of the cave, just past the door, was wide enough for someone even taller than myself to stand upright. It took some time to accustom our eyes to the dark and coordinate ourselves to try not to flash our headlamps into each other's eyes. Once used to the complete absence of exterior light, the reddish folds and crags of rock came into focus. The cave smelt slightly damp but didn't have that stale smell I had expected from such an enclosed space. As our guides would later tell us, even though the cave is closed off, air continues to circulate. Carlos and Elena pointed out the first images and symbols close to the opening and I could immediately see why it had taken so long to notice them. Because if you aren't deliberately looking for them, they are actually quite hard to make out, especially for someone like me with a certain degree of red-green deficiency. As I had suspected, Carlos happily scampered off into the dark, urging us without words to keep pace and keep to the strict time limit we were allowed in the cave. Elena trailed us, making sure no one got left behind or lost, even though there were no tunnels that branched off the main route. The tunnels themselves that connect the galleries were quite low and at times rather narrow and we had to walk in single file, crouching somewhat most of the time and at times even crawling through the smaller access areas on hands and knees. The farther we ventured into the cave, the more my mind began to dwell on just how closed off and isolated we were. I have never suffered from claustrophobia before and, even though this could hardly be considered spelunking, I had to stop several times and take a few deep, reassuring breaths through my mask to calm my quickening heart rate.

After some time, we came to a gallery where Carlos told us that a den used by giant paleolithic cave hyenas was discovered. These were not your everyday Disney movie bad guys but terrifying, predatory creatures that were around three times larger than those seen in Africa today. The remains excavated from the den revealed a complete picture of the animals that were prevalent in the area at the time. Strangely enough, no human remains had been found in this area, making me wonder just how organized the groups of people were at the time. Did they have elaborate burial ceremonies that would prevent scavengers from stealing their dead? Did they always move together in armed groups so they themselves wouldn't become prey?

The blackness was intense notwithstanding our six bright LED headlamps piercing it here and there. It was almost impossible to envision someone crawling through the dark, possibly wriggling along with some sort of torch that would only add smoke to the oppressive blackout. The pinched, tight spaces and complete absence of light made me wonder if prehistoric humans had used these spaces as homes or maybe as part-time shelters for some sort of ceremonial purpose, shadowing the huge hyenas also tracking migrating animals. Carlos mentioned to us as we ducked down once again through another tight tunnel, "One of the false clichés we still have is to think of prehistoric people as 'cavemen' or cave dwellers. But think about it: a narrow, damp, unventilated cave, perhaps shared with animals who would be happy to devour you, is not necessarily the most practical place to call home. In this cave, there is not a single piece of evidence that humans ever inhabited it. We know they entered to hunt, to make art, and to bury their dead, but not to live." Carlos was stressing the importance of not confusing cave artists with the idea of cavemen. Whatever the case, it was certainly hard to conceive of someone crawling home through this after a hard day's hunter-gathering out on the savannah. Leaving them having to guess at each turn if they were going to run into a 200-kilogram hyena in a pitch black tunnel that was too narrow to turn around in. Yet, even with all of that against them, all throughout the cave over fifty hands reach out to you, high-fiving you and emboldening you to push on into the nothingness. It's the unknown story of the hands that draws you further in and guides the way. That and Carlos's enthusiasm, of course. Crawling through one of the tightest spots yet, he encouraged us onward: "Isn't it a privilege to crawl through a crevice and see fossilized rhino bones still in situ! I never tire of repeating this, here in the darkness and silence, illuminated only by a flashlight, performing perhaps the same movements of that Neanderthal ancestor who risked going deep inside to leave the imprint of his or her hand, so similar to mine."

The imprints themselves span many different periods and more than ten thousand years can separate some in the same gallery. The technique, however, remained more or less the same over the eons. Oxidized reddish ore was plentiful in the area, and they would mix the materials and then spit them through a reed or even straight from their mouths. Prehistoric photographs that gave birth to the negative outline of their hands. One of the added mysteries is why many of the handprints have only four fingers, deliberately leaving the pinky finger out. This wasn't unknown in other sites, but their predominance here was curious. Again, scrawled messages whose real meaning we can only guess at. With advances in DNA sampling, questions have been raised about the possibility of extracting a paleolithic clue from around the hands, making it then possible to, if not put a name to the artist, perhaps a face.

We reached the end of the line and the biggest gallery yet. Just beyond the area where we were allowed to access lay the frozen remains of an excavation on pause, marked off by little flags. A treasure trove of potential information lying in wait, on hold until the regional government decided if the researchers would one day be allowed back. As we stretched our backs and took advantage of the higher ceilings, Carlos continued, "The research here in Maltravieso has never stopped offering up fascinating stories and clues to our past. Through it we can reconstruct almost half a million years of history of the landscape, fauna and, of course, human presence in the area. And there is still much to do! Only that, since 2008, the regional administration has decided that more archeological excavation inside the cave is incompatible with the conservation of the paintings." Yet here we were, among some of the oldest representations of art on the planet, and if you asked random people out on the street, few would even be aware of their existence.

I asked Carlos if he thought more should be done to raise awareness about them. "In order to approach this issue, I think a mantra should be repeated: 'What is not known is not valued, what is not valued is not preserved.'" He stopped for a second and searched out our eyes between the flashes of our headlamps, and once he was sure we were following said, "What I mean is that a genuine effort to inform people about what lies beneath their feet needs to be made. Information needs to be spread and therefore help people feel that these remains belong to them, that this story is their story. This sense of ownership is essential to conserve whatever is left. It is not enough to just bolt the door, nor is it enough to have loads of scientific publications in libraries. The Spanish word 'patrimonio' can be translated as 'patrimony,' but the sense I mean is closer to 'heritage,' and this is our heritage. The word comes from the Latin, to keep your parents' inheritance, and this means that the concept of heritage must contain a sense of property or ownership. How am I going to feel that something is 'my own' if I do not know anything about it, if it remains something hidden from me?"

It was here, with his words echoing in my mind, where I found myself lying on my back in the red dust, in the deepest part of the cave. Here I was, face to face with what might be the oldest artistic representation on the planet. Here was a voice reaching out over the eons with something to tell. The importance of the find overwhelmed me, as did the need for our ancestors' voices to be heard. Here at the deepest point of the cave, they had decided to leave their marks and their message and let us guess as to why.

We had reached the end of the line, but the real story had only just begun. What had driven these people into the farthest reaches of such an uninviting cave? Why had they left some of their marks in the least accessible of places? Were they just passing through, or were they part of the waves of hominins sweeping out of Africa at the time? Is it possible they settled in the area permanently? Were they trying to tell us something, or were they just trying to say they were here?

Our time was limited and we had to head back. Without so much as saying so, everyone's pace was much faster than when we had come in. We scrambled back towards the entrance in almost complete silence, everyone lost in processing what they had just experienced. We had seen what we had come to see. Now it was time to leave, the fresh air and light above beckoned.

As we stepped out into the bright sunshine, I had the same disorienting feeling I used to get when coming out of an after-hours club into the morning light. The disconnect between what was behind those doors and everyday life out on the street was intense. Two completely distinct worlds separated by a simple door. Just moments ago we had been crawling deep under a parking lot examining some of the oldest artwork ever discovered, and now we were crossing a busy street. Carlos's shift was over for the morning and there was still some time before we both had to pick up our kids from school at 2 p.m., so we decided to duck into a bar along the way for a quick beer.

The word "bar" might be a cognate in both English and Spanish and alcohol plays a part in each, but the similarities end there. The Spanish simply do bars right and this was just the kind I love. The kind without pretensions of being anything other than what it is, a bar. A loud, echoey place where cheap reflective materials cover every possible surface for easy cleaning at the end of the workday. A place that means different things to different people throughout the day. A place that throws up the squeaky metal shutters early in the morning to serve strong coffee, churros, and toast to sleepy people heading to work. The same place that later converts into a makeshift championship domino centre for retired folks who no longer need to get up so early but who still like to take their first or second breakfast with their neighbours. A place that then slowly fills up again towards midday as people of all ages grab a quick bite to eat and a *caña*, or small glass of beer served throughout Spain, so they never get too warm before heading off to lunch proper. There are those, of course, who decide that one small beer is not quite enough and use the bar as a midday refuge from the brutal noon sun. These regulars often stretch out their *tertulias*, or informal discussions on putting right what's wrong in the world, well into the late afternoon until it's somewhat more bearable to brave the heat outside. It's a place where people get their news from neighbours or by leafing through the sometimes soggy, coffee-stained local and regional newspapers that sit next to the steaming glass-covered display cases filled with *tapas*.

My head was still reeling and I quickly ordered two *cañas*. We sat on high stools at the metal bar and I immediately realized this was one of those neighbourhood bars that knew the devil is indeed in the details. The woman carefully pulled our beers and made sure there was just enough foam to make them just right. She then asked what kind of *tapas* we wanted to go with our beers. Extremadura is still a place where the *tapa*, or little snack, comes free with each drink, and the experience in the cave had made me hungry, almost ravenous. This wasn't one of the fancier hipster gastrobars you encounter more and more these days, desperately trying to reinvent the wheel. No, this was one of those places here in Extremadura that almost takes offence if you don't finish and enjoy what you are offered alongside your drink. Avocado toasts are a rarity in such places, but cured Spanish ham, freshly grated tomato, and pâté will always be close at hand. Thick Spanish omelettes, cured meats on bread, deep green olives, anchovies in extra virgin olive oil, local goat and sheep cheeses, stewed pork snout and tripe, fried calamari and ham croquettes all await your next drink. The menu may waiver little, but as the saying goes, if it ain't broke... The hard-working staff innately understand that if a local isn't happy with the service, they often won't complain, they just won't come back.

Carlos could see from the look on my contemplative face that the experience had dramatically impacted me. "So," he smiled, "was it worth it?" I drained my beer and before answering him ordered two more. "It's unbelievable," I began, "living here, I have always felt the close presence of the past. In a place like this each successive wave of peoples have left some sort of palpable mark. It's always there and I'm conscious of how it influences the present day. You know, from my window I can see the layers of history, their stories are left in stone. I look out onto the Roman foundations of a twelfth-century Almohad Caliphate wall decorated with medieval Christian motifs and modern-day graffiti. All of this is framed by the now useless TV antennas of the '60s, '70s, and '80s that still sprout from the rooftops. I've always known I could peel back the layers of thousands of years of history right below the floor tiles of my house, but this...these prints trace back to the very beginnings, our beginnings. Now the only thing I can think of is what do they mean, what were they trying to tell us?"

Carlos ordered the next round and encouraged me to eat the last piece of Spanish omelette. "Posing the question is the first insurmountable paradox. I am sure that what the hands mean 'to me,'" he said, using his fingers as air quotes, "as a historian in the twenty-first century, is not what they meant to the person who made them sixty-seven thousand or so years ago. If I do not even fully understand the thought system of two generations ago, of even the people who discovered the cave, how am I going to possibly understand the thought processes of someone living sixty-seven thousand years ago who was not even from my species?" And here he was right. We don't even have to look back so far as two generations. Social media echo chambers were creating disparate and opposing clans every day that could no longer communicate with each other, even if they supposedly spoke the same language. Truths had become lies for some, up was now down, and opinions, no matter how far-fetched, had become other people's facts.

Carlos continued, "There are rock hands in places as far apart as Patagonia and Borneo that are almost ten thousand years old. Jump ahead and the Navajo in North America were doing them three hundred years ago, and we have handprints from almost contemporary Australian Aboriginal Peoples. Within Maltravieso itself we have hands dated at sixty-seven thousand, forty-two thousand, and twenty-seven thousand years old. How can it mean the same for all of them?" I myself had seen some of these sites he mentioned, along with etchings in Yemen, and petroglyphs in places like Azerbaijan, Zimbabwe, and Canada in British Columbia and at Writing-on-Stone Provincial Park in Alberta. Each place with its own story, and each place with its own possible interpretations. Here Carlos gave his opinion, "I believe that any attempt at interpretation must humbly start from this single certainty, that archeology is a science and therefore it can only be based on empirical truths. There have been many attempts at interpretation, or perhaps I should say elucubration, of all types and colours. From psychoanalytic interpretations based on supposed elemental masculine-feminine principles, to esoteric ones based on sympathetic magic, tribal marks, and appropriation of a place."

He stopped for another sip of beer. He spoke somewhat passionately, his voice urgent. "Art is art because of its symbolic capacity and symbols are cultural conventions. Let me give you a somewhat silly example, yet one that is effective all the same. If someone asked you to draw the sun, how would you draw it? You would almost certainly draw a circle with lines around it. But if you look up in the sky, the sun is not really like that. It's only because we have been taught since childhood to symbolize it that way. If we don't have the 'Rosetta Stone' to teach us to read them, we will never understand the full meaning of these symbols." And while interpretation may be complex, the symbols they chose to represent are telling. Carlos was surer about this. "What can better symbolize the essence and presence of a human than the imprint of his or her hand? The hand with which we make tools? The opposable thumb and fingers that differentiate us from the animals around us? Give a baby some paint and the first thing he or she will do is plant his hand or footprint on the wall." As if to prove his point, he placed his hand in the pool of water that had collected under his glass of beer and left his mark. "I think the more elaborate our attempt at interpretation, the more likely we will be wrong. That's why, personally, I do not go beyond considering them a sort of 'I was here.' The same thing the kids have always done over at the secondary school or those who sneaked into the cave when they could and engraved their name or erect penises!"

Time was running short, so we ordered the "penultimate drink," as they say here in Spain, and I wanted to know what Carlos had come away with after ten months of taking the small groups through the cave. He reflected for a moment. "Throughout the visits I have come to realize how the decades of closure of the cave had resulted in the loss of social memory of what it is and what it means to the community. Yes, older people have anecdotes, real experiences of either being in the cave or hearing about people who were, but people who are about fifty years old and under have lost a personal connection with it. The little knowledge they do have is generally reduced to things seen in the press or at the interpretation centre."

I knew exactly what he meant. When I had told people I was going to visit the cave, they were surprised it was even possible, assuming they even knew what I was talking about. We finished off our beers and Carlos concluded, "The visits have been a success, even considering the few people able to enter over these past months. They have in some way reconnected the people of Cáceres with the heritage that lies beneath their feet because they have experienced that it is real. This has also made the visits more enriching experiences for me. Many have shared a personal connection or family memory that links them to the cave." He took one last drink of his beer and smiled. "One visitor told me his father was a worker in the quarry, while another told me that as a teenager he used to sneak into the cave every time he escaped from high school classes. Then there were the people who told me about the urban legends and myths that resounded in their homes around the cave. How people would say that there are passages that connect Maltravieso with the mines of Aldea Moret more than two kilometres away. These people will no longer allow Maltravieso to fall into oblivion. They will demand that politicians take care of her." With that, we both looked at the time and had to rush off.

It's impossible to know for sure what all the handprints in Maltravieso are trying to tell us, or if indeed they were an attempt by the ancestors to communicate with this side of their spirit world. It is possible they viewed the rock as permeable, the threshold to the supernatural, and the handprints are reaching out to those on the other side. It's a past we can step into but one we can no longer read. The time that separates us from them and each epoch from the next is measured in geological terms rather than in passing empires and religions. What is even more mystifying, if the hypotheses are indeed correct, is that these messages even cross between species. If the uranium-thorium dating holds true—the oldest of the handprints dates back some sixty-four thousand or sixty-seven thousand years—the difference is negligible but the meaning is profound. This would strongly suggest, as there is no other evidence of Homo sapiens on the peninsula at the time, that the earliest paintings were done by our close cousins, the Neanderthals. This would raise a lot of questions about our own story as a species and how we have always viewed our hominin cousins. We now know that we share about 2 per cent of our DNA with them, which means there was obviously some intermingling going on after hours down in the caves and it can't have all been forced relations. What if there was some shared storytelling? Shared symbols, beliefs, and ceremonies? The word "shamanistic" is often associated with prehistoric art, but this seems to denote that our current religious ceremonies are, if perhaps more elaborate, more correct. Reducing the beliefs of the artists to those of soothsayers, we presuppose that, with all our knowledge, we know the correct way to approach god and that we know exactly what it wants and demands. In a country that until only recently was compulsorily devout, what kind of a challenge do revelations like this represent? How do these finding accommodate the tenets of Christianity? Why had the monotheistic god only made his existence known to one branch of humankind some four thousand years ago when others from his flock had been huddled, cold and frightened in caves, for some sixty thousand years prior?

While the exact meaning of the ancestors' messages and symbology may never be known, they had a story to tell, a shared need to leave their mark in a place that obviously held great meaning. The Iberian Peninsula has always served as a bridge between continents, between worlds, with people like me constantly moving through and trying to find their place. Here in Extremadura they left their mark all over the region. There are nine sites listed on the Council of Europe's Prehistoric Rock Art Trails, five of which are in the province of Cáceres. While many people at the time probably migrated with the seasons and game, some chose to settle here for a reason. The stories behind what has led us here are the handprints of today. While some of the marks left behind are decipherable, many that can be seen around us in the rocks, carved into the stones that make up the palaces or in the solemnness left behind in the wrinkles surrounding someone's eyes, are hazy, hidden, and ambiguous to someone looking in from outside. After so many years here, I continue to learn. It would be reckless to claim that art and storytelling began here—we are only a discovery away from finding a site with paintings somewhere else that are slightly older. What we can now say, though, with some certainty, is that here we can immerse ourselves in the beginnings of humanity's oldest tale and trace its path towards today. It's a tale that will forever be entwined with the stories of the people who have made these lands their home. And I wanted to explore them.

Avenida de Antonio Hurtado
leading to the Plaza América and
the Cruz de los Caídos.

CHURROS FOR BREAKFAST

2

IN THE TWENTY-FIVE-MINUTE WALK from the bar to my daughters' school, you can see the city's evolution over the past 150 years roll up in front of you. Randomly grouped single-family homes and townhouses that have only recently been built quickly turn into a jumble of modest eight-to-twelve-story tower blocks whose shadows fall over the cave's entrance and lead towards the city centre. The tree-lined Avenida de Antonio Hurtado eventually runs to where all roads seem to lead in Cáceres: an enormous, yet at the same time somehow squat, heavy-set granite cross plonked in the middle of a rather chaotic roundabout. It's an extremely divisive monument that symbolizes the culture wars stewing here since the fall of the dictatorship. Any mention of *"la cruz,"* as it is known to all, has a dog-whistle effect on supporters from each side of the argument. Originally raised back in 1938, it served as a monument to the fascists' victory in the Spanish Civil War. As the mayor at the time, Narciso Maderal Vaquero declared at its unveiling that it was meant to symbolize the redemption of Spain and served as a stark, daily reminder for all to see of who was now in charge. With the restoration of democracy, it was posthumously rebaptized as a symbol for *all* of the fallen during the conflict. This way assuming, I suppose, that those from the losing side had somehow also been redeemed in the intervening forty-odd years the dictatorship lasted. The Historical Memory Law that passed in 2007 includes a provision that states the government must remove monuments from public places that exalt the coup, the war, or the Francoist repression that followed. Yet there it stands.

From here, a wide, heavily treed boulevard traces back in time to the older parts of the city. The heavily used *paseo* that, up until the beginnings of the twentieth century, had been lined with imposing mansions, now looks like the centres of most cities around the country. A diverse, somewhat motley row of tower blocks from the '60s, '70s, and '80s flanks this central green artery. High street shops on the ground floors give way to the offices above. Lawyers, psychiatrists, psychologists, doctors, podologists, English academies, mutual insurance companies, and the delightfully sounding profession of stomatologists all advertise their services with signs and placards in the windows and entranceways of the buildings, each of differing shapes, sizes, and effectiveness. The curtained windows above peer into the private lives of those who make their lives in the city centre.

The last remaining turn-of-the-century mansion on the boulevard sits on a corner just up the street from where my kids go to school every day. Its early-twentieth-century gilt opulence makes it look slightly cartoonish as it struggles for air between the completely forgettable buildings surrounding it. It looks distinctly like that metaphorical '80s-movie property that refused to sell out to land developers and gives you an idea of how different the city would have looked with the avenue lined with these mansions just fifty years ago.

Nowadays, rather than hosting well-to-do families, the old house controls their money. A few years ago, one of the region's rural credit unions decided to up its presence in the city. It redid the deteriorating building and it is now one of the ever-shrinking number of bank branches found on Spanish streets. After the financial crisis of 2008, the country's banks were precariously overextended. To avert the collapse they presaged, they were gifted a generous bailout by the central government. It was a rescue package that was sold to the public as a temporary loan. A loan that has never been repaid and more than likely never will be. Once the flood of carte blanche public funds rolled in, many entities fused, giving them the perfect excuse to pull down the shutters of around 50 per cent of their branches, shedding tens of thousands of workers in the process. The effect is noticeable in the cities, but it's in the smaller centres that you really feel their absence. In smaller villages, people, many of whom are retired pensioners, have to travel thirty or forty kilometres just to access their savings.

As you leave the *paseo*, the street narrows considerably and becomes the Calle San Antón. Here a distinct change in the surrounding architecture takes place, transitioning from taller buildings to those on a more human scale. Going down the hill, you reach another landmark in the city, the refurbished Gran Teatro, or Grand Theatre, that was built in 1929. Along the way, the sidewalk becomes more crowded and city buses pass by so close you can feel their draft as they bump and jar over the manhole covers. Opposite the theatre, a pedestrian street then brings you towards San Juan and its namesake, pocket-sized Gothic church of ochre stone. It's the first instance you get of the building blocks that, like sand chameleons, change colours depending on the light of day, foreshadowing the buildings that lie beyond. In the middle of the square stands a small statue lost in a sea of tables from the surrounding restaurants. A bronzed, elderly newspaper vendor, proudly selling the last newspapers of an extinct profession.

Here the way splits into two. You can veer right and walk past the square that shares the name of the church or left into the even narrower street that has historically served as the city's main commercial area, the Calle Pintores. Terraced, nineteenth-century buildings with the odd modern protrusion line the street on both sides as you walk down it. Until relatively recently, international franchises rubbed shoulders here with pharmacies, tobacconists, booksellers, and independent retail shops. The street has seen a steady decline, though, ever since people began migrating out of the centre and the tentacles of online retail shops wormed their way into everyone's homes. Seemingly meaningless scrawl, like the graffiti I saw around the cave, metastasizes steadily over every flat surface. Empty shop windows papered over with posters of pretty images now come close to outnumbering those with life inside. The posters are a benevolent initiative, but one that only covers up the ugly truth of the slow death of brick and mortar shops and independent sellers.

The Calle Pintores is short. It might not even be two hundred metres long and you don't really realize you are in the main square until you are actually in it. The tightness of the Calle Pintores and the shade of the buildings that line it make your eyes grow accustomed to the relative sombreness along the street. Then, when you suddenly drop into the brightly lit square, you find yourself momentarily blinded. It's when your eyes refocus that you fall in love.

| My wife, Conchi, and I had been living abroad for many years in disparate places like Yemen, Azerbaijan, and Laos and decided to come back to her roots and settle, at least for a time. To take some time to reflect on the experiences we had lived and figure out what was going to be next. A time to create a home base after years of living out of backpacks and carry-on suitcases. Back to the town where she was born and back to where most of her immediate family still lived. This was the land of sparse holm and cork oak groves she still pictured when she closed her eyes and thought of her happy place. We chose to migrate back to a region whose principal export has been people since locally born conquistadors went searching for gold and plunder. A place that has been marked by travellers since Art as we know it began in those nearby dark caves. My wife had come back home and in a way I had found one. After half a life on the move, I had found a place to pause, at least for a while, and become immersed in its story. A story that would become part of my own and go on to shape my life for the past fifteen years. My children were born here, their stories began here, and I've seen how living here has influenced the way they see the world. Coming from the prairies of Western Canada, a place where the oldest building was built around 1875 and where most date from well into the twentieth century, I still pinch myself when I drop into that square again and again. My grin gets even wider when I consider the fact that the Romans, like me, were relative newcomers to a land that has hosted humanity and its close cousins for so long.

I had lived in Spain before and looked forward to settling in a place where I at least had a modest grasp of the language. I was tired of feeling like the outsider, always looking in and observing societies from the outskirts through the sole perspective of the privileged eyes of those who spoke English. I had felt welcome in most places that I had lived, but without a grasp of the local language, you can only delve so deep into the local mores and you can only understand so much. As a natural bridge between continents, the Iberian Peninsula has been hosting outsiders, welcome or not, since those handprints were imprinted on the walls of the caves. Travellers who had passed through well before the Romans left their lasting imprint. Extremadura is a place where, if you make even the slightest effort to integrate, you are welcomed as one of its own while still being able to make your own print, your own mark. Hard as some may try, you will never be the first foreigner the locals have come across and you certainly won't be the last. That said, foreigners tend to blend in. They settle here for reasons apart from the sun, sand, and sangria that act like a magnet for tourists and make Spain one of the most visited countries in the world. The closest thing here to an "expat scene," like those you find down on the coasts or on the islands, are probably the English language academies whose signs you can see up in the tower blocks. Stray away from these faux-Britannia centres, though, and Extremadura is still a place where you find yourself turning your head when you hear another language on streets like the Calle Pintores.

From previous experience, I knew what summers here could be like in a small apartment. Dante himself considered including a stay in a dark, poorly insulated flat during the Spanish summer in his circles of hell. And Spain is indeed a country of apartment dwellers. But even if the majority do live in apartments, many dream of moving into detached houses with a small yard and a swimming pool to escape or at least seek some relief from the intense heat of the long summer months. However, those that do manage to live the detached home dream most often find themselves cheek by jowl to the next person who had the same dream. The intense social side of Spain is hinted at even in the way the detached homes are built. So closely bunched together.

These dreams became even more poignant during the COVID-19 pandemic when the Spanish government introduced some of the most draconian lockdown measures in the world. In a dramatic attempt to reduce the dreadful number of cases, the entire country was locked down in their homes for the brief Spanish spring. Only those who worked in essential services were allowed to go to work, and we were only allowed to leave the house, one by one, to pick up essential items. Children around the country remained indoors for more than six weeks. Many, cramped in thirty-square-metre interior flats, were only able to catch a glimpse of the sky through the edges of their windows. The summer of 2020 offered some respite when restrictions were somewhat eased, but with the economic crisis that came in the pandemic's wake, many could no longer afford to escape those four walls.

This social nature, added to the generally good weather, has had a big influence on the style of life here. As a general rule, the Spanish socialize and live a big part of their lives in the street. From the afternoon *paseo* back and forth along public, bench-laden promenades and boulevards like Cánovas, to the quick beer and *tapas* before lunch, the street is everyone's comfort zone and a neutral area to meet. Even the way the Spanish use the language reflects this. I remember when I first started teaching teenagers English I would start classes with the typical, "What did you do this weekend?" and invariably the answer would be, "I went to the street with my friends." And it wasn't an error. It was exactly what they meant to say. *La calle*, the street, carries a much deeper meaning here than simply a place for cars to schlep us from point A to point B. The very Anglo concept of loitering simply doesn't exist on these streets. If you look the word up in a Spanish–English dictionary, you will find words that are vaguely associated with it but whose translations would be closer to "drift," "linger," or "hang around." For the Spanish, *la calle* is public and a place for everyone. Groups of people gathering on sidewalks might mean the slight inconvenience of having to walk around them, but it's no reason to call the cops.

The first thing we needed to do was find a house. We had one thing clear: if we were going to live here, we wanted to take advantage of what made it so special and different. I knew if we were going to make this decision, it had to be in or at least around the old city. Little did I know we would buy a house because the one beside it had come crashing down.

We had been looking for a place in the UNESCO World Heritage Site core of this small, provincial capital in southwestern Spain for some time and weren't having much luck. We'd stalk the balconies and windows of the old town on our walks, looking for little for sale signs, but there weren't many to be found. The places we did find within our modest price range were mostly dark, burrow-like warrens that had been divided, subdivided, and subdivided again with each successive generation. The inheritance history of each family was written into the strangest distributions you can imagine, with bathrooms in kitchens and bedrooms without windows that acted as passageways to rooms beyond. Most of the places that were for sale had seen some renovations sometime in the early 1980s. Faux-granite floors, popcorn ceilings, and stucco walls were in fashion at the time and were some of the more ambitious yet modest attempts to "modernize" these age-old homes that people had turned their backs on. Just as they had turned their backs on everything else that reminded them of the recent, darker past. Most of the water pipes ran outside the walls and the electrical wiring was artisanal at best. Some sort of rubber-soled footwear was advisable when unloading either the washing machine or dishwasher, unless you were looking for a slight electrical jolt to get your day started. The future means progress and progress was apparently not where these homes were at.

These dwellings smelled strongly of the past—literally. They were built without foundations and their adobe-like construction draws up damp from the ground like a sponge in the winter that then dries out in the summer, leaving a crust of minerals on the walls as avant-guard art reminders it was time to paint, again. Convenience, functionality, ease of living is what people were looking for, and if these homes were one thing, it certainly wasn't convenient. The houses that hadn't undergone one of these polyester makeovers were simply too run down to be moved into immediately, and while my in-laws are some of the most understanding, accommodating people on the planet, we didn't want to impose for the time it would take to renovate and completely refurbish one. There were, of course, much bigger homes to be had, some that had even been done up with tastes suiting the millennium, but these were priced far beyond what we could afford. So we continued searching and even expanded our search to the historical homes that rung the walled city but came up with similar finds. Our walks continued until we were at the point where we were ready to give up. That is until one day when we were exploring a lesser-known neighbourhood of the old town, a corner somewhat off the tourist trail. We followed the Almohad wall as it circles the UNESCO core of the old city and then saw them. Up above us in the fading light, we could make out a pair of trussed beams spanning a void. A gap in the whitewashed, continuous line of housing left by a building that had collapsed.

| Admittedly, the trussed beams against the darkening blue sky were somewhat ominous. The empty lot underneath them stuck out like a gaping wound from the line of irregular terraced houses opposite the Almohad defensive wall. The scarred, raw walls of the houses that remained standing on each side of the slash looked almost indecent, a reminder they were never meant to be seen like this. These structures had been leaning on each other in some shape or form since well before records had been kept. The house we were looking at was the most modest along the street. While all of the other buildings had three floors, this one had only two and it would have to stay that way. When the city became a UNESCO World Heritage Site back in 1986, it was as if a Polaroid had been taken. No major changes would be allowed from then on and this part of the city was to be frozen in time, a postcard from the 1980s. Europe's third-largest intact medieval city would remain "as was," even if much of what you saw was far from being in any way historic.

Teresa lived in the house on the other side of the yawning gap. She was born and raised in the house. She then went on to raise her own family under the same roof. An impressive feat considering that, while it was indeed three stories, it was basically three single rooms stacked on top of each other with a narrow staircase connecting the three. Changing rooms meant changing floors. In the eighty-plus years she had lived on the street, she had seen mules carry goods up it and now watched as electric tuk-tuks carry tourists past her door from all over the world. When we first met her, she was edging into her eighth decade but showed no signs of slowing down. Most days she purposely walked up the steep hill to help her "kids," as she called them, at the Cruz Blanca, a home for people with severe intellectual disabilities run by an order of Franciscan monks tucked away behind one of the ochre-coloured walls of the old town. At the Cruz Blanca, Teresa did everything from preparing meals and ironing clothes to mothering anyone needing a band-aid or something more. She then came home, climbed up and down those stairs, and did it all over again. She was the street's unofficial memory and its official sentry. Very little happened in the neighbourhood she didn't know about. She remembered when running water finally reached the street in the late 1960s, around the time one of her children was born, and she clearly remembered every unkept promise from the town hall since. As we were about to go inside, she intimated, "It would be nice to have some new blood in the neighbourhood," and then she added, "I can't remember the last time we heard kids playing in the street. Probably since mine were bouncing balls off of the wall. A few couples have come to look at the house, but then they see that," and her voice trailed off as she pointed up at the trusses between the homes. "By the way, if you're going inside, let me know how the lemon tree is doing."

The house we were looking at had never really received a full-blown '80s makeover. It was definitely venerable with the scars of years of neglect but wasn't a total wreck either and sat, slightly out of place among its taller neighbours. It had been lived in until relatively recently and, aside from the fact that most of the bedrooms had been painted in eye-scalding reds, greens, and blues, it was livable. It was definitely a fixer-upper. Yet it wasn't in much worse shape than the Khrushchev-era flat we had lived in in Baku, Azerbaijan, and at least here we wouldn't suffer the wicked winter winds blowing off the Caspian through the warped window frames. The ground floor had lovely *bovedas*, vaulted brick ceilings passed down from Roman times that are often found in these old homes. Even though plastered over with mortar, the irregularities and lack of harsh straight angles made the place seem more human and certainly more exotic. The plumbing worked, at least at surface level, and the roof, while shaky, would last a few more years before raining down on us in bed late one night. All of this led off into what made the place so different from most of the places we had seen, a patio in the middle of town and, of course, the lemon tree Teresa had asked about.

It had been a few years since anyone had lived in the house, probably since the accident next door and ivy had run wild on the patio. The plant had grown so much it was at least half a metre deep, which made it hard to even open the rusted-out iron frame door that opened onto the patio. It was difficult to get a grasp of the actual size of the place, and it was only as we pushed our way through the undergrowth that we discovered there was a large square well in the middle of the patio. Under the deep green of the ivy you could just make out the mismatched tiles covering almost every surface, which made the scene even more disorienting. There was a storage room off to the right and some stairs leading up to a terrace that could boast of having the world's largest canary cage embedded into the wall of the house. The patio looked on to a four- or five-story wall that gave on to the monastery behind it. Seeing as the nuns were cloistered, not a single window or opening looked down and out onto the scene. And there next to the wall was the tree Teresa had asked about, heavy with bright yellow lemons. Here, smack in the middle of the city, was a private little oasis. Even if the mishmash of different-coloured tiles did make you feel a little queasy, they could always be stripped or painted over. There was work to be done, but this was definitely a place where we could start a new chapter. It may have been romantic, but the metre-thick walls inspired confidence. You knew the same hands that had built them would later live within them.

We stepped back out into the cobbled street, our heads reeling a bit with what we had seen. Trying to take it all in, I began to think of reasons to justify paying a price that was too high for what it really was, trying hard to overlook the fact it was somewhat beyond our budget ceiling. It was much more expensive than one of those kudzu flats on the outskirts, but the difference was obvious. What we had seen up until then in our price range had been apartments cubed out of larger homes, albeit with metre-thick walls, but apartments all the same. This was a house, a home with a lemon tree, with a private, open-air space. A space that would become a sanctified refuge years later during the harsh COVID-19 lockdown when children weren't allowed out of the house for more than six weeks. Little did we know our children would be able to lie out under the stars when others couldn't.

Spying us from where she keeps her daily vigil, Teresa asked again after the lemons and I told her the tree was full of them. "That tree used to keep the whole block in lemons," she enthused, hurrying back down the stairs and out into the street. "Did you see the orange tree that's growing on the other side of the wall? Its oranges also used to get shared around with the neighbours, but that, of course, was before the house fell down." I told her I had indeed seen the top of a tree, but as they weren't in season, I hadn't known it was an orange tree. It seemed the perfect opportunity to ask about the house that had fallen down. As we would come to learn, Teresa loved any chance to tell the story.

"Oh, it's a bit of a sad story, one you almost can't believe. I myself wouldn't have believed it if I hadn't lived through the whole thing," she explained as her outstretched index finger punctuated the air (something I would learn she often did when she got excited or upset). "It was a young couple too. I think they were from Madrid or somewhere like that but had roots here in Extremadura. I think they had a little girl and were expecting another when they bought the house and started renovating it, but I can't remember for sure." She paused for a moment, adding just the right dose of suspense, and then drew herself up a little higher and continued, "Then it started to rain. It was one of those autumns where the rain starts falling in September and doesn't stop. They had hired one of those shady architects and constructors who didn't have legal licences, though of course they didn't know that at the time." Here Teresa really began shaking her head while muttering a few insults under her breath we couldn't quite catch. She then lamented, "After everything happened, their insurance wouldn't cover the damage, and on top of that they had to pay for the demolition and removal of everything, all the while still having to pay for a house that was no longer there!"

The story was indeed tragic and I was reminded that, even today, there were still many different types of hyenas lurking in caves, tunnels, and beyond when looking for a home. "That's awful, Teresa. Do they know how or why it actually happened?" I asked, wondering if there was a chance it could happen again. "You mean you don't know?" Here's when Teresa got really animated. "I can't believe you don't know. It was in the paper and everything! I was the one they talked to," she added proudly. "So, as I was saying before, it rained a lot that fall and, one day, Dolores, who used to live next door on the corner, had some churros. The three men who were working on the house were really nice and attentive and were always asking if the neighbours needed anything or if they could do anything to be less bothersome." This spirit of lending a hand to others was important to Teresa. She was always the first to offer to help out with things like putting up and taking down the curtains that protect the doors from the merciless summer sun. "So it was just before ten in the morning and Dolores knew they would be taking a break, so she called them over for some of the churros. The three men happily came out of the work site and chatted on the corner with Dolores while they finished their churros. Just as they were about to go back to work, there was a sudden rumble and then, boom! The whole house just crumbled and came crashing down." Here she got so spirited she actually jumped as she demonstrated how the house collapsed. "They say that all the rain had weakened the back wall and it just came down, but some people also say that the rotten architect told them they could remove one of the *bovedas* (vaulted ceilings), and everyone knows those are really what holds up these old houses." I suppose she would know. After all, she has been living underneath them her entire life. She turned to go back inside but then turned around just as she was opening her door and added, "Just imagine if they didn't like churros, the three of them wouldn't have made it under all that rubble. Good thing everyone likes churros, especially Dolores."

A panoramic view of the medieval castle of Jarandilla de la Vera that isn't in ruins.

A TRIP TO
LA VERA

3

A SMOKY TANG spreads across the southern slopes of the Sierra de Gredos as the changing leaves put on their annual display. This imposing high mountain chain forms part of the Central System that runs south-west from just north of Madrid and then dives deep into the midriff of Portugal. The massif splits the Meseta Central of the inner Iberian plateau in two, like the minute hand of a clock marking twenty to the hour. The pleasant aroma rolls and wafts along the valleys that cascade out of the mountains that rise up on your left and reaches you through your open window as you wind along the narrowish EX-203. It's a raw, earthy smell you can almost see. Immediately conjuring up images of chorizo, paellas, sizzling Spanish-style shrimp, and Galician octopus, all with a backdrop of smoked oak. It's distinct and definitively local.

What is even more unique about this smell is that it unites an entire nation. The storyteller and poet Rudyard Kipling once said the first condition of understanding a country is to smell it. In a territory as vast and varied as Spain, few things bring together all of the regions and lay bare its shared commonalities more than this. Football may be the country's new faith, but within that there is division. Without exaggeration, in each and every kitchen across the country, from the restive regions of the Basque Country and Catalonia to Galicia and the distant Canary Islands, you will find *pimentón de la Vera*. It's rare that a specific area or region imprints its name so indelibly on a spice, but here in La Vera it's done just that. Browse any Spanish recipe and it will not only call for *pimentón*, but precisely *pimentón de la Vera*. What sets it apart from similar spices like the *pimentón* from the region of Murcia or the paprikas of Eastern Europe is that, rather than simply drying in the sun, the peppers here are smoked over the oak and chestnut wood so abundant in the area. While this area can bake in the summer, once autumn falls, and if the rains don't fail, it can be quite wet. Definitely not ideal weather for drying in the sun. It's a spice that is one of the essential flavours of Spain, and it comes from the southern skirts of these mountains. Just over an hour's drive north from Cáceres, I had made the trip to talk to someone to get a better understanding about the housing trends and the way people house themselves in this part of Spain. But first, breakfast.

One of the first Spanish phrases I can remember being aware of is *"mi casa es su casa."* Long before I had even the slightest grasp of the language, I recall hearing it in completely non-Spanish-speaking contexts. I remember seeing debonair, leisure-suited, '70s movie stars using it while offering drinks from padded, well-stocked bars that overlooked the Californian coast. It even pops up in places like *Pulp Fiction* when John Travolta asks for a place to shoot up. Without being completely conscious of the significance of each word, the meaning behind the idiomaticity of the phrase is clear: make yourself at home. It wasn't until much later that I would learn it was a saying that is far more frequently used south of Hollywood down in Mexico than it is in Spain, but it does repeat one of the most widely recognized Spanish words outside *hola*, *adíos*, *gracias*, and *siesta*. Spanish, like English, uses two words to describe a place to live, *casa* and *hogar*, and like English they have two distinct meanings. *Casa*, or house, is a physical dwelling, a place made up of wood, bricks or, in the case of the old houses around Extremadura, stone masonry. *Hogar*, or home, is more of an abstract concept, much less centred on simply a place and much more focused on feeling. It can be a country, a region, or even a particular landscape, but it's more than just a GPS coordinate. It's an idea, a notional place you create with thoughts and feelings rather than brick and mortar. It's a place many are dying to leave when they are young and one that you can never entirely come back to after having been away for a long time. We make our homes in houses and these come in all kinds of different shapes and sizes. Tastes differ around the world and here in Spain, the preference is clear.

One of the first things you notice in Spain is that there are apartment buildings everywhere. Bigger cities are built up almost entirely of apartment blocks, with single-family dwellings appearing like rarities on the fringes of the outskirts. But it's not only a big city phenomenon; smaller centres also have them, with even the smallest villages sporting rings of four- and five-story blocks surrounding their historic cores. Long before buzzwords like "sustainability" and "ecology" became associated with vertical living, the Spanish had strongly decanted for collective housing and, in fact, are only second to South Korea in choosing to live this way. If every home has some *pimentón de la Vera* in it, it is more than possible that home will be found in an apartment.

Since this is a situation that is an anomaly in Europe, I wanted an insider's view on how some of these developments had come about and some insight into why the Spanish housing trends were so different from their neighbours'. I turned to a specialist in the field, Marcelo Sánchez-Oro Sánchez, a social worker and professor of sociology at the University of Extremadura. A mutual friend had introduced us and we had arranged to meet over breakfast in the Parador hotel, in Jarandilla de la Vera. A hotel set in a thirteenth-century castle where it serves a wonderfully varied breakfast buffet in the central courtyard with fairy tale cylindrical towers rising up in the corners. The scene is idyllic; perfect almost, good enough for a king or even an emperor and just right for a pair of commoners. In this setting I found a kind, generous man with a serious love of the songs of Bob Dylan. Over some coffee, *migas* (fried breadcrumbs with chorizo and *pimentón de la Vera* topped with a fried egg) and Dylan anecdotes, I asked him to tell me about himself. "Well, what can I say? I'm fifty-nine years old, married, and have two children who really aren't children anymore. Irene and Nacho are now twenty-six and thirty-three years old and they both work and no longer live at home. I am part of what is known here as the 'baby boom' generation, the Spanish one that is." He smiled at that and continued, "Those of us who were born in the '60s during the heyday of the 'developmentalism' of Spanish capitalism that went hand in hand with the pro-Franco technocratic elites. You might not have heard, but one of the slogans of the Francoist regime, Franco being a confessed Catholic, was that families should have *many* children. For example, we are four siblings, and in my wife Auxi's family they are five. That was the usual thing at the time."

It was remarkable how the pendulum had now swung completely in the opposite direction. Whereas just a generation or two ago it was normal to have four, five, eight, or ten siblings, Spain is now just behind Italy in having the second-lowest birth rate in Europe. Primary schools in smaller villages are being closed down one by one and those that manage to stay open have to resort to multi-grade classes to stay alive. A declining birth rate that is only set to worsen with the uncertainty that the COVID pandemic has ushered in. I asked Marcelo if he was from Cáceres or if he, like many who migrate to the provincial capital, was from somewhere else. "I live in Cáceres but come from a village very near here called Jaraíz de la Vera. It's a beautiful place. Like here, oak and chestnut tree forests run out from the mountains and crystal clear waters flow down from the mountains into gorges that form natural pools you can swim in during the summer. Farther down, on the banks of the Tiétar River, there are huge tobacco plantations that give you an idea of what the climate in the area is like in the summer. Is it your first time up here?"

It wasn't and I understood why he was so proud of where he came from. When I was just getting to know my wife and her roots, we decided to do some camping there. I was perpetually on the move at the time and carried a small, two-person hiking tent, but I only had one small sleeping bag. It was August and the days were extremely hot and I was sure we would be fine without anything other than the light, one-person sleeping bag I had. What I hadn't counted on was that we were sleeping at about 585 metres (1,919 feet) and that the nights next to the river cooled off considerably. After a long, cold night, my tired future wife called her blues-loving oldest brother who was living and working in nearby Cuacos de Yuste and asked him if he could please bring us a few blankets to get us through the next couple of nights. He came immediately and, as he pulled up, I could hear the tortured string bending of Chess Records-era Buddy Guy blasting from his car's stereo. He stepped out of the car, tall and lanky and baby-faced without the beard he wears now. I could tell he was concerned yet cautious. After all, who goes camping up on the mountainside without anything to keep them warm? He gave us all the blankets he had in his rented flat, wished us luck, and reminded us he wasn't far away. I'll always be thankful he gave me the benefit of the doubt and didn't whisk his kid sister away from the crazy Canadian who, at least at that time, was not prepared. Not the most auspicious first meeting of my future brother-in-law to be sure, but at least we had our shared love of the blues that would make things all right.

Marcelo continued with his story. "My family, parents and grandparents, made up what sociologists call the local petty bourgeoisie. Most ran small businesses while some even had larger ones. My paternal grandfather, Don Marcelino, was a canning industrialist and had a registered trademark 'Monastery of Yuste.' It was the nearby monastery where Charles V, the last Holy Roman emperor, spent his last days before dying of malaria." He pointed up the way to where the monastery was and said, "With his trademark, my grandfather was able to maintain commercial links throughout the 1920s and 1930s of the last century. He had suppliers in Barcelona, Valencia, and Seville and he would travel there frequently. They sold all kinds of canned goods, mainly peaches and pears but also quail and other meats. With the Spanish Civil War of 1936, his business, like others throughout the country, collapsed."

We had finished breakfast, but there was still a lot more I wanted to ask Marcelo. As we left the castle and were walking through the park under the impressive topiary of curated trees and bushes that looked like castles themselves, I suggested, "Why don't we continue this talk up in the monastery?" "Sounds like a good idea to me," said Marcelo. "It's been ages since I last visited and that way I can pick up some *perrunillas*, cookies made of almonds, at La Soledad in Cuacos."

The EX-391 leaves Cuacos de Yuste, the village from which the monastery takes its name, and winds its way farther up one of the folds of the skirts of the Sierra de Tormantos until the sixteenth-century complex appears out of the thick chestnut forest on your right. Back in 1908, the influential educator, philosopher, and author Miguel de Unamuno wrote after walking up from Cuacos and visiting the site that was still in ruins,

"You do not see remains of the monastery until you are in it, and you suffer, in a certain sense, a disillusionment, even if this is later rectified." Today, the sensation is completely the opposite. Step inside the grounds of the completely rebuilt compound and a monastic peace surrounds you. On the horizon, descending wrinkled hills run southeast into the ozone-filled distance past the unseen Tiétar River as it winds its course towards the Tagus River and the hazy plains of the Campo Arañuelo. Behind you, two very distinct structures emerge. On the one side is the monastery with its five or six Polish monks, while on the other side stands what became the residence of the last Holy Roman emperor, Charles V.

The well-tended gardens surrounding the monastery were the perfect place to continue our talk, so I asked Marcelo to resume his story. "My maternal grandmother, Doña Adela, was widowed very young with three children. She was also a dynamic woman who ran a furniture and clothing trade until she passed away in 1969. The Spanish Civil War marked the generation of my grandparents, who at the time were around thirty or forty years old, but it's my belief the post-war left an even deeper mark on their children, my parents, Don Marcelo and Doña Marti." He slowed for a moment, reminiscing over their names, then continued, "They were born in the '30s and, above all, were socialized during the period of the most radical time of Franco's regime. Franco's ideology, in essence, was order, stability, work, family, God, country, unity, and savings. That is, authority and restraint, almost a Calvinist creed. Of course, when we speak of family, the model was the patriarchal family in its strictest sense. The Francoist ideology was well in tune with the values of the local bourgeoisie, which was made up of small landowners, service companies, mid-level officials like teachers, bank employees, pharmacists, doctors, judges, and, of course, landowners. Adherence to the Franco regime this sociological component was total and absolute." He emphasized this last point, then added, "In my opinion, the essence of what is still known today as 'sociological Francoism' has its basis in this socializing process, suffered so intensely by the younger generations between the 1940s and 1950s. This era marked them profoundly, and in part left a mark on us, their children, too."

Keenly aware of the hagiographic potential of the site, the regime began to undertake the reconstruction of the monastery during the extremely austere years following the civil war. The monastery had been practically destroyed in 1809 during the Spanish War of Independence when the convent was set ablaze by retreating French troops who had just lost a battle in Talavera de la Reina. In the early 1940s, the General Directorate of Fine Arts began the restoration of the monastery, attempting to respect as much as possible the original design. It was a difficult task, though not only for its enormity. Due to its complete abandonment, some locals had built homes using the remains over the years. The ruin of the last Holy Roman emperor's final retreat had become a de facto free quarry. The architect in charge of the enormous task of the reconstruction, José Manuel González-Valcárcel, had to negotiate with those who had scavenged pieces of the monastery to build their homes. The architect agreed to replace and repair their homes in order to recover the original material and was able to piece together what can be seen today.

In 1958, the Hieronymite order of monks, who had originally welcomed the emperor on his ultimate retreat, reoccupied the reborn monastery and lived in relative peace and quiet. That is until Patrimonio Nacional took a renewed interest in the building in 2004. An edifice of such historical importance had sat silent in a depressed area for too long and its tourism potential lay inert on the fringes of these mountains that are within easy reach of the nation's capital. After complicated negotiations, the monks ceded and agreed to allow around 10 per cent of the sprawling complex open to the public, even if at the time the monks numbered less than ten. In 2004, the long-standing regional president at the time, the effective yet somewhat garrulous Juan Carlos Rodríguez Ibarra, promised in an interview in the national newspaper *ABC* that "first and foremost are the monks who live here." He then went on to swear,

> *this agreement guarantees the continuity of the Hieronymite monks of Yuste, who live with the aspiration of trying to offer people what Yuste is and what it can provide. Consider that Charles V came to the shelter of a monastery to die a holy death, atoning for his sins. He strengthened the*

monastic life, respected it and built his palace attached to the Church. He
was an extraordinary man, respectful of the monastic life, while enriching
the level and numbers of confessors, preachers and musicians among others.
What's more, some additional personnel of the Order were incorporated.
The monastery is for prayer and contemplative life, with all that this entails
in terms of cloistering and what not. Charles V came to live a monastic life.
He was a politician who came to participate in the monastic life and the
Monastery of Yuste offered a place of prayer, peace, tranquility, study and
silence. And everyone who comes must assume this life.

A few short years later, the few remaining aging Hieronymites that
were left were gone. After a toxic mix of politics and infighting, the monastery once again found itself orphaned. The Hieronymites made the
decision to leave and regroup in the monastery of Santa María del Parral,
Segovia. At the time, only eleven monks remained, the last in Spain. In
the nineteenth century, there were about one thousand spread out over
forty-six monasteries. In a country of aging and empty seminaries, the
orders found themselves forced to turn to foreign-born seminarists to
keep themselves somewhat relevant. Rumours flew that the medieval
monastery was going to be turned into a luxury hotel when an agreement
was reached, somewhat reluctantly, with a Polish order of monks to
repopulate the empty cloisters that tourists were unable to visit. Before
the agreement, monks of the Order of Saint Paul the First Hermit, or
Pauline Fathers, used to only stop in nearby Plasencia long enough to
pick up some Spanish en route to their more lucrative missions in Latin
America. Now these devotees of the Black Madonna of Częstochowa,
patron saint of Poland, were tasked to maintain the monastic flame in
the place where an emperor who dreamt of a united Europe had passed
away.

The emperor—I of Spain and V of Germany, son of Philip the
Handsome of Habsburg and Joanna of Trastámara, who was daughter of
the Catholic Kings Ferdinand and Isabella, and otherwise known as
Juana la Loca—could have chosen anywhere in the world. His realm
stretched from Manilla to Madrid, as he ruled over one of the first
empires where it could truly be said the sun never set. His life had been

spent travelling around his sprawling empire, putting down rebellions and dealing with the expansion of both Protestantism and Islam under the Ottoman Empire. He saw his dreams of a united Europe fade after conceding the Peace of Augsburg in September 1555. It was a treaty that would allow rulers to choose either Lutheranism or Roman Catholicism as the official confession of their state, effectively bringing an end to Christian unity around the continent.

Shortly afterwards, in October of the same year, he abdicated, dividing his reign between the Spanish Habsburgs and the Austrian Habsburgs, deciding to live out the rest of his life in relative seclusion. In his abdication letter, he speaks directly about movement, foreshadowing the globalized, interwoven world that has grown out of these beginnings:

> The campaigns I undertook, some to begin wars, some to make peace, took me nine times to Germany, six times to Spain, seven times to Italy, four times to France, twice to England, and twice to Africa in a total of four great journeys, not to mention the less important visits I paid over the years to my individual realms. I have crossed the Mediterranean Sea eight times and sailed the Atlantic Ocean twice, not to speak of the journey I made from Spain to the Netherlands.

With such an extensive empire at his disposal, his gaze became fixated on this corner of the northern province of Cáceres. A place that his friend the Count de Oropesa had spoken wonders of but had never seen during his many visits to the country. The world's most powerful man was drawn to a monastery far from the main arteries of power. One that was not in any way the most lavish of all the monasteries controlled by the Hieronymite monks in Spain. For two years he fished for tench in the pond below his window, shot pigeons, and listened to Mass from his bed overlooking the main altar of the church surrounded by the most modern machines of the time. All the while suffering from the gout that tormented him, a condition that had dogged him since 1530 and was caused by his insatiable appetite. According to accounts of the time, the emperor drank four litres of beer per meal and was served around twenty dishes, most of them meat. On September 21, 1558, he died from malaria, perhaps bitten by a mosquito from the pond he fished in. His corpse remained in a chestnut wood coffin in the crypt of the palace for almost seventeen years until it was transferred to the palace of El Escorial in the Sierra de Guadarrama north of Madrid.

The emperor first arrived in Spain a foreigner, unable to speak more than the most basic Spanish. Like many of us since, he found a place so different than the land of his birth, yet at the same time a place that accepted him as one of its own. Marcelo and I walked up the ramp and through an open-air colonnaded portico into what was once the emperor's bedroom. According to the information available, the emperor designed the bedroom himself. The word "austere" and its associated synonyms seem to be mandatory when describing it. The room itself is a cobbled-together pastiche of odds and ends, collected from here and there, all centred upon the bed where he is said to have passed away. Though, unless it had been stored elsewhere after his death, it is hard to imagine it would have survived the fire or that during the ensuing years the locals had only appropriated masonry. We turned into the living room with a fireplace and a wide bay window overlooking the fishing pond, and Marcelo reflected, "I have always wondered about the locals' reaction when the imperial court arrived. I mean, just imagine a small, isolated village suddenly being turned upside down by the arrival of an emperor and his court. Imagine the relationship of the local 'Veratos' with the 'Flamencos' who were part of the emperor's court. Spanish by then was the language of the court, but even still I wonder about the communication. It is said there were very close contacts with the villagers. The fact there are so many 'blond' people in that area, particularly in Cuacos but also in Losar, probably has something to do with all of these... close contacts. Some say the surname 'Cano,' which is common in the local villages of Jarandilla, Losar, and Cuacos, refers to that past lineage."

We were both looking out over the valley when Marcelo stopped to collect these thoughts. "You know, the people of La Vera have always considered it an honour, a kind of a sign of distinction that the emperor chose Yuste as his final retreat, but there must have been a counter reaction too. Have you ever heard of the legend of La Serrana de la Vera?" I told him I had. It's a myth that follows an oral tale born in these mountains and that has been written down many different ways, even showing up in the plays of Félix Lope de Vega. It tells of a young woman, generally blonde and beautiful, who is forced to leave the village and exiles herself in the mountains in one of the caves located in the Sierra de Tormantos, near Garganta la Olla. All of the different tales insist on the Herculean strength of this woman, but perhaps it would be more accurately described as Athenian. The locals in nearby Garganta la Olla still remember the legend of the "Tiro de la Serrana," which is a hollow in the ground in the village they say was made by an enormous stone she once threw. Legend also has it that the baptismal font of the church was fashioned from the gigantic stone La Serrana used to close up her cave at night and, even though it was gargantuan, she handled it as if it were an orange.

The legend goes that for years she tempted men she came across on the slopes of the sierra. She would seduce them and take them back to her cave where she would offer them partridges and rabbits she had hunted for dinner. Once dinner was over, other carnal pleasures were on offer. Once the travellers had rested, she forced them to pay for the services rendered. She then killed them in revenge for the suffering she had endured, transforming their skulls and bones into day-to-day utensils. Marcelo thought about it a while longer and said, "The myth dates back to the beginnings of the seventeenth century, or at least that's when it was first written down, in the years after Charles V arrived. What has been transmitted through popular memory and conscience is a myth with great feminine power, the reaction of a woman to abuse she had suffered. It's just a first thought, but perhaps this legend has a different reading, one in relation to the reaction of the locals to the 'flamencos' that accompanied the emperor?"

As Marcelo and I stepped out of the emperor's chambers, we spoke of the contrast he must have felt, abandoning the seat of power and retiring to these lost mountains. This made me think about how Marcelo had made the transition to the city from a village up in these mountains. That, while being only 175 kilometres away from Madrid and less than one hundred kilometres from Cáceres as the crow flies, is still relatively isolated today. Marcelo said, "That local bourgeoisie I spoke about out in the gardens aspired, above all, for their children to maintain the social status acquired through the efforts of several generations. The most common way to do so was to maintain or even expand their businesses. This duty used to correspond to the older children and the second born used to study. Even though in the 1940s or 1950s access to the university was expensive and problematic, mostly due to the distance between the village and places that had a university. In our case, the closest were found in other provinces in Salamanca, Seville, or Madrid. A common way for the children of families from the villages with less means, who wanted their children to 'study,' was to enter the seminaries that were in Cáceres, Coria, Plasencia, and bigger towns in the region."

I had first-hand experience of this as my own father-in-law, who is from the village of San Martín de Trevejo in the northwestern corner of the province, had begun his education in a seminary and thus was able to make his way from there.

We continued our conversation and I asked Marcelo what his house had been like over in Jaraíz de la Vera. "Contrary to what happened in the 1970s and onwards, and of course nowadays, when studying away from home, the idea was to return afterwards. This was because, in the village, there was the family and the house and the family businesses that had to be passed on. Ever since they were little, my parents had always lived on the same street and in the same house. The houses, like the older ones we saw in Jarandilla, were obviously huge. Both my mother's family and my father's had great big homes." This was something I had trouble under-standing. Given that these great big homes were still standing, as I looked around us I wondered why so many apartments had been built. Why had people turned their backs on the big houses? Marcelo added, "When they got married, in the '50s, a whole floor in the house of my paternal grand-father's family was set up to accommodate the new family being formed. In that house, in Calle Herradores, Nº 13, there was also the family busi-ness that was a large clothing and furniture store. The back rooms and the cellar served as warehouses. It's hard to imagine now, but up to eleven people lived in the house: my parents, Marcelo and Martiria, and their four children; my grandmother, Doña Cándida, a widow, who was a pri-mary school teacher until she married in 1924, and an assistant, Encarna.

My uncle José Antonio, my father's brother, also lived there until he married. Oh, and there were two employees, who we called dependents." He paused and thought, then continued, "Of course, when you consider a way of life like that, you could not live in a flat or apartment. When my mother and father were the last ones left in that house, in their eighties, they simply couldn't be convinced to move to somewhere more manageable. My father died there, in the house where he was born, at the age of eighty-five, in 2018. It was an afternoon in January. He got up from his siesta at 4:30 p.m., and he sat in his armchair, had a decaffeinated coffee and a figurine of marzipan, and, as my mother sat opposite, he quietly passed away."

So if this was the case of Marcelo's family and others like his, I still wasn't clear as to why things had changed so much, from big family homes to tiny, poorly equipped flats. Was I just being a romantic wanting to buy an old house? What had caused the shift? Around 66 per cent of Spaniards live in flats, far more than any other country in Europe, where the average is about 40 per cent, reaching as low as around 20 per cent in Holland and even lower in the British Isles. Here in places like La Vera, in villages like Jaraíz de la Vera or those that are even smaller, where you'd think the cost of land wouldn't be so much of an issue, you find dreadful Frankensteinian, appendage-like apartment buildings sticking out from partly abandoned blocks of whitewashed homes. The country cousins of those you see in the bigger cities like Cáceres. Each and every picturesque, and not-so-picturesque, *pueblo* in the country has its share of clapboard-looking monstrosities irregularly protruding from their older, inner cores.

Marcelo observed, "My generation, the 'baby boom,' is very different from that of our parents. To begin with, the middle-class family was made up of many more children, largely because the Francoist health system made it possible to reduce the terrible infant mortality rate that existed in Spain in the first decades of the twentieth century." We turned a corner and he became more animated. "And, of course, there was no family planning policy of any kind. That would have gone against the regime. At the time it was common to say you 'had the children that God sends you.' So something like sending four or five children to university was difficult, even for middle-class families. Franco's scholarship system was effective with low-income families but not so with middle-income families. At the same time, in the 1970s and '80s, job opportunities in the towns were increasingly scarce, even for middle-class families. Before then, in the '60s, the problem of unemployment and the precarious conditions of the agrarian sector in Extremadura and Andalusia had already forced people to move away from the towns." Marcelo took a moment to gather his thoughts and said, "We're talking masses of day labourers, peasants without land, and unskilled workers all belonging to the working class. This was the phenomenon of immigration to the industrial expansion poles of Spain, like Madrid, Valladolid, Barcelona, Bilbao, and later to Switzerland and Germany. Something similar happened with the rural middle classes in the 1970s and '80s, and in fact is still happening."

The apartment craze then had its roots in the mass exodus of people from the countryside to the cities in search of work, and in many cases bread, after the Spanish Civil War. A city like Madrid doubled in size from a city of barely a million people in 1930 to more than two million people just thirty years later. With so many internally displaced people (IDPs) pouring into the cities, cheap housing had to be put up quickly and, during this rush, speculation became rife. It got to such a point that in 1957 an order had to be issued that banned people from getting off the trains in the capital if they didn't own a house. *Hagamos un país de propietarios, no de proletarios*" (we will create a country of property owners and not proletariat) became one of the propagandist slogans from the virulently anti-communist fascist government of the time and this sowed the seeds for the fierce homeowner instinct that remains prevalent today. "If anything, at least we can leave our kids something" was the dream that drove many to accepting such usurious terms. Usury aside, the regime's housing minister at the time, José Luis de Arrese, freely married home ownership to Christianity and the ideals of the fascist revolution, blending them all into the regime's hagiography. To reinforce this link, ribbon-cutting ceremonies became open-air masses, and priests would bless new buildings as their new tenants picked up their keys. Blessed indeed were the developers.

Addressing real estate agents in 1959, the minister went on to say,

We do not want, and we consider it evil, although sometimes a necessary evil, that construction derived generally towards renting and/or leasing. Not even towards the access to the property, when the due dates for payment are so distant that they might affect the lure to buy. Urban renting or very long-term access [to a property] can be a mandatory formula in certain situations such as being in transit or homelessness; thus, the Ministry must continue to practice such formula. But the ideal formula, the Christian one, the revolutionary one from the point of view of our own revolution, is the stable and harmonious formula of property, where such logic and human goal, though still reserved almost exclusively to those with the privilege of wealth, is that the home belongs to the one who lives in it.

The wording may have been purposely oblique, but the message was discernably clear: good revolutionary Christians buy property and at the rates and terms we dictate.

The low-density housing that had been so important in the immediate post-war construction, especially in the three hundred *pueblos franquistas* of the Instituto Nacional de Colonización, or what have become known as the colonialist villages, had begun to seem "backward" to some in the regime. These *pueblos* were modernist creations that had been adapted from plans from the Second Spanish Republic before the war and were built in twenty-seven different provinces (half of which were in Extremadura and neighbouring Andalusia). These eased the demand for housing in some of the more underdeveloped provinces, but the vast majority of IDPs were headed to the larger urban centres. Besides, high-density housing was a powerful symbol of progress and the future—the past was actively forgotten. Small private homes reminded some of the misery, infighting, and instability they had endured before the war.

This shift in tastes came as manna from heaven for unscrupulous developers who happily feasted on the endless stream of easy prey coming in from the countryside. The figure of the countryside dupe was so common he became a staple character of the film industry at the time: the peasant worker who comes to the bright lights and big city and ends up building the tiny flat he would later buy at rapacious credit rates from the very same banks that were fuelling the developers. This represented a prime example of the supposedly paternal fascist state tutoring its less fortunate because, after all, it knew what was best for you. All the while it was taking full advantage of the peasants' toil to fill the coffers of those who collaborated with it. Since then the regime may have changed, but the last names of the principal actors that pull the strings mostly have a familiar ring. The means and methods also bear a remarkable resemblance, but question the system and you are immediately reminded of the "pact of forgetting" and amnesty law that eased Spain's transition towards democracy. Ask me no questions, and I'll tell you no lies. Indeed.

Marcelo told me how these demographic shifts had affected Extremadura. "When you visit towns in the region like here in Jarandilla, you are immediately struck by the deterioration of the traditional housing and how these kinds of homes have suffered. These homes, generally ground-floor or two-story houses with large cellars, a backyard, or orchard, were common. They were generally owned by the local middle and upper classes. In general, vast swathes of the rural population, who had fewer resources, lived in what today we would classify as sub-dwellings. Places without electricity, without toilets, and certainly no heating. Overcrowding, humidity was frequent." I was shaking my head as I followed his thread, and he checked to make sure I was following him before he said, "The social housing policy of the Franco regime encouraged the construction of homes in the villages and towns that would respond to the needs of so-called decent housing in the 1950s and 1960s, depending on the value of the land, of course. This combined the construction of blocks of flats of up to five floors with the building of single-story houses with patios. Back in Cáceres, there are examples of both types in the Plaza de Italia, San Blás, and especially the area called the 300's. This alternation of 'social housing' in blocks and in single-family houses has also continued throughout the democratic period in Cáceres. In Aldea Moret, for example, there are the abandoned, ghostly apartment blocks on the Calle Germán Sellers de Paz and the single-family houses in Cerro de los Pinos."

I knew exactly what he was talking about because I used to walk to work every day past some of those four-story flats in the Plaza de Italia that he mentioned and they had always struck me as curious. They looked somehow out of place, and in fact reminded me of whitewashed, southern versions of the smaller blocks of flats found in the old communist blocks of Eastern Europe. Dwellings with just enough floors to be profitable but not too high so the extra cost of an elevator would have to be included. That said, I also remember a "modern" block of flats that was being built during those years, and I watched in horror as they went up with basically zero insulation between the thin layer of bricks and the southern facing wall. I kept on telling myself they would install the insulation the next day, then the next and the next...it never happened. The fascist flats have been standing for decades. These "new" flats? Only time will tell.

Marcelo concluded, "The important thing is that, instead of adopting a policy of renovating and rehabilitating the historic centres of the towns, the Franco regime transmitted the message that modernity implied that traditional houses were a burden, something that had to be demolished, and in the villages they could build those horrendous blocks of flats and there was no consequence. The builders and the people never forgot these messages, and the result is the true urban horror we can see today. In fact, urban planning, respect for classical buildings and the environment, didn't really begin to develop until well after Franco's death, in the 1980s, when Spain became a member of the European Union."

The regime's original housing plans were based purely on brute functionality, but as time passed and the speculators gained power and influence, the quality of the building materials became less and less important. One of the regime's housing ministers was even quoted as saying, "Housing first, then urban planning." Well before the tourism boom became so vital to Spain, construction solidified itself as one of the main engines of the economy. Edifying the notion that, at least up until the economic meltdown in 2008–2009, Spain has "lived by the brick" (*España vive del ladrillo*), as the local saying goes. I asked Marcelo what this saying meant to him. "The construction sector is and has been important in our society. In the years leading up to the 2008 crisis, which had a devastating impact on Spain due to the implosion of the real estate bubble, it was striking to contemplate the skylines of any town or city in the country. Each and every town was strewn with cranes that were raising large buildings and housing estates. Today, many of these are semi-abandoned spaces and skeletons of unfinished floors, with a decadent, almost sinister, look. Of course, the end of the real estate bubble has had enormous economic and social consequences in our country." I can remember news reports at the time of more cranes and more concrete being poured here in Spain than in China. Due to the boom, there were more real estate agencies in Spain than in any other country, even those with double its population. But they kept on building.

Marcelo explained its effect locally. "Even here in rural, mostly agrarian Extremadura, the crisis had dire results. And this is if you consider that we are less dependent on this sector than other regions. Some towns, and many families from Cáceres, were entirely dependent on this sector. There is talk that in nearby towns like Arroyo de la Luz, Malpartida, or Casar de Cáceres, there were crews of masons who travelled to other parts of the country during the week to work, particularly to the Community of Madrid, and then returned to their villages every weekend. Rumours have it these workers came to earn around €3,000 or €4,000 per month, three and four times what most people were earning. I don't know, maybe it was an exaggeration, but there is definitely some truth to it." Here I told him that I, too, had heard this. My other brother-in-law ran a video store when such places used to exist, and I clearly remember a day when one of his regular clients chastised me, "Why bother with writing, teaching, guitar playing, and all that? Come work construction with me for a while and you'll only have to work half the year!"

Marcelo finished off his thought by saying, "The concrete answer to your question is that, yes, the 'brick' continues to be an important sector here in Spain, though less than it was up until 2008. And, yes, it will continue to be important, as long as the foundations of the welfare state do not guarantee enough security for the people. That and real estate, a house of your own, which can serve as a safety net against the uncertainties of life." His words rang true. Soulless cardboard cut-outs with paper-thin walls and zero insulation spread over the country like kudzu vines, engulfing entire villages, towns, and cities. Heaven forbid your neighbour was a reggaeton fan or had a prostate problem, because you were going to know all the lyrics or every time they flushed.

Stepping out of the monastery, we passed under an avenue of enormous eucalyptus trees. I looked up at their stringy trunks and remembered something my Australian friend, Jules, had told me after a recent visit to the monastery with his family. "After the visit, I thought about how Anglo-centric our education had been. The Holy Roman Empire had been just another passing name in a long list of empires. Then I looked up and saw these trees. Like us, these were Australian and therefore unknown to this continent until something like two hundred years ago. It's hard to conceive really, but it meant these huge goliaths were also a part of the globalization that Charles V sparked. Here were towering trees that looked like they were eternal and had always been, when really they were in some way the newest things there."

Laneway in the old town of Cáceres.

NEIGHBOURIZATION

4

LATE AUTUMN MORNINGS can be surprisingly cold in Cáceres. The sunny Spain of the tourist brochures certainly exists through the long summer months, but it's far from tropical. The long hot days and warm nights come to an end in mid to late November when there's usually a sudden change in the weather. Flowers abruptly stop blooming and the leaves begin to turn and fall. It's also a time of year when thick banks of fog can lie for days over large swathes of the region. Gauze so thick that, when it's really socked in over the creek valley, I can't see anything beyond the Almohad wall in front of our house, let alone the Roman arch just down the street. The wall hasn't had a real military purpose for years. Its principal enemies now are drivers blindly following Google Maps, plowing through streets too narrow for their cars. Its rich earthy colour also gives off a different warmth by creating a micro-climate for those who shelter behind its embrace.

One of those very same foggy mornings, my daughters and I were making our daily commute to school in the woolly light of the low-rising sun. A walk that takes us straight across the length and breadth of the old town. Every day we pass a twelfth-century cylindrical stone tower. Tour guides continuously debate over whether its origin is Arabic or Christian, but to us it has Rapunzel written all over it. We then hoist our overly heavy backpacks as we walk past the Gothic *concatedral*, or co-cathedral, and the bishop's palace opposite. Above the palace's entrance are crests that act as reminders of all the gold that flowed here from the Americas. The pockmarked façade is littered with more recent scars left by shrapnel from a bomb that fell in the Plaza de Santa María during the civil war.

We were turning into the narrow Calle del Arco de la Estrella when a metallic clanking noise came reverberating along the stones. The skewed arch that runs out into the main square at the end of the tight lane was indefinite and indistinct in the murky light. Then, out of the mist, came a column of soldiers fully armed and dressed in medieval-looking armour. The line marched past us while my young daughters continued chatting away as though the soldiers were nothing but a car passing by. That is until one of them suddenly broke formation and jumped in front my girls and gave an elaborate salute worthy of two princesses. My girls stopped briefly, laughed for a second, and then returned to their conversation about who had the better snack. Just another day's walk to school.

Life behind these ocher stones. There are days when your footsteps and the clack-clacking of storks nestled among the spires are all you hear. Others can present every possible corner crammed with people enjoying open-air concerts or medieval markets. While on foggier days, like on our walk to school that morning, you can see extras from *Game of Thrones* being filmed marching past you through a living, breathing movie set. There are mornings when I step out my door only to be nearly clipped by sweaty, Lycra-wrapped people running half-marathons through the cobbled streets. There are other days that find all vehicle access has suddenly been cut and no one had thought to tell residents that former Queen Sofía was coming for lunch, leaving us all unable to access our homes, some of us with a car full of groceries and melting ice cream. Modern problems in medieval settings.

These sets of stone represent something different for everyone. Cacereños who live beyond the walls most often use it as a quiet place to stroll after dinner on the long, sultry summer evenings. The authorities, however, use this medieval assembly as their window to the world. For them, it is an elaborate stage to host everything from macro-concerts with twenty thousand people heaving, elbow to elbow and drink to drink, in the main square, to a backdrop for televised padel tournaments, to foot races and just about anything you can think of if it means a chance to project the beauty of the city afar. Somewhat controversially, production companies are given free rein (in all senses of the word "free") to transform the stones into medieval Barcelona, Columbus's starting point, a Netflix period piece set in Italy, or, as my daughters saw that one morning, King's Landing in *Game of Thrones*. The message is clear: Cáceres is open for film business.

I had heard the city was planning to better place itself when attracting new film productions and arranged to meet up with Jorge Villar Guijarro, the socialist city councilman in charge of tourism. After what seemed like months of back and forth messaging, one morning he suddenly said he was free and invited me to his office up the Calle Amargura, the street of bitterness, to the Calle Tiendas. Just as I was about to send him a message asking how to get into the building, he rolled up on one of the most space-aged electric bikes I had ever seen. We entered the building and came to a set of beautifully restored offices made up of exposed vaulted brick ceilings. In fact, the renovations were still taking place and, as we squeezed past some of the drywall, Jorge turned to the workers and said, "Shouldn't you be using the green drywall, the one that is moisture resistant? Oh well, I'm not the surgeon of this operation." We then walked past a rather jittery-looking intern staring into his screen and Jorge motioned for me to sit down as he opened the large, barred window that looked out onto the narrow street. "It's a bit sparse at the moment, but as you can see, we just moved in," he said as he smiled and straightened his smart yet casual sport jacket.

I got straight to the point and asked him what he thought Cáceres had to offer production companies. "Look, starting from the basis, it's our understanding that Cáceres is one of the greatest film settings possible. A setting that has not only been used before but one that also has everything necessary for the content creation sector. With the growth and development of all the audiovisual platforms, it has everything you need. It does so for many reasons, but let's start with the obvious ones." He raised his right hand and started to enumerate on his fingers. "First, because we have a natural setting combined with an amazing medieval architectural setting that allows us to, well, always be one of the best options if you are going to film something medieval, or if you are going to recreate Italy it also works. Same thing if you want to film a Renaissance piece. Therefore, here we have weapons, powerful weapons to attract production companies. That said, we also understand Cáceres is not just the old city and therefore we have the capacity to attract other types of productions. What we have is unique, perhaps digitally replicable, but that wouldn't make sense when you have access to the real thing."

He smiled for a moment, feeling he had made his point, and then continued, "It's also a city that has considerable experience in these matters, and this invaluable experience allows us to speak the same language as the networks and to create relationships with the people who do this type of location scouting. Therefore, we do things, or we try to do things, as much as possible, in a way that is easy for the production team. We do so effectively, accompanying them throughout the whole process, both when they first arrive and during the filming itself. Us, the administration, in our role and them in theirs, obviously, but I understand that with us it is easy to film because we will tell you what to do at all times."

I wanted to know how pleased he was with the recent super production that took place in the city, where the old town was once again turned into King's Landing for a few weeks, this time for the prequel to *Game of Thrones*, *House of the Dragon*. Here his smile grew wider. "We are talking about an event that has had an extremely significant economic impact on the city. An event that not only benefitted the more conventional sectors, which of course did some very good business. When we think of *House of the Dragon*, the crew rented somewhere between six hundred and one thousand hotel rooms and tourist apartments. And not just for a weekend—they were here for a month and some more because Cáceres is their European operations base." This phrase had obviously been well rehearsed, but he had more to say. "As I said, there were other sectors that benefitted. We saw, for example, the fabric store in the new Jewish quarter that's been there forever, Manolo, and the other fabric store, you know, the one above the Tambo supermarket? They say they are already fixed for the year. What I mean is they have already sold more this year than any other year thanks to the thousands of metres of fabric that were used for the wardrobe and scenery."

It was true, the economic impact couldn't be denied. The production was simply massive. It employed everything from a small army of private security guards to an entire fleet of sleek black vans that acted as runners between the different bases and sets. For weeks, the dark hoodies and knee-length shorts of the crew became the de facto uniform of those you saw in and around the old town who weren't tourists taking selfies with the props from the sets. But that's just the thing; it wasn't a Hollywood movie set. It's a living, breathing neighbourhood, even if it does look like an oil painting from the sixteenth century. And here's where things get complicated. How do you balance a super production with people dropping off groceries and taking their kids to school? There's a worrying trend around the world where UNESCO World Heritage Sites are emptying out. Overvisited sites becoming beautiful empty shells, bereft of local life and victims of their own success. If you add film productions to a steadily growing number of visitors to the city, then the balance between the economic benefits and the day-to-day life of the neighbourhood becomes more difficult.

I raised this question with Jorge and asked him about how the town hall planned to balance these issues. Here he became slightly more serious: "From the very beginning, trilateral meetings have been held between the production company, the neighbourhood association, and the city council, which acted as mediator. I myself am a neighbour of the old town and I understand we are all creatures of habit. If at a given moment you have to make a five-minute detour because you live in one of the areas where they were filming, well...even though there are really few who live in the actual part they are filming in. But if they are filming right in front of your house, you always have, on the one hand, information and, on the other hand, if you live in the area they are filming, an usher accompanies you through the set to your home." He shrugged his shoulders and raised his palms up in a gesture that suggested there was nothing more to say.

"What about charging the production companies a cannon or some kind of fee that would in some way offset the inconveniences?" I asked.

"What we really ask of the productions is that, as much as possible, all the expenses that can be made within the city should be made within the city. What I mean is that if you need to hire a caterer, please do it in Cáceres. If you need a tent, please rent it from here, if you need cranes, please do it in Cáceres. If at any given moment you need something like saddles, the same. As an anecdote, there is a company in Cáceres that sells saddles, and it told me that during the filming of *Games of Thrones* it had never sold so many saddles in an entire year. It sold more than thirty saddles, and these are things that cost a lot of money."

"So, in your opinion, what's the overall balance?"

His reply was surprisingly sincere. "The majority of the complaints we have received are from people that have had to change their routine, and, as I have said, I understand that the change of routine can be complicated for some. But I also understand that, in this relationship with the shootings, we can also feel tremendously proud to see our own backyard on TV in such a major production that is going to be seen by millions. To me, it seems to be a tremendous honour."

| Tourists bring their own notions with them of how they imagine places to be. They create an image in their minds and this has a direct effect on what the old town then becomes for them when they actually encounter it. Castles in Spain have been inspiring travellers since long before Jimi Hendrix's "Spanish Castle Magic," and travellers and tourists alike continue to return to find that dream. Many travellers want to find the reality of foreign lands but get mired in the uninformative, if pleasurable, orbit of the tourist industry that works hard to feed them what they believe they expect. Places like Cáceres, nearby Los Barruecos, and neighbouring Trujillo represent for many the dream world of the *Game of Thrones* seven realms, and now with it being the setting of the series prequel, *House of the Dragon*, this is what many come to see. Indeed, there are few places in a country and a continent overflowing with castles that can compete with the near-intact medieval experience as Cáceres can. I immediately fell under the spell of the Torre de la Yerba in the main square as it morphed from a dun-coloured brown tower to a glowing orange work of art as the sun set opposite it. It fascinated me that a town in Europe could so resemble the imperial cities of Morocco, like Fez and Marrakesh. That is until I became aware that its towers had the same architects. Like

everyone, I had brought my experience of other places, and what I had seen before, as baggage, and this had a direct influence on how I first experienced the place.

My experience now as a resident is completely different than it was as a visitor, but after all these years, I still stop and make time for the sunset on that tower at every chance. Now, as time has passed, it has taken on different meanings. I now am aware of the lives going on behind those walls, which has given them new meaning. The privilege of living some-where, rather than the fleeting glimpse of someone passing through, is seeing the light change as the days get longer. It's catching the first rays of spring creep over the crumbling walls and light up the newly blooming bougainvillea. It's seeing the tower enveloped in mist. And later in the year, it's looking concerned as crowds gather around the burning of an effigy in the main square under the surveillance of the Torre de la Yerba. The *pelele* figure that represents winter and the hardships that washer-women used to face during the coldest months of the year is burned both in protest and remembrance. It's walking home from work and noticing quarry marks and hidden inscriptions on the stones you have passed by hundreds of times just because the angle of the sunlight that falls across them has changed.

Life among and beyond the stones is what I wanted to find. The stor-ies of the people living in the shadows of the churches, palaces, hotels, and restaurants that have been silent for so long. The day-to-day narra-tives the production companies and tour groups were not hearing. Even some Cacereños are unaware of the lives behind these walls and believe that these are just beautiful stones with no life or tales behind them. It was the stories of everyday people who have left their mark here, and who have also been marked in some way by the spirit of this place, that I wanted to uncover. Their handprints were here and always had been. Like those in the cave, you just had to look. Time didn't stop in that Polaroid in 1986, and life has continued behind the curtains since these palaces were raised. I knew if there was one place to start, it was with the man responsible for the recent rebirth of that awareness. He was the one to breathe life back into the moribund neighbourhood association of the old town—its presi-dent, Juan Manuel Honrado.

Juanma, as everyone calls him, is an official driver for the regional government by day and a miracle worker in WhatsApp groups by night. Rarely have I seen someone with such a natural, innate ability to reconcile people with such diverse and often divisive opinions in just a few kindly worded posts. He's a gentle yet persuasive lion tamer with those who don't get the point that not everyone loves being spammed with cute kitten GIFs. He's also a kind yet strict nurse to the angered and injured whose social media bubble blinds them to the awkwardness of sharing borderline fascist messages in a public neighbourhood chat group. He's equally at home with the more extreme progressive wing of the group, as he is with the elderly widows who work to maintain the more folkloric and religious customs of the neighbourhood. He's an innate politician with too much sense to get into such a dirty business.

His house is just up the hill in one of the many hidden cul-de-sacs and passageways that branch off from the main ways of the old town. His "cave," as he calls it, backs onto some hidden remains of the Almohad wall. He described it to me: "My house is an old one from around 1900, and it was divided into two parts in the middle of the last century. The area I live in now is the lower part, the part that was formerly used to keep animals. Following the advice of my late neighbour, Antonio Fernández, who was an Imaginist sculptor, he always told me that houses had to breathe, just the same as people. With this in mind, I chipped off the years of mortar that choked the arched ceilings and vaults. I did the same with the mortar that covered the base of the Torre del Aire that makes up part of the back wall. I also re-exposed the rocky outcrop in the bathroom and hallway. All of which gives the house a cave-like appearance." His traffic-less porch of sorts serves as the perfect place to conjure up spirits and recite incantations while brewing a *queimada*, a Galician fire drink, on nights like the eve of All Saint's Day. An open place to meet with your neighbours while fusing age-old customs like roasted chestnuts with sugared-up kids in made-in-China Halloween costumes.

On one of those nights I asked him where he was from and what brought him to Cáceres. "I was born in Valencia de Alcántara back in 1968, a small town on the border with Portugal and by that I mean right on the line. There, I spent my childhood in what I guess you would call a country house. Whenever I wasn't studying, I spent my time working in the fields." Extremadura and its people have long been very closely tied to the land and I asked him about the work he used to do. "I am the fifth of seven siblings and we all worked on the small fifteen-hectare farm. My parents started as employees working on the farm and after a lot of hard work and effort ended up buying the land and becoming owners," he added proudly. Extremadura also has a long history of often-absent land-owners tying the local workforce to their land and making it difficult for them to emancipate. Their power has been so great at times they have been able to stop the construction of railroads and even motorways that would run near their lands because this chance at mobility might rob them of their serf-like workers. The dream of owning your own piece of land was akin to those living in cities struggling to buy flats and, in some way, become their own masters.

"What kinds of things did you grow back then?" I asked.

"On the farm there was a little of everything. In the irrigated area, we cultivated all kinds of vegetables and fruits. On the dry land and pasture areas, we had dairy cows, pigs, goats, sheep, chickens, and mules that we used as a transport tool." He stopped for a second and then remembered, "I said that when I wasn't studying, I worked in the fields, but even when school was in, before going, we milked the cows and then the milk was taken to the cooperative. And when we came home from school, after a short time for homework, we continued with the multiple tasks in the field until it was time to sleep." He said all of this very matter-of-factly, and I could see his life experience had made him the extremely dedicated, hard worker I had come to know. He then smiled and reminisced, "It wasn't all work, work, work. In the summers the farm became an impro-vised summer camp for our city cousins who came from Madrid, and even some of their neighbours would come along with them. We all worked together pulling weeds, watering the garden, harvesting pota-toes, harvesting alfalfa for the livestock, feeding all the livestock, and cleaning the stables. That said, there was also plenty of time to have fun by taking a swim in the pool or playing tag. You know? Things kids used to do."

"When did you come to Cáceres from Valencia then?" I asked. He kept his eyes intent on the blue flame flickering in the bowl as he stirred the *queimada* and told me, "I finished my vocational training when I was nineteen, and then I had to do my compulsory military service for a year in Madrid. I briefly went back home to Valencia but had itchy feet and took off to Barcelona. Back in the summer of 1990, I met a girl from Gerona who came to spend her summers in Valencia. She was from there but the daughter of immigrants. Or I should say that her mother was born out here in Valencia de Alcántara and her father was from a small town near Gerona up in Catalonia."

"Immigrant": a word you often hear in this context here in Extremadura and in neighbouring Andalusia. Even though the people were moving from one place to another within the same country, the sense of displacement and detachment from their deeply embedded roots infused the move with this significance and meaning. Between the mid-1950s and the end of the dictatorship, around 40 per cent of the population of Extremadura immigrated to other regions, mostly Madrid, Catalonia, and the Basque Country. In 1959, when the dictatorship decided to crack open the border and allow people to leave the country, many went even farther afield to France, Germany, and Switzerland and became actual immigrants, as Marcelo had told me in the valleys of La Vera. These were men who left their families behind and would often go years without seeing their children. This steady hemorrhaging of people has had a profound effect on the demographics of the region, with often the elderly and infirm being the ones left behind. Today more than 750,000 people who were born here, a region of around a million people, now live outside its frontiers in search of prosperity and work. Since the times of the civil war there has been talk of two Spains. And now, with the culture wars, those on the left and those on the right have reigned over this feud. But if indeed there are two Spains, they may well be the ones that are forced to migrate and the ones that are not.

He lifted the ladle and let a stream of fire lick its way back down into the bowl. "I fell in love with her, so a couple of months later I took advantage of a job offer that came up over there and dropped everything I was doing, the job I had in the village included. This all basically happened overnight. There I was, embarking on an adventure to a far-off city like Barcelona, where I had never been and, to be honest, where I had a hard time adapting. A year and a half later, I returned to Cáceres and this time the girl came with me." This was only a few years after the old town had been declared a UNESCO World Heritage Site. I asked him why he had chosen to live in the old city rather than the newer flats that were being built everywhere. Flats that were the spreading kudzu that signalled the initial wave of the housing boom that would eventually lead the country to ruin twenty years later. "I started living in Cáceres because I passed a competitive exam to become a civil servant with the regional government, the driver I am today. At that time, the rental market was completely overrun by university students and finding a decent home to live in with my girlfriend was nothing short of impossible. During my second year working in Cáceres, my older sister put up her little house for sale, this one, to go to live in the suburbs because there just wasn't enough space for her three kids. I bought it basically because of all the easy terms she gave me to pay for it, and from that moment I began to enjoy soaking up the heritage around me." So far, everything had sounded positive, but there must have been some hiccups along the way. I asked, "Have there been any downsides to your decision to live here?"

He chuckled. "There was a time that all Cacereños and even most Spaniards will remember, when they used to celebrate huge *botellónes* in the main square every weekend. The after-effects would spill over into every nook and cranny of the old town and those years were hard."

If you visited Spain sometime in the 1990s, you probably saw, and may have even participated in, one of these "big bottles," as the direct translation so poorly reflects. What they basically consisted of was large numbers of young people, roughly from thirteen to twenty-five years of age, who would gather in public squares around the country to talk, dance, and drink. It was the now almost inconceivable Ryanair, low-cost version of a Saturday night out with your friends. I can remember being fascinated by the laissez-faire attitude people demonstrated and couldn't believe that the police, while usually present, were generally there to intervene only if things got out of hand. That or to get the overzealous drinker—who would never be able to look at vodka again—to the hospital in case of alcohol poisoning.

The local people's genuine unwillingness to get into another's business, even if it caused so many headaches for them, amazed me during those years. A friend of mine who had a flat looking out onto the very central square of Tribunal in Madrid wasn't even able to walk her dogs outside because of all the broken glass the army of sweepers were unable to clear. Even still, she staunchly defended the young people's right to enjoy themselves and have a good time. Attitudes change, though, and the *botellón*'s negative effects on communities could no longer be ignored. The government completely changed its position and proposed the surprisingly harsh *"ley antibotellón"* law in 2002. Under it, Nordic-style prohibitions on the consumption and selling of alcohol were ushered in. Overnight, Spain went from trusting the civilized behaviour of responsible adults being able to have a beer in a public square while they ate their *bocadillo* sandwiches to becoming another so-called nanny state pushing carbonated, sugary drinks on their citizens. Beer disappeared from vending machines in places like train platforms, and you suddenly felt like a criminal if you tried to buy a bottle of wine after ten o'clock at night.

Unsurprisingly, the measures didn't work. In communities like Extremadura and Andalusia they created *botellódromos*, which were in effect outdoor arenas on the outskirts of town where young people could BYOB. Tacitly approved stadiums of sin beyond sight of the average citizen, and hopefully out of earshot of people trying to get some rest. Out of sight, out of mind, I suppose, but that much-anticipated, ice-cold beer from the vending machine on your commute home in August was to never return.

"How are things here now that the *botellónes* have been pushed out of the city centre? Do you have any real regrets about living in the old town?"

He sighed deeply and said, "You have to be aware of the plain fact that living in a space like ours has its limitations. All the advances that society has achieved are quite complicated to apply here, and those that are possible are much more expensive, things like decent internet coverage and natural gas. These—let's call them inconveniences—have pushed residents out of the old town." Here he pointed to beyond the line of terraced houses and said, "Some have moved to the outskirts, looking for larger areas and things like schools, nurseries, and medical centres. Then there are the cars. These-centuries old streets weren't made for SUVs, and parking and access can be a real problem. Any investment that has been allotted to the old town has been directed towards the palaces, leaving the places where people actually live largely abandoned, with very few policies that encourage investment in them."

"So is that why you took the step and decided to revive the neighbourhood association?"

"After my divorce, I found it difficult to integrate the life of my three-year-old daughter into the rest of the neighbourhood. I observed how the vast majority of local residents with children had to go to other neighbourhoods to do the kinds of things kids need to do. Like go to a park, attend after-school activities, and things like that. Then I met up with some friends from the nearby Aguas Vivas neighbourhood, and I took part in some of the neighbourhood parties their association put together and it was great." He smiled at the thought and continued, "This coincided with the neighbours in Adarve del Cristo and the Calle Amargura starting to mobilize through a network of residents because of increased vandalism in the area, combined with the prevailing lack of civility during the events programmed in the old town. All these ingredients led us to begin to piece the puzzle together and reactivate the long-dormant association. The group of people we were finally able to get together to form part of the board did it with more heart and plain will than the actual know-how to put together an association, but in the end we did it and here we are."

The night wore on, neighbours came and went, and the kids continued to burn off the sugar, but a gathering like this is not complete without food. Juanma nipped inside and grabbed some bread and home-made chorizo to pass around and soften the effects of the spell the *queimada* had started to put us under. The neighbourhood behind the stones was indeed alive and well. I knew Juanma had a great respect for his surroundings and its history, but I also knew he was fervent in the belief that our streets shouldn't turn into a museum with the only life being shops selling swords and questionable *paellas* to tourists.

I asked him, "How do you think these stones can be kept alive, warm with the lives of families behind them, and not become a bunch of empty apartments for tourists?" He let the ladle drop into the bowl and began to get excited. This was, after all, his real passion. "Remember back in May 2017? It was the first time the association really participated in the festival of birds that is held here in the old town every year." And indeed I did. Our street had been chosen to be decorated by my youngest daughter's class, and we spent the entire afternoon with her whole class trying to hang up the artwork they had done all along the street. People from all over the city came to see the decorations, and some began to realize there were indeed families living in the shadows of the palaces. "We decorated so many houses with crafts the residents themselves had created during the many workshops held in the different corners and public spaces all over the old town. The grassroots movement was somewhat revolutionary in that so many residents were working together and getting to know each other. Suddenly, public spaces that had hardly been used by the people who actually live here were being used to produce, create, and beautify their own neighbourhood." He paused a moment and reflected, "I remember when I was posting something on Facebook about the activities, the word '*vecinificación*' came to me, literally, 'neighbourization,' and I immediately called María Bris and proposed we baptize it as such and use it until it went viral. For me, it's a word that transmits a more positive message than gentrification. For me, *vecinificación* can be defined as the use and occupation of public spaces by local residents in order to undertake different recreational activities that help to promote a healthier balance between the local residents, tourism, business, and the local government."

It was getting late and it was time to go, but before we left, Juanma turned to me and said, "If you're really interested in prehistoric rock art, you really need to head out to my village, Valencia de Alcántara. There are many different sites with paintings in the area, along with the dolmens they built. Not only are there many of them but the setting is truly spectacular."

"Do you mean the ones that are part of the Council of Europe's Prehistoric Rock Art Trails?" I asked with surprise and rising interest.

"Yes, those very ones, and in fact I know the man who rediscovered them. I can give you his number."

I was excited about the idea of following the trail of the handprints I had seen in the cave. It was the perfect opportunity to follow the art that has been left behind and see if its message was similar to that which I had seen in Maltravieso. With my mind spinning, we decided to take the long way home, through the narrow passageway that connects Juanma's street to the Calle Caleros below. I thought about what Juanma had said and realized it was just that which the re-birth of the association was bringing about. Neighbours who had never known each other now could put faces to places. Blank white walls and stone entrances now had names, names of the people living behind them. Through the association, they were also making their voices heard in the town hall. Asking to be heard and consulted when decisions were made about the very streets in which they lived. The stones had once again found their voice.

A panoramic view of the Sierra Fría near Valencia de Alcántara on the Spanish–Portuguese border where some of the cave art can be found.

THE CRACK BETWEEN PORTUGAL AND SPAIN

5

AS YOU LEAVE the tiny village of Las Huertas de Cansa, a jagged grey shark fin rises out of a patchwork of changing green. The bluff cuts across the horizon like a megalithic dorsal fin of craggy granite, making the way seem impassable until a chink in its sharp, serrated teeth appears and allows the two-lane highway to slip through. Trees and undergrowth, like willows and birch, that wouldn't look out of place in the milder Atlantic regions of the country, cluster around the multiple courses of water. These sculpt the valleys and feed into the Rivera Avid while, higher up, cluster pines embroider the hills. The Sierra Fría, in the western reaches of the province of Cáceres, is a colossal rock formation you feel instinctively drawn to. It's a prehistoric landmark, the kind that resounds somewhere deep down in our DNA, somehow answering our evolutionary needs and desires for resource-rich environments that promise food, shelter, comfort, and, of course, beauty. Juanma was definitely right; it was more than impressive, but standing at its feet, it seemed more like a wall than a hike. My brother-in-law, Juan, turned to me and said with a note of concern in his voice, "You said to bring comfortable shoes, but you didn't mention anything about harnesses and ropes!"

This is La Raya, the sometimes-imaginary rift that marks the border between Spain and Portugal. This geological singularity has been attracting people since the hominids that spread out of Africa to leave their mark in places like the Maltravieso cave. In their wake they left a rich trove of prehistoric graffiti and dolmens around the province. Out here, hidden among these stratified rock folds, like the cave in Cáceres, you find art from some of the first Europeans. And the chain in front of us is the westernmost stop in the province along the Prehistoric Rock Art Trails.

Before coming west, I knew I had to speak to someone who knew the region inside and out. José Ramón Alonso de la Torre Núñez is a teacher, director of the School of Dramatic Arts of Extremadura, essayist, and colleague who also writes for the regional newspaper, *Hoy*. Alonso de la Torre, as most of his readers know him, is perhaps one of the most prolific writers I know. His pieces cover everything from lost recipes in even more lost villages to *saudade*: that Portuguese feeling of loss that forced emigration can produce. They can range from light-hearted and fun to deeply insightful and even tragic, but always with the underlying undercurrents of empathy and discovery. He's also one of those people I see almost every day, simply because a smallish city like Cáceres is like that. Even though it is a provincial capital verging on one hundred thousand inhabitants, it often feels like a small town because you come across the same people every day, as they, like you, go about their day-to-day routines.

We sat down at a terrace off the square because we didn't want to be interrupted. Before asking him about La Raya, I wanted to know how he got his start writing. He tilted his head back and said, "It was in Galicia, up in the northwestern corner of Spain. Back in 1986, I started writing a column in *La Voz de Galicia*, and it was there where I began to travel and, more importantly, to tell the stories of all these travels. In fact, I still write a column on the back page for them every Sunday."

"But are you from Galicia?" I asked.

"No, I was born in Cáceres in 1957. I'm from here, and my parents, almost all my six siblings, and most of my family on my mother's side still live here. The thing is, my father came down to Extremadura from Asturias in the 1950s and started working here as a civil servant. He met my mother, got married, and they stayed here. I lived in Cáceres until I was fifteen years old, and then they sent me to secondary school up in Zamora, which as you know is more than 250 kilometres to the north, and with what the roads were like back then...well, I didn't come back until I was forty-four."

"Did you stay in Zamora then?" I asked.

"No, I studied Hispanic philology in Salamanca, and when I was twenty-three I took the competitive exams to become a secondary school teacher. I scored well and was the first to choose a position. Even though some of the options available to me were schools just thirty kilometres away from Cáceres, my requests seemed like a brochure from a travel agency that specialized in the sea and mountains. I had chosen schools on the coasts of Galicia, Asturias, Murcia, Andalusia, and even the Canary Islands. Then I also chose schools up in the mountains in the Picos de Europa and over in the Pyrenees. It made sense really. Throughout the year I was preparing for that competitive examination in Salamanca, I had a map of Spain in front of me for motivation. It really seemed I was studying to travel and not to be a teacher. In the end, I was assigned to a secondary school in Vilagarcía de Arousa (Pontevedra), where I lived from 1981 until 2001, when I returned to Cáceres."

Once again, I was witnessing the idea of people migrating from place to place. As I have often encountered here in Spain, there is a desire to see the world, but there is always a deep down desire to return. Many if not the majority of the emigrants Marcelo spoke of eventually return home from places like France, Germany, and Switzerland. In Spanish, there is a common expression, *"la tierra llama,"* literally my homeland beckons. I asked Alonso what his reason was for coming back, and here he shrugged his shoulders. "My family was here, and it was either return at the age of forty-four or I simply was never going to come back. It was quite easy, really. All I had to do was ask for a transfer and I was guaranteed a secure position. When you live far away, there are moments when you feel you are not in your place: the songs at the end of a night out, traditions, the absence of the family...Little details that fill you with melancholy and, in the end, you return. Keep in mind my wife and her family are also from Cáceres and live in Extremadura. In fact, when my son was born, even though we lived in Galicia, my wife came to give birth here. That says something."

Even if he did choose to return, I still wasn't seeing a direct relation with his past and why so much of his writing was set in La Raya. I asked him about his travels throughout Extremadura and whether they were more about work or passion. He thought about it for a minute, then said, "Yes, I do travel a lot around Extremadura and the Spanish–Portuguese border. My journeys are a mix of passion, interest, and I could say work, because then I write about them in books or on the back page of *Hoy*. But I have never considered writing a job. It's something fun and exciting that stimulates me. It makes me forget everything around me. It's an abstraction I enjoy."

It was through Alonso's writing I had discovered many things in the region, yet I remained curious about why so much of it focused on this specific area. His reply was immediate: "La Raya is a vital space for me. It's a place around which I have spent my whole life. You have to take into account that I lived in Badajoz, where I spent two years of my life with my wife while she was finishing her degree. At the time, we were engaged and very young. Since then, I have lived in Cáceres, in Salamanca, in Zamora, and in Pontevedra. That's to say in five of the seven Spanish provinces that share a border with Portugal. In addition to that, my mother is from Ceclavín, a village in the province of Cáceres that is famous for being the town with the most smugglers in La Raya. When I was a child, my mother would tell me stories of smugglers and *carabineros*, and those adventures fascinated me. My mother tells stories very well. She is very literary and that has influenced me a lot. Then there was the gastronomic part. My parents would go to eat with friends in Elvas in Portugal, and on the way back they would tell us about their meals, which seemed like a feast to me. Those stories were something that marked me and gave me an appetite for Portuguese food."

I laughed when he spoke about food. If there was one thing the people in Cáceres always mention when referring to their neighbour, it was the food. Trips across the border might have once been about buying towels, visiting churches or castles, or going on hikes, but they almost always ended up somewhere at a lunch table enjoying the differences of a cuisine that lay just ten kilometres away. That invisible frontier marked a world of difference in their food. I asked Alonso what some of the main differences were that he saw. "There are curious differences such as the use of parsley in the cuisine in Extremadura and coriander in Portuguese cuisine. Another difference is that, across the border in the Alentejo region, the garnishes include rice, perhaps influenced by their colonies in China, and pinto beans, because of their relationship with Brazil. Here in Extremadura perhaps the most common garnish is potatoes. Then there's the *gazpacho* here that is blended and pureed. Across the border it is more in the old style of the shepherds of Extremadura, with chunks of vegetables mixed with bread, water, oil, vinegar, and salt. There is also a significant difference in the *migas*. In Extremadura the bread is crumbled, whereas in Portugal it's a mass of bread alone or sometimes with vegetables, forming a kind of compact puree."

As he spoke, he followed his words with his hand, making crumbling gestures and then creating the more solid Portuguese version. His voice changed slightly and he became more serious. "One of their faults in Portugal is their cuts of meat. They just do not cut it well. Though recently they have been starting to offer Iberian meats with different cuts (*pluma*, *secreto*, *lagarto*) due to the influence of Extremadura. Another difference is that in Portugal their charcuterie is smoked. Then I think about the humblest black puddings. The *farinheira* in Portugal and our *patatera* here in Extremadura are very comparable. When it comes to cheese, there are many similarities. There are also comparable elements in the *chanfaina*.

"If we look at the cuisine on both sides of La Raya, it is based on subsistence and the use of leftover bread (soups, *gazpachos*, *migas*), or the use of local products: pork, asparagus, olive oil. Another curiosity is that the Alentejo and Extremadura regions could form a cross-border territory of soups, be they tomato, garlic, or vegetable. In Alentejo they are somewhat heartier, but the essence is the same. Cod also unites both sides of the border. It's definitely more present in Portugal, at least with a wider recipe book, but it's still very present in Extremadura's cuisine and on the menus of restaurants throughout the region. With wine, the change and evolution has been similar, although with more momentum and success in Alentejo. On both sides of La Raya, bulk table wine and strong wines were produced thirty years ago. Today, high-quality wines are bottled and the Alentejo region has become a reference for Portuguese wines."

It was a pleasure to talk to someone who obviously enjoyed exploring the intricacies of the gastronomy of each place. He stopped for a moment and added, "These are perhaps the origins of my passion for La Raya and why I have written three books on the subject: *The Border That Never Existed*, *R&R: Restaurant Guide of the Raya*, and *A Trip along the Raya*. The latter is the first book I know of that details a complete journey through the entire Raya from the mouth of the Guadiana between Ayamonte and Vila Real de Santo António to the mouth of the Miño between Caminha and A Guarda."

Back in Cáceres, there was a sign that always called my attention when I walked farther up the Avenida de Extremadura to the edges of town: "Portugal 100 km." There in Cáceres the border felt close, but here it was obviously much closer. Yet it's a border unlike others I had crossed in my life, each having their own peculiarities. My first border crossings were with my grandpa across the US–Canada border. He would drive his Winnebago caravan with the hollowed-out aisle across the border with me in the passenger seat to distract the border guards while we returned with a hidden load of cheaper beer, vodka, rum, and cheddar cheese. I remember the convenience stores on the other side being filled with mountains of unknown, exotic-looking candies and chocolate bars that were mysterious just three kilometres north across the line. Still as a young boy, I remember first becoming aware of completely different worlds when I walked across the border with my family into Tijuana, Mexico. In my later travels, I once again saw worlds completely change walking across the bridge from Zimbabwe to Zambia, Azerbaijan into Iran, or from a lush green Thailand into the clear-cuts of Cambodia. But here in La Raya the contrasts are subtler and the border more diffuse, giving the impression that, even before the EU lost its borders, the line was completely artificial. While there are differences, they don't run as deep as they do in other places and the contrasts are nowhere near as stark.

With these contrasts in mind, or perhaps because of the lack of any clear ones, I asked him what La Raya meant to him and how he felt it differed from other regions in Extremadura. "La Raya, geographically, is a space that extends between ten and twenty kilometres from the border into the interior of Spain and Portugal. It is a region, or rather a territory, marked by human and commercial relations. It's a space where languages are not a problem and where, if you wanted to buy something, you went to the next store, whether it was in Spain or Portugal, and nobody considered smuggling. Being the poorest border of the earliest version of the European Union, and also the longest and least populated, as well as the oldest, it preserves some very particular traditions and customs that have not yet been lost. This is one of the advantages of poverty and underdevelopment: it favours the survival of traditions and ways of life. In La Raya there are frequent mixed marriages, joint cooking recipes, similar festivities, pottery, charcuterie, cheeses, and even solidarity. This has been especially visible throughout difficult times such as during the civil war in towns like Barrancos and in Elvas, although the latter is less well known."

The solidarity he was referring to is deeply entrenched in the collective memory of Extremadura. It forms part of a living memory still held by the very few remaining who experienced the horror first-hand. In the early months of the civil war, rebel troops swept out of Africa and up the ancient Vía de la Plata (Silver Way) after they took Seville. After taking Mérida, General Juan Yagüe's "column of death" turned its sights on the city of Badajoz. Word of the scores of summary executions en route spread, creating widespread panic. Republican militia, trade unionists, village mayors, councilmen, elected deputies, and women and children began to flee towards the border with only the clothes on their backs as thousands of rebel troops, along with their Moroccan mercenaries, lined up to take the city. Once it was over, thousands were dead. The arrival of the refugees surprised the Portuguese authorities. Portugal at the time was under the rule of the like-minded dictator, António de Oliveira Salazar, who took sides with the rebels. As a result, the border became a trap for those trying to flee. The army and the Portuguese Republican National Guard placed troops along the border and were ordered to turn the refugees back, many to certain death.

But some had made it through. In the area of the Coitadinha Hacienda, in the municipality of Barrancos, next to a meander of the Ardila River, groups of refugees began to gather. They made it there from places like

Oliva de la Frontera by using routes traditionally taken by smugglers from both sides of the border. Soon there were almost eight hundred of them, mostly men but also women and children. An infantry regiment, GNR (National Republican Guard) troops, and a mobile brigade of the PVDE (Portugal's secret police) and the Fiscal Guard were deployed in the sector. Reluctantly, the commander of the military region ordered the creation of an internment camp on the site under the army's surveillance and placed the lieutenant of the Fiscal Guard, Augusto Seixas, and another lieutenant of the GNR, Oliveira Soares, in charge. Here, the refugees were only guaranteed water and freedom of movement in the enclosed area. The military, however, would not take responsibility for feeding the refugees. This was where the humanity and solidarity that Alonso spoke of began. The people of Barrancos saw people in need and took up collections among their meagre stores and helped feed those who had managed to escape.

During the first days of their stay in Coitadinha, the refugees were not even safe in Portugal. Groups of Falangists stationed on a hill on the Spanish bank of the river located in front of the camp continuously took pot shots at them. That is until Lieutenant Soares crossed the stream on horseback and warned the rebels they were shooting at Portuguese soil and that if they continued to act so cowardly he would order his troops to open fire. News of the existence of a concentration camp eventually reached the International Non-Intervention Committee, which then began a political negotiation to evacuate the refugees from the ranch.

In the meantime, people fleeing from as far afield as Andalusia continued to arrive in Barrancos. Seixas, knowing the government would happily send them back to what could amount to a death sentence, decided to relocate them to a farmhouse a few kilometres to the south without informing his superiors. Around three hundred people ended up in the clandestine camp of Hacienda Russianas. The situation came to an end when, in October, the Non-Intervention Committee managed to have the official refugees evacuated from Coitadinha. They were taken first to Moura and then on to Lisbon, but by then they numbered one thousand. A figure that exceeded the capacity of the trucks, so Seixas paid for the additional transport out of his own pocket. In the Portuguese capital, the contingent was joined by a group of prisoners from Lisbon's Caixas prison, most of who were military personnel. On October 10, 1936, the refugees left the port of Lisbon on board the ship *Nyassa*, bound for Tarragona that was still held by the Republicans. On the thirteenth they arrived at their destination and immediately after that Portugal broke off its relations with the Republican government.

Hounded by snipers and on the verge of starvation, those that escaped were the fortunate ones. First-hand journalistic accounts of the atrocities committed by the rebels that followed the capture of the city make your blood run cold. Reporters from Portugal, the US, and France let the world know about the massacre that was taking place. Some accounts claim that up to four thousand people were murdered in the aftermath. René Brut from the French-based *Pathé Journal* was able to smuggle out photographic evidence of the war crimes, but the great powers remained "neutral," and publishing them only succeeded in encouraging the incoming regime to tighten its censorship net.

Observing the never-ending column of putrid smoke streaming out of Badajoz from twenty kilometres away across the border in Elvas, the young reporter Mário Neves from *Diário de Lisboa* wrote, "The bonfire has been burning for ten hours. A horrible smell penetrates our nostrils to such an extent that it almost turns our stomachs." The smells and images were horrendous, but perhaps the most chilling account is Jay Allen's "City of Horrors" for the *Chicago Tribune* in August 1936. His moving, in-depth account begins with this opening: "This is the most painful story it has ever been my lot to handle. I write it at 4 o'clock in the morning, sick at heart and in body, in the stinking patio of the Pension Central, in one of the tortuous white streets of this steep fortress town. I could never find the Pension Central again, and I shall never want to." His story is heart-rending and the scenes he paints are cruel and difficult to erase once read. The events he describes are horrendous and his observations bleak: "There is more blood than you would think in 1,800 bodies."

The solidarity that Alonso mentioned was a bright light during a very dark time. The people of the village ignored the dictates of the cruel Salazar regime at their own peril and helped their neighbours in need as best they could. Neighbours from across the border, across La Raya, but neighbours all the same. An imaginary line that stands clear in Allen's words: "We shall go away, as soon as it is light. People who ask questions are not popular near this frontier, if it can be called a frontier."

The civil war in Spain officially ended in 1939, but the intense trauma it created still reverberates throughout the country. The war may have officially ended, however, some say the last shot was fired when the artist Francisco Cedenilla Carrasco inaugurated his moving work, *Sierra y Libertad*, in 2009 on the slopes of the Traslasierra and the Sierra de Béjar in the Valle del Jerte north of Cáceres. A series of nameless, almost face-less, figures stand and blankly gaze out across the stunning valley. The absence of any clear identity denounces the fact they have been for-gotten, abandoned in nameless mass graves throughout the country because of the lack of courage for accountability on both sides of the con-flict. The figures quietly scream that the so-called pact of silence that paved the way towards the beginning of the Spanish democracy had left them forgotten. A pact that may have been taken in the belief that looking forward and never looking back was the only way to peacefully move on after Franco's death.

It's an odd, unbalanced silence, though. The "butcher of Badajoz," General Yagüe's name, along with other war criminals, still shouts out from street signs around the country. People born generations after the war ended still speak as though "their side" won or lost, when in truth there were only losers among the masses. The idea may have been to remain silent, but as the award-winning documentary by Almudena Carracedo and Robert Bahar on the topic well documents, it's a *Silence of Others*. All the while thousands of families on both sides of the conflict have had to forget, by obligation, that relatives were murdered after their euphemistic "forced disappearances" and still lie unclaimed in ditches. Countries like Cambodia, Vietnam, and Iraq may have more unidentified bodies lying in mass graves, but only dogs hide their bones. The country is now mature enough to give them peace.

It was clear that La Raya was very dear to Alonso, so I asked him what he enjoyed most about it. "I associate the Raya with tranquility, with its cafes, with surprising stories of survival, with the beauty of the land-scape, with the indefiniteness," he said. "I especially like the spaces that are neither from here nor there: Casas de la Duda in Valencia de Alcántara, Couto Mixto in Ourense, the double villages of El Marco–Marco, A Rabaça–La Rabaza, Rionor de Castilla–Rio de Onor, and the mixed villages of Ourense such as Soutelinho da Raia or Lama d'Arcos that have been both Spanish and Portuguese. Then there's Hermisende, a village in Zamora that was Portuguese, but after the Portuguese war of independence and the restoration of the House of Bragança on the throne, it was decided, like it or not, that it would remain Spanish and here it stayed."

I was intrigued that he hadn't mentioned the rock art in the area I was going to see, or the dolmens, and asked what he thought of them. "I'll be honest," he confessed. "I'm not very interested in rock art. The truth is until the arrival of the Romans, the history of the people who inhabited La Raya does not really interest me. What does interest me, though, is the fact the rock art is similar on both sides of the border, which offers historical proof La Raya has had a development similar to that of other regions of Spain and Portugal, just that back then there were no borders. Later, with the borders and the five wars between Spain and Portugal, La Raya suffered brutal impoverishment. This was because the wars were declared in far-off Madrid and Lisbon. The battles, however, were fought in La Raya. The impoverishment and the economic and cultural stagnation of Extremadura and the Alentejo can be traced directly to these wars."

With that thought, he paused a moment and advised, "But if you are going to see the rock art, when you finish you should have lunch at the nearby En Cá Milio in the tiny village of Aceña de la Borrega, not only for its great food but for its history and its literature. I will never forget when it was also a small grocery store where you could eat at a brazier table and buy everything you needed. Back then, in addition to having a drink and taking home soap, canned foods, or oil, the parishioners at the bar could buy tickets for the rabbits Mari and Emilio raffled off during the hunting season. With time, Mari began to cook the rabbits for those who won them. From there, she went on to cook them for other hunters in the area and then ended up feeding everyone else."

| A shiny blue EU sign welcoming you to Portugal stands among a past that has since been left behind. The derelict border post that once registered everyone's coming and going between countries is now a hollow shell of broken windows and tattered posters announcing bullfights on both sides of the border. The abandoned buildings of what used to be a hard border stand disused and moldering by the sides of the road. Stark reminders of how unnecessary they are between countries that share so much in common. Just up the highway on the Spanish side we found the trailhead to the four-hundred-metre, well-marked trail up to the paintings. You have to hop over the guardrail to access the well-marked trail, complete with an information panel at the bottom, but thankfully traffic was light. The trail immediately starts to climb sharply through a dense stand of fast-growing pines that look somewhat out of place given the surroundings. While the trail is well kept, it quickly became clear that at times we were going to have to use our hands along the route as it zigzagged up the stone shark fin. The pine forest quickly gives way to bare rock, and the way forward was up the stratified rock face decorated here and there with the broom and scrub managing to cling to it. The view expanded and became more impressive every twenty metres until we came to some guide ropes that helped lift us even higher. "Time for another selfie," joked my brother-in-law, Juan, as we both struggled to catch our middle-aged breaths.

The evening before, Juan and I had been sitting on a terrace drinking gin and tonics when I told him I wanted to see another stop along the Prehistoric Rock Art Trails route. His convinced bachelor's face instantly changed and he agreed to drive out here. Public transport in the area is close to nil, and it would have been impossible to get here without a lift. A little farther up we came to what seemed like a dead end. Between deep breaths, Juan laughed, "I told you I didn't bring any climbing material. Not that I actually own any to tell you the truth!" Juan was in much better shape than me. He's been known to play pickup basketball games with friends, and if he was suffering...well, let's just say my breaths were even deeper. For a moment it seemed we weren't going to be able to go any farther when we noticed a small metal ladder fixed to the rock to help us overcome the obstacle. Farther up, a few narrow defiles of rock forced us to use our hands to make our way, but while the climb was somewhat challenging, we both found ourselves thinking about how we would help my eight- and ten-year-old children up on our next visit.

In less than half an hour we came to a slight alcove in the rock with all of Portugal spread out in front of us. Portugal is a country of supernatural pageantry, as the Nobel Prize-winning author José Saramago describes it in "The Sermon of the Fishes" in his travel book, *Journey to Portugal*, and this view proved his words true. We were standing on a rock shelf big enough to accommodate several families. The alcove itself didn't offer much protection from the elements, but it would have been very easily defended as you could see anyone or anything coming for miles around. The 974-metre Sierra Fría across the valley was scarred by forest fires and was sliced up in cross-sections by fire cuts. The northern slope is Spanish, while the southern slope falls away into Portugal with a thicker fire cut drawing the line that divides the two.

The sun was bright and half of the rock shelf fell in the shade, making it difficult to adjust our eyes to the contrast. My eyes were drawn into the deepest recess in the rock and there I saw the first motif, looking like a stitched-up reddish wound on the rock face. Down below it I also made out other symbols, though these were less clear. The brutal onslaught of seven thousand summers had taken their toll on the paintings, but many were still clearly visible. I scanned the rock for more, sometimes mistaking irregular patterns of iron ore left behind by eons of dripping water that had stained the fissures and cracks in the rock for paintings. Neon green lichen covered honeycombed sections of the rock in the shadier areas, adding another hue to the pallet of reds and greys. "Look at this one," Juan shouted excitedly, "that's not just a symbol!"

There, arms almost akimbo, a frog-like human form in red stood out from the granite. A Neolithic portrait that had seen the passing of the copper, bronze, iron, and internet ages still looked out over the valley. Like those that can also be found in nearby Santiago de Alcántara and Albuquerque, the schematic paintings here represent symbolic motifs and animal representations, but what interested me most was the representation of people. Like the handprints in the Maltravieso cave, it's impossible to know for sure what the art is trying to say. It could be totemic hunting instructions, good or bad magic spells, symbols of a tribe tagging its turf, a simple love letter to a partner, or even art for art's sake. What you can't do with these paintings is disassociate them from their surroundings. Without the setting and the landscape that surrounds them, they lose context. The handprints on the cave were not only symbols but symbols that had been placed in a specific place. The oldest handprints in the deepest reaches of the Maltravieso cave were not put there because someone happened to be passing by. There was a specific purpose. Up here on this rocky outcrop, the same was true. The artists had chosen to leave their mark here, for the sights or even for the sound, but it had been a conscious choice. No matter the exact meaning, what I understood is that beauty was equally important to them.

After an equally complicated descent, Juan drove us back to Valencia de Alcántara. True to his word, our neighbourhood lion tamer Juanma had put me in touch with the man who discovered these paintings back in 2012, firefighter and archeological enthusiast, Juan Carlos Jiménez Durán. We had agreed to meet at the Bar La Serrana. As my eyes adjusted to the contrasting dark inside, I saw some of the same bullfighting posters we had seen peeling off the abandoned border control buildings just off the trailhead. I ordered three bottles of beer and was served one of the two national Portuguese beers, Sagres and a *tapa* of *callos* (stewed tripe). Another reminder of just how close we were to the border and the constant flux that exists between both sides. We sat at some plastic tables just off the Plaza de la Constitución, the town hall, and the Iglesia de la Encarnación that seems to be turning its back on the square, deliberately shunning the constitutional elements they represent.

Juan Carlos had arrived just before us, and when I brought the beers and *tapa* out to the table I asked him, "Are you originally from here?"

"I was born in Cáceres but have lived in Valencia de Alcántara since forever," he answered with pride. "Valencia de Alcántara has been included in the health area of Cáceres since the late '60s, and every mother, or I guess I should say almost every mother, has their children in Cáceres. I was born there, but I have always lived here." I knew that, being a firefighter, and particularly a forest firefighter in Spain, could mean having to move around until they secure a fixed position, so I asked him how long he had worked in the area. "I first worked as a wildfire watchman in Monfragüe National Park and then was transferred here and have been a forest firefighter with the heliborne brigade here in Valencia de Alcántara as second team captain for the past thirty years."

The climb was still fresh in my mind and I couldn't help but wonder how he had come across the paintings. After all, it isn't every day you simply choose to climb up a rock face like that. "I'm really curious, Juan Carlos. How did you find these paintings? As they say here in Spain, what was it you lost up there to get you to climb all the way up to that alcove?"

"To be honest, I have always been attracted to ancient history. You know, prehistory, the great civilizations, and especially archeology. Here in the area of Valencia de Alcántara there are so many archeological remains of so many different historical periods. The area is especially known for the dolmens, but it seemed odd there were not any other traces of the people who built them. They hadn't found any cave paintings, as they had in similar areas around the province, and it seemed strange to me. Encouraged by this idea, I started my search in the area, starting with the cliffs of Puerto Roque very close to the border with Portugal." He drew a map in the air with his hands and continued, "I know the area very well, because of my work as a firefighter both on the ground and in the air. I have flown in helicopters many times over many corners of the area and I like to explore. As you could probably see when you were there, the shelter can be seen from the highway, once you know what you are looking for. This particular formation had always attracted my attention so that was where I started."

He shaded his eyes, then pointed in the direction of the sierra. "So, on March 26, 2012, on a very sunny morning, I decided to climb the crags with the aim of reaching that rock shelter. I was alone and the only companions and witnesses I had during the climb were the great griffon vultures that usually circle over the area." But, even still, I reflected, I knew from recent experience that if I hadn't of known the paintings were there, I'm not sure I would have seen them. He smiled. "Once I got there, the brightness of the day prevented me from seeing clearly what was there, but I had a feeling. Little by little my sight adapted to the shade of the shelter, and then I began to see clearly the reddish tones of the paintings. It was an unforgettable moment. I can't really explain in words what I felt, but it was a sensation that changed my life. I stayed up there for a couple of hours taking pictures and enjoying the environment and every detail represented there. I believe our ancestors saw in this place a strategic site to dominate the area, either as a sacred place where they did their rituals, or to control resources such as hunting or keeping an eye on other human groups.

"At first, I had my doubts and thought they could be from a more recent period, but after looking closely I realized they could be prehistoric since the symbolism represented was typical of schematic art. That, together with the wear and tear due to erosion and the passage of centuries, made me think they were cave paintings. In the areas where the sunlight hits them directly, the paintings have obviously degraded more than others. But paintings like these ones on rocks are like tattoos. They are difficult to erase and are embedded in the rock itself, which is why they last so many millennia."

I still wasn't sure just how he got up there, though. Without the ropes and ladder, my brother-in-law and I would never have made it. "How did you get up there that first time?" I asked in bewilderment.

"I approached it from a different way. I started the search from the other side of the border and went through the crags because it was easier going at medium altitude through the ridges. The most difficult part was reaching the shelter, where I had to climb a little, you know, where the ladder is now. Then, when I finished documenting everything, to get down I had to make my way through thick mountain scrub until I reached the pines and then get down to the road. The whole path was completely covered with vegetation. It certainly wasn't like what you see now. That was later cleared to open the route. The town hall is in charge of that."

"So what happened next?"

"Well, the first thing I did was to contact a Portuguese archeologist, Jorge de Oliveira. He's a specialist in prehistory. I sent him some photos and explained where I had found them. A few days later, he and an archeologist showed up and, after seeing them, they certified their authenticity. Then came technicians from the Junta de Extremadura, the National

Heritage Board, and archeologists from the University of Alcalá de Henares, who also certified the find."

"In general, how is your relationship with the people on the other side of the border? It's curious that the first person you contacted was someone from across the border."

"In Portugal I have very good friends. We have always had a very good relationship. In general, I think they are more concerned about caring for and valuing heritage. We have a common project that hopefully will be developed over the next year. The idea is to join two rock shelters with rock art via a trail—the one you saw in Puerto Roque with another just across the border called Nido de Búho. They are about eight hundred metres apart and the trail would run parallel to the rocks. As far as we know, it would be the first international rock art route. Unfortunately, this link with nature these people obviously had has almost been completely lost as we have become more urbanized. The abandonment of work in a natural environment has meant we have lost much of the link with nature. Although, there are still some people who can feel this connection. I think seeing these paintings can help reinforce that long-lost link."

The Torre de los Espaderos in the Plazuela del Socorro
in the old town of Cáceres.

TAKING CHANCES

6

I FIRST HEARD IT ECHO around the Plazuela del Socorro, a small, shaded square on the edges of the walled city. The sound then ricocheted off the circumscribed, or perhaps more precisely *circumcised*, Torre de los Espaderos. This is a fairy tale-looking defensive tower rising above the square, or rather a stone giant, complete with machicolations, ready to dump hot oil on invaders and hapless residents who throw out their garbage before the bins are set out. It had been emasculated back in 1477, along with all the other military towers attached to the individual fortresses in the medieval city, save one. That year, Isabel the Catholic passed through town as she was consolidating her reign. During her visit, she dictated an ordinance "for the pacification of the land and repression of the factions of the town." The defensive tops of the towers were pinched off to quell any further uprisings against her rule, very effectively nipping any real chance of insurgency in the bud and in the process creating what would become the Spanish nation.

The echo then bounced off the postmodern, prison-like annex of the provincial archive that squats next to the tower like some sort of drunk wedding-crasher. It was a monstrosity that was built in the late 1980s when the region was heady with EU funds flooding in and grandiose projects were springing up around the country. Its sheer ugliness is even more surprising given the city had by then obtained its protected

UNESCO status. Not that this always means a lot. I had seen my share of architecture fails in UNESCO cores around the world, and this was yet another to add to the list. This fail was no different from the embassies of supposedly woke northern European nations disfiguring homes and palaces in places like the old city of Baku, all under the supposed guise of preserving them. UNESCO's red list of World Heritage Sites in Danger is almost entirely made up of countries from the global south. Nations that are either too poor to fund preservation or, perhaps more concretely, lack the political might to keep their names off the list.

That's not to say more powerful nations have never been warned. The fact is only three sites have actually lost their World Heritage status since the list began in 1978. The first site to be removed was Oman's Arabian Oryx Sanctuary in 2007 due to the government's decision to reduce the sanctuary by 90 per cent. Then the Dresden Elbe Valley in Germany was kicked off in 2009 for building a four-lane bridge in the heart of the cultural landscape, which meant the site failed to keep its "outstanding universal value as inscribed." Recently, Liverpool lost its status for an "irreversible loss of attributes" due to a new football stadium that ate up much of the city's waterfront.

The echo I had heard carried over the ruins of one of the historic Roman gates to the old town. La Puerta de Coria was one of the four Roman arches that gave access to the walled city. Back in 1879, an esteemed member of the liberal party, Joaquín Muñoz Chavez, who happened to live in the street that led to the arch, petitioned to have it torn down to allow "evil winds" to "freely exit" the walled city. In his opinion, the millennial arch was completely devoid of any artistic merit that would advise its conservation. He further argued that, in the nearly two thousand years it had been standing, it had accumulated large deposits of dirt in its corners that were incompatible with the cleanliness and good hygiene of the residents of the area. Perhaps somewhat subconsciously, he also allowed that its heavy arches constituted a formidable obstacle to the expansion and proper decoration of the area where it was located. He was candid enough to leave out the fact that, by tearing it down, his carriage could deliver him straight to his door, but I imagine everyone at the time got the point.

Here, in one small out-of-the way square in the city, you could observe five hundred years of politicized urban disasters. Evil winds, indeed.

I continued walking down the hill and caught up with the sound again. It was an indistinct amplified voice, but as I drew closer a few words became clearer. One word seemed to be repeated again and again: "*fuera*" (outside, out, away). I stepped down the stairs leading towards the Calle Caleros, and it wasn't until I had just about reached the Plaza de Santiago that I realized it wasn't coming from a neighbourhood *verbena* or fiesta as I had originally expected, but, instead, a political rally. Being a foreigner from a country that isn't particularly reviled (yet), I don't remember feeling nervous at the time. But in times like these, the 'other' is increasingly flogged as the scapegoat of all the county's problems. I didn't necessarily relish the thought of coming face to face with a jacked-up crowd, drunk on the idea that Soros-inspired atheists from abroad were going to ban Christmas and force everyone to add chorizo to their *paellas*. Thankfully, the Spanish are notoriously nonviolent and, in fact, for the most part, abhor violence, often taking out their ire on garbage bins and shop windows rather than bystanders. A fact you can see any given Saturday night as people pour out of bars and you notice the almost complete absence of fist fights so common in other countries.

Unfortunately, the extreme right-wing movements smoldering steadily around the world have also found fertile ground in Spain. Opportunists taking advantage of the gurgling discontent left behind since the terrible economic crisis that brought the country to its literal knees in 2009 and had yet to fully recover from before the COVID-19 pandemic struck. Their numbers are thankfully still relatively small but are a growing presence in all levels of government. Whatever the case, I wasn't particularly keen on being singled out as being one of those from *fuera*, even if I wasn't wearing socks with sandals.

I cautiously turned the corner and, somewhat to my relief, saw the president of Extremadura, Guillermo Fernández Vara, framed by the traveller's scallop shells on the Iglesia de Santiago that gives its name to the square. A man who had ruled Extremadura since 2007, minus a somewhat short interlude in the opposition from 2011 to 2015. A man

A political rally in the square next to the Iglesia de Santiago.

whose socialist party had ruled the region since the autonomous community was formed back in 1983. This was as "establishment" as you can find in these parts, as the chances of anything new, let alone revolutionary, coming from them or their followers was slightly less probable than snow in August.

A modest, mixed crowd of pensioners, locals, and the party faithful rocked on creaking fold-out chairs in the late afternoon light as he presented the team the socialist party, Partido Socialista Obrero Español (PSOE), was running in the upcoming local elections. In all my time in Spain, I had never really experienced anything like this before and the traveller in me wanted to see if the often-repeated tales of political parties offering free sandwiches to those attending their rallies were true. That, and there was that word I had heard back in the upper square ringing off the decapitated Torre de los Espaderos—*fuera*—that had piqued my curiosity.

As I got closer, I heard the president excitedly repeat, "*Hemos traído gente de fuera*" (We've brought people from outside), and my intrigue grew. Was it possible the endogamous power structure here in Extremadura was opening itself to the world? It was true it was fielding a relatively young candidate, one who would become the youngest mayor to ever govern a provincial capital in Spain if he was successful. Maybe this was revolutionary? It was going to include assessors with different perspectives to complement its team? Had the party sourced people with the necessary experience from around the world to bring their skill sets to help shift the inertia of the "same old, same old"? Then I heard him boom, "*Hemos traído gente de incluso fuera del partido para complementar este equipo*" (We've even included people from outside the party). Suddenly, it was like a train had smashed into the Romanesque arches of Santiago and any hope I had of real change was buried deep beneath its steaming rubble. True, the hermetic party structure was letting in some outside air. There were "outsiders" in the candidacy, but as special exceptions rather than being the rule. Real change had been put off once again.

And then I started to laugh.

It was a laugh that came from deep down inside. A laughter that resounded like the profound blues motif that intones that you have to laugh to keep from crying. It seemed nothing had changed and no one else was laughing. The partisan blinders that have for so long stifled change and growth here had converted people who weren't card-carrying members of a political party into outsiders, people *de fuera*. Blinders that also seem to filter and block out humour. An international malady that extends the humourless cynicism we see all around us, the symptoms of which include the inability to perceive irony and to see the bizarre humour of their own colours. To be blind to the incredible weirdness of the different acts we were seeing lately: protests against the measures the government had taken against the pandemic by fervent nationalists; and, protesting in Japanese cars, waving made-in-China flags was definitely ironic if not completely laughable. Or the dystopian fairy tale that happened during the worst months of the lockdown in Madrid, when the mayor had the idea to outsource school cafeterias and stuff at-risk kids with pizza for months on end. Disturbingly transforming herself into some sort of blend of Cruella de Vil and the old woman in "Hansel and Gretel."

Then there was the Orwellian realism of one of the vice presidents of the government at the time, one of the six or seven of them that seem to multiply like rabbits depending on the need. It was a tale of a perpetually frowning, self-professed communist from Vallecas, a very working-class neighbourhood in Madrid, going against his professed word. A case of someone finding out what it really was like to have money and which saw him move from his humble base in Vallecas to the affluent suburbs in the mountains that lie just north of the capital. It's a creeping cynicism that reeks of a world devoid of irony, or at least the ability to recognize it. If it's something someone else does, tweets galore denounce the fact. But if it's something someone does on my side of the spectrum, then for some reason it just isn't funny. Highlight the obvious to the respective flocks and the last thing you'll find is a laugh. It's a humourless polarization that only seems to worsen with every passing year.

There was someone I knew, though, who had been able to keep a smile on her face throughout much of this. Precisely one of those from *fuera* who had joined PSOE's team and who eventually won the local election. An outsider who has bravely jumped into the political fray knowing that, as an outsider, hers will surely be the first head to roll if and when things go south. She's one of those distinct people you can spot from afar in this, at times, seemingly small provincial capital of about one hundred thousand people, and someone I bump into almost every other day on the street. There was even a time when I would know she was coming before I could even see her. During those morning walks to school, we would often hear the blue notes of a chromatic harmonica presage her arrival in the square, as her young daughter Zoe livened up the morning's soundscape with her inspired playing. Fernanda Valdés Sánchez was another traveller who had found a home among these stones.

Cáceres is a city of hills, a place where you feel you are always climbing and rarely going downhill. What little bicycle culture it does have is mostly limited to the weekend Lycra crews that widely roam the secondary highways and mountain bike trails that radiate from the city. Fernanda's ride, though, is a different speed that matches her character, and when she isn't walking her daughter to school, that's how I usually see her. She uses her bike almost everywhere she goes, either with her young daughter sitting behind her, or on her way to a rehearsal with her accordion hanging off her back. She's one of the growing number of people you can see using bikes as a form of transport rather than exercise in the city, something that's slowly changing, but just that: slowly.

I can't exactly remember when we first met, probably during one of the informal Irish music sessions held in the Lancelot tavern a few hundred metres from my house. We have been friendly ever since. I had heard she was getting into politics a short time before the presentation in Santiago, and I remember running into her one of those times and asking if she knew what she was getting herself into. I still recall her words: "We can stand around complaining that nothing happens around here, but if no one takes the initiative and tries to do something new, something different, nothing will ever change. So I guess I have to take a chance."

And take a chance she did. She was now the town councillor in charge of culture and festivities and had been in the position for just about a year when the COVID-19 pandemic slammed the door shut on just about everything. The city's biggest celebrations of the year, both secular and religious, became impossible while everyone was locked down in their homes. We watched what was normally the most culturally active time of year bloom and take shape through our windows. I knew Fernanda had lived in Cáceres for quite some time, but on one of those times I ran into her, I asked her where she was originally from. "I was born in Almendralejo, a smaller town about one hundred kilometres south from here, but I feel like I'm from the world. I think I could live anywhere and feel like I'm from there. That said, Cáceres welcomed me warmly, and as long as I feel good here, I'll stay. I don't know if I'm answering your question, but I don't believe in nationalities or borders." With that, she raised both her hands in the air and continued, "Everything seems to me the result of chance, although this luck gives some of us privileges that others don't have."

With the movement of people in mind, I wanted to know what brought her to the city. "I follow my instincts a lot and I adapt to situations and try to do my best in each of them. Since I left home at sixteen and moved to Mérida to study at the art school, I have made a living working in all kinds of things. I worked for ten years at a craft stall in the Christmas market in the centre of Cáceres in Cánovas Avenue. I've also worked at a play centre in Aldea Moret, in associations, cleaning houses, taking care of children, painting, doing restorations because I also took a carpentry module, and, of course, music." We sat down for a moment outside the library. Some people mulled around the entrance waiting for it to open, while others sat on the silver ledges outside the windows and caught the free Wi-Fi signal from inside. I asked her how much her life had changed since she took the position at the town hall. "Now I'm a town councilwoman, but I'm still a musician and gig when I can. Right now I'm also involved in a local production of the play *Hipolita*. It's 100 per cent from Extremadura, and we toured quite a bit with it when we could. Through it, I get to tell stories with music. But above all, first and foremost, I'm a mother, Zoe's mother," she affirmed as she patted the back seat where Zoe often sat.

One thing was to come and live in Cáceres, but another was to choose to settle in the old town. I knew what had brought me to the old town. I knew if I was going to live in a small, provincial capital that is somewhat isolated from the rest of the country, I wanted to take full advantage of what it had to offer and what made it special. With this in mind, I was curious about her reasons for choosing these stones. "I have been here since I was eighteen years old, so about...twenty-seven years, more than half of my life. I came to study music teaching, and when I first moved, I lived in the next street over in Calle Caleros. After that, I lived for almost a year in Mexico and then came back to Cáceres. I looked for a house in the old part and I found my house and I have lived here ever since I was twenty-three years old." I think I understood why she had chosen Cáceres, but I pressed her, as I was particularly curious as to why she had chosen the old town. "I guess you need a special character to live here. Almost everyone likes to park at the door in front of their house, or have a garage, things that most of us who live here cannot do. Then there are things like having a fireplace, something I would love, but which I just can't have in my house. Other things like central heating or a fibre optic internet connection would also be nice to have, but they aren't currently available. That said, I hope they will arrive soon," she added with an ironic smile that at the same time showed optimism. "Whoever chooses a house in the old city to live in knows they have to pamper it. Almost every year I have to repaint the rooms at home because the humidity that rises up from the ground is simply unforgiving. But our neighbours, in general, usually consist of quite particular, or perhaps peculiar, people who value things—something perhaps not very common nowadays. This may sound a bit romantic, but sometimes it actually isn't, you know what I mean?"

I did.

The idea of ritually cleansing and whitewashing your house every spring may look attractive in travel brochures, but after the fourth or fifth time, the glamour tends to wear thin. There was even a trend among some of the residents to forego the whitewashed look and leave the stone uncovered, exposing the adobe-like look of the homes. But even then eventually the damp would show itself. As Fernanda then highlighted, "If I had to choose the single biggest disadvantage of living in the old city, I suppose it would have to be the damned humidity, inside and out. It is just so extremely difficult to fight against. I guess there's also the odd uncivil neighbour who can make life impossible for the rest, but that can happen anywhere. We are very centrally located. I always move around by bike, and we have some of the most beautiful places in the world just outside the front door. What more could I ask for, really?"

I could deeply sympathize with Fernanda's battles with the ever-persistent damp that slowly creeps up the walls like egg white in a frying pan, leaving its crystalline trail behind. It's the bane of these houses that everyone who lives in them suffers to some degree or other. One that is responsible for all of the green or white mosaics you can see on the lower parts of the walls throughout the older parts of the country. The cool, damp earthiness of our sometimes metre-thick walls can be a welcome refuge when the thermometers outside tip 40°C, while inside they read a somewhat cooler twenty-five degrees. But once the fierce summer gives way to autumn, then winter, and the temperatures drop, the rising damp stops evaporating and mold can start to appear in the most unexpected of places.

"Just a couple days ago I moved a piece of furniture from a room and behind it there was mold. I felt somewhat overwhelmed and even went so far as to look for houses to rent. Later that night, though, I reflected and spoke with one of my neighbours, Pablo, an endearing architect who always gives me a hand with anything. We met and I told him my problems and he offered some simple solutions, if not exactly cures. That afternoon I painted the room and now we are looking at ways to remove the relative humidity from that room, because even though I did a lot of renovations about four years ago, the house is below street level and humidity enters from all sides. So now I have a dehumidifier on and, well, I want to give it a try because the hardest thing about living here is the winter. As you know, it's wonderful to live in these naturally air-conditioned homes during the summer."

There was still that question of *fuera* running around in my head and I wanted to ask her more about what led her to politics. I remembered what she had told me about wanting to effect change, but I thought I would see if she would go a little deeper. "I was never really involved in politics, although now that I think about it, in the end I realize I have always been involved in NGOs, associations, and I have participated in many social movements. In the end, everything is politics. What moved me, after thinking about it a lot, was the opportunity to be able to do things for the city that had welcomed me so warmly. What I enjoy most in life and, in fact, what my life is, is culture. Since I was seven years old, when I started playing the accordion, whenever I had the opportunity, I have enjoyed cultural events. Getting involved was also an act of responsibility, because the future I was foreseeing at the time was not very conducive to a thriving cultural scene."

For decades, the regional government here in Extremadura had made a very concerted effort to "bring culture to the villages." Vast amounts of money were spent in an attempt to give people in smaller communities the same opportunities to enjoy concerts and theatre productions that people in larger centres had. A few production companies did very well for a while, and apart from bullfights and tribute bands, alternative cultural options like jazz, blues, fado, and new plays were seen in small towns. Something that would never have happened otherwise. All of this has come at a cost, though, to private promoters without the privilege of the seemingly unlimited budget the regional government enjoys. Culture and all it represented was now seen as "free," something the state brought in. Few if any private promoters can compete with the state's resources, and while people are happy to enjoy cultural events, they are less keen to pay for them. That was the case until the economic crash of 2009, when one of the first things to be slashed was the budget for culture. It was an attack from which the cultural scene never fully recovered. Then COVID brought its mortal blow.

I realized I had asked about what had convinced her to dive into politics, but then it dawned on me I hadn't asked her about what had led politics to her. "The party, and especially a certain friend who is also a militant, believed in me, and from there everything has been all about learning, and learning a lot. I believe I now have the responsibility to do everything I can to bring culture to all parts of this city, not just the old town, and for artists to be able to work, and that's my day to day." Aside from being a well-known and respected musician in the region, what perhaps she was best known for was founding and running one of the most successful, and certainly distinct, international music festivals in the city, the Irish Fleadh. It's one of the fall highlights of the festival season here and a festival that attracts people from everywhere, including the Irish ambassador most years. I asked Fernanda what made the festival so different. "There really aren't any festivals like this in the rest of Europe, with the exception of Ireland, of course. There, almost every city has its own fleadh. That's why it is so important and distinct, because not only do people come to the concerts, they come to play with the musicians who give the concerts, before, after, and in the sessions. They come to learn from them in the workshops. I never thought at first we would get to where we are now and that there would be so many people counting the days when one fleadh finishes until the next."

I was curious as to how it came about. How did Irish music find such a receptive home so far away? "The fleadh was born out of necessity. It was born out of a desire and a need to learn music from great musicians and to share a few days with them. Although I am not in the association anymore, I can tell you that, when the fleadh began seventeen years ago, we were only two groups, one of Italians and another made up of some Irish musicians and, of course, those of us from Cáceres. Nowadays the festival fills the Plaza de Santa María in the old town with ten thousand people. Cáceres has gone from being a lost city on the map of Spain to being the city of the Cáceres Irish Fleadh in Ireland, and for many musicians around the world. And the most important thing is musical and emotional ties have been created here that last. Every year it provides us with a reason to get together and meet again."

Fernanda's handprint on the city was now indelible and, at least for the near future, it would be impossible to disassociate her story from the fleadh. The music and the musicians have also left their echoing marks on the community, and I was curious about how she saw the Irish and how they felt here in Extremadura. "The Irish and the people from Extremadura are very similar in that we both love music. Proof of this can be seen in the respect you experience during the concerts and after them in sessions." This was certainly true. The Spanish are very social people, and it is often the case that many come to talk as well as listen to the music at concerts. This can obviously cause tensions among those who really want to listen. But at the fleadh, most come to listen and dance and many come with their entire families. It's not uncommon to see groups of young kids whirling around to the music off to the edges of the stage.

"In addition, the quality of the workshops each year has been growing, reflected in the growing participants. Both cultures like music, the good life, and lasting friendships. I don't know how to explain it exactly to you, but I can tell you that, when I go to Ireland, I feel at home. There are times when I go to a session and know almost everyone there because most of the musicians have played at the festival in Cáceres." She paused and then underlined, "If you look at the fleadh programs, you can see the best musicians in Ireland have passed through the city, not to mention all the groups that play traditional Irish folk in Spain that have also passed through. Groups like Rare Folk, Boj, Kila, Dervish, Mairtin O'Connor, Mairtin Hayes, and Dennis Cahil—so many legendary figures have played here. Then there are the three or four days of coexistence that have fostered collaborations, concerts, and many, many friendships, as well as other types of closer relationships that will remain secret."

Every autumn, the old town fills with people as they take advantage of the lasting good weather, and the stones resound with music. There are pop festivals, blues festivals, and, of course, the fleadh. Juanma and the neighbourhood association had taken surveys to see which festivals rate highest with the people who live behind the stones, and the fleadh always comes out on top. I asked Fernanda what she thought about the people we lived among and she reflected, "In the last few years, the monumental city as it is called, has become a small village of very valuable people whose main aim is to try and help each other. During the lockdown, being able to go out and sing, clap, say hello, and have a beer with the neighbours on the street got us through this extremely challenging time. Things like an anonymous neighbour setting out lemons for those who wanted to come and pick them up. If someone has a problem, there are many neighbours, like Antonio the architect, who try and lend a hand. For me, this is the real meaning of *vecinificación*. The value of being human, and it is so important that, under the value of these centuries-old stones, there are souls who fight for these stones to continue breathing life."

Time was running short as we both had to run off and pick up our kids from school, so I quickly asked her how she foresaw the future of the old town. What did its future look like to her? "I once had a dream where they put a big, glass bell jar over the old part and it was only accessible by one entranceway, like a gigantic museum. There were stones and beautiful ones at that, but they were inert. It was like a plastic city. Of course, for me there has to be a balance. Tourism is very important because a large portion of Cáceres lives off it, but it has to be compensated in some way to lessen its impact on those of us who live here." Here she became more serious and said, "Culture and art will always adapt to circumstances and will continue to do so. Culture and the artists that produce it will always be present. Cáceres is a city of many treasures, and I suppose those who left their hands in those caves you were fortunate enough to visit fell in love, as we all have, with these landscapes. I imagine they stayed here for the same reason many of us do. Sometimes I wonder if there is an energy, the granite below us, a force that makes us want to stay in this land."

| The sonorous nature of the stone that makes up the old town gives it a soundscape all its own. The palaces built out of toasted, warm stone, sometimes the colour of a crumbly mature cheddar, reflect and refract the slightest murmur in all directions. That is until the sound reaches the confining stone barrier of the defensive wall that encircles the old town and is then bounced back in a different direction from where it originated. Early in the mornings, the crack of stiletto heels striking the flagstones that pave the square in front of the Concatedral de Santa María reach you long before you see the elegantly dressed civil servant they belong to walking to work. Depending on the cadence of the clacking, you can usually tell the time and if the workday is about to begin, or if they are returning from their second or third coffee break. The seat of the provincial government sits in what used to be the convent of Santa María de Jesús next to the fifteenth-century church. It is one of a handful of Renaissance palaces in the old town that have been converted into public buildings. The civil servants and bankers who work in them add their own hushed undertones to the scene. That is until 3 p.m., when they all call it a day. The bells I use to mark the passing of the day roll along their walls and then ricochet through the narrow streets, making it difficult to tell which church each knell is coming from. Occasional irruptions that starkly contrast with the generalized hush blanketing the city's core throughout the day.

Once the few cars on their way to work finish rumbling over the cobblestones, the quiet is restored to the real protagonists of this soundscape: the birds. Extremadura is one of Europe's great bird watching areas and several species have adapted to the peculiarities of the city over the centuries. It's a seasonal soundtrack that evolves over the year as the migrating birds pass through en route to and from Africa. Taking the same route our ancestors did so many millennia ago. The year starts with visits from what is perhaps the most emblematic bird of the region, the stork. The local proverb, *"por San Blás, la cigüeña verás,"* means that by February 3, the saint day of Saint Blaise, the storks will have once again returned. More often than not, though, you hear them before you see them. Their distinctive bill clattering reverberates off the stones like the sound of far-off machine gun fire. A characteristic that gives them their more onomatopoeically accurate name in Arabic, Lak-Lak. It used to be that, as you walked through the old city, you would see them perched on seemingly every spire, making their enormous nests in the corners of the roofs of these Renaissance palaces and churches. Nests that get so big I once saw a car crushed by one that had outgrown its perch and came crashing down, flattening the car parked below. Their numbers, however, have sharply fallen in recent years. So much so that at one time they began to pipe in pre-recorded clattering to replicate how it used to sound, lending the old town the vibe of an ornithologists' karaoke in the process.

The storks are followed shortly by the swifts and swallows taking advantage of the crumbling adobe-like walls to make their nests. Those that find a "no vacancy" on the wall by the time they arrive build their mud sculptures under the eaves of the Arabic tiles that roof these old buildings. These winged kamikazes, or "crazy-fliers" as my kids have dubbed them, circle and screech overhead, adding just a sprinkle of danger to the pleasantly brisk spring mornings. Between the shrieks, a closer listen reveals one of the shyer year-round inhabitants of the trees and tiles—the owls. Birds that blend in so well with their surroundings you usually only catch a glimpse of them as shadows fleeting past the street lights at night.

On those same mornings while we walked to school, my daughters and I would often hear a different voice ring across the main square as we left the birdsong of the walled city. On many mornings, the first man-made sound we would hear was an uplifting, "Good morning to you all!" in the softened tones of an Irish accent of someone who has long been abroad. There are few more positive starts to a day than running into people like Brian Mulcahy and his two daughters in the early morning. Brian is one of those people who seem to be smiling even when they aren't. A smile that is ever-present, no matter how difficult it may have been to get out of the house on time that morning, or how hard the rain was falling. And while it doesn't rain here very often, when it does, it can come down hard, and it's rare in these parts to see someone as prepared for the rain as Brian and his family. Decked out in rain gear, they would always be ready to dodge the murderous umbrellas wielded by inexperienced users on the narrow sidewalks ahead.

As our kids are around the same age, we have both watched each other's youngest kids migrate from strollers to the independence of walking on their own over the years. Both our kids had certainly inherited some of our features, but what they also had inherited was our respective accents. Whether they were talking about movies or "fillums," they would interchange each other's vocabulary. In other words, mornings were simply more fun when we coincided. "Great craic," as Brian would say. The tiny English-speaking spectacle would suddenly vanish if we bumped into other kids, and our world would meld back in with our surroundings. Brian and I would be in awe at the ease with which the girls would seamlessly shift between English and Spanish, and even code-switch their conversations depending on whom they were with. For them, there was no "between worlds" or "between cultures." They were simply creating their world as they lived and experienced it.

Brian was another fellow migrant who found himself raising a family in a time and environment completely different from his own experiences. We had both slipped our own cultural moorings and were navigating waters that were at once unknown yet had begun to feel familiar before having kids and were introduced to another layer of Spanish culture. On one of those mornings, while the girls ran ahead up the Calle Pintores, I asked him about his memories of childhood. "I'm from Tipperary in Ireland. I come from a fairly typical Irish family with four kids, but what was a bit unusual for Ireland was that due to my dad's job, we moved around every four years. My childhood was fairly simple. We didn't lack anything, but there was no ostentation either. My mum basically ran the house as was typical, and her philosophy was that we should spend as much time in the fresh air as possible." I could definitely see that. I had met Brian's mum on many occasions, as she would often fly down to help out when Brian had to travel abroad for work. An energetic woman in her eighties who had no problems navigating life in Spain, even if she didn't have a strong grasp of the language. Like Brian, she knew a well-intentioned smile could go a long way, and she had two little, yet fully proficient, translators to help if needed. Our kids ran ahead even farther, and I had to quell my instinct to run after them. I asked Brian about the differences he saw between his commute to school when he was a kid and the one we now took every day.

"There was a lot of freedom, and we would have cycled country roads to school from the age of ten. I was the third of four kids, so I lived in a happy anonymity. Keep in mind, Ireland in the '80s was a grim place economically and socially, with the Catholic Church maintaining a firm influence on political policy. But we were oblivious to that situation. As I grew up in a rural area, about five miles from a small market town, life was simple and uncomplicated."

"What about school itself. What was your school like in Ireland?"

"The school I attended had two years per classroom and a really enlightened headmaster. He ensured we were exposed to a rich variety of sports, as well as getting involved in vegetable growing in the schoolyard, carpentry, butter making, and art. The GAA [Gaelic Athletic Association] was the fabric that bound Irish society together. I played hurling and Gaelic football for the local club as did anyone with any level of sporting ability in the parish."

Even if our experiences were literally oceans apart, as we talked it sounded like our schooling shared more in common than the few differences. Definitely more similar than what we had found over the years as our children have progressed through the Spanish public school system. It's an education system with very little supervision of what actually goes on inside the classrooms. A system that looks modern on paper yet is atavistic in practice. One where happenstance has more to do with whether your child will have a good, productive year than anything else. You may get lucky and have an empathetic educator, equipped with the knowledge and understanding of what education is in the twenty-first century, but you also have a chance of getting saddled with a teacher whose most innovative move in the classroom is to do the exercises in the course book in a different order from which they appear on the page. Educators whose vocation is either well past its due date, or had been beaten out of them after years of inefficient, haphazard management.

Due to the very nature of the Spanish civil service sector, it is nearly impossible to weed out those with little or no vocation who go on to torment children for their entire careers. Principals and heads of studies are basically administrative posts, and even if they do want to effect change in certain classrooms, they are close to helpless to do so once a teacher has become a fully-fledged civil servant. The moment they pass that all-important test, they become de facto emirs, with near absolute rule of their classroom taifas. Any criticism or attempts to investigate malpractice are almost always overruled by hiding behind the legal mechanism and fundamental right of academic freedom that public school teachers here enjoy. A misused protection that has an unfortunate knock-on effect on the majority of professional teachers who do have a vocation, leaving them to pick up the broken pieces their less enthusiastic colleagues leave behind. Until, that is, they too eventually burn out in resignation and a feeling of hopelessness, faced with a system incapable of recognizing and rewarding their worth.

Successive attempts have been made to right these wrongs. Wrongs that not only result in burnt-out teachers but also have led to one of the highest dropout rates on the continent. In fact, there have been no less than eight complete overhauls of the national education laws since 1980, but they have been an example of a dog chasing its own tail. In every attempt, they ignore the enormous elephant lazing in the room. You can have the most up-to-date, cutting-edge laws in the world, but if you don't source the people with the skills and management to put those laws into practice, the result is the obsolete, black and white equivalent you find in a startling number of the classrooms across the country.

School starts here at nine o'clock and we still had some time so slowed our normal pace and continued our conversation. I wanted to know what had brought Brian to Spain, and more specifically to Cáceres, so I asked how he ended up here. He flashed that smile once again and said, "I met Carolina, my future wife, in Ireland in 1994. We stayed in touch and had met up from time to time in the intervening years. I had first travelled to Spain in '94, exploring Cantabria and Asturias, and a little bit of Castilla y León. I loved it. It was completely different from the generalized Irish perception of Spain as the *costa* (coasts) or the islands.

"In '96, I travelled with friends to Portugal, and we made an excursion to Cáceres, driving over from Castelo de Vide and into Cáceres via Malpartida de Cáceres, which is a village quite close to the city. I recall we bought a watermelon from an old lady on the side of the road. Watermelons were expensive in Ireland, and we thought we had gotten a great deal until we saw the old lady had a large smile on her face as well!" Brian laughed as he looked back on how naive he was when he first arrived, knowing now old women at the markets might look harmless, but looks can be deceiving.

I asked him what he remembered about his first impressions of the city.

"We stayed in the wonderful Pensión Carretero in the Plaza Mayor where we were looked after by Carolina's *abuela* (grandmother) and *tía abuela* (great-aunt). This was when you could still park in the Plaza Mayor before the major remodelling of it. Though the cultures were completely different, both Des, my friend, and I could see many similarities between the kindness and warmth of the Spanish and Irish granny. That evening, Carolina gave us a tour of the old town, which she was immensely proud of. We were bowled over. We finished the evening with a few beers in El Corral de las Cigüeñas." Brian stopped for a moment, then stressed, "You have to realize that, for two country lads from Ireland, to be having a beer under palm trees, in stunning surroundings, in your T-shirt at nighttime was something we were very unaccustomed to! I dreamed of coming back some day, and the memories of that first exploration of Cáceres sustained me during many a dull morning driving through the Limerick traffic on my way to work in Shannon.

"We returned to Spain again in '98, travelling to Madrid and Galicia, and again marvelling at the richness of the country's heritage—our arrival in Santiago de Compostela coinciding with the big Santiago el Apóstol celebration. With each different region visited, we found a real warmth of welcome for the Irish and left with a feeling we were genuinely privileged to see and taste a Spain that most outsiders were oblivious to."

Brian looked up the street to see if he could see the kids, and when he felt comfortable continued with his story. "When having completed five years at the company where I worked, I decided to try living abroad in the year 2000 and Spain was the obvious choice. Carolina had invited me to come to Cáceres to see first-hand the Semana Santa (Holy Week) celebrations, so I got into my battered old Saab 900 in Limerick with my bike, a clunky computer, and all the books I had never read, and set off. I took the ferry from Rosslare to Le Havre in April of 2000, driving down through France and on to Spain via the Pyrenees, Burgos, Zamora, and Salamanca, arriving in Cáceres on April 16, 2000, just in time for the Semana Santa of that year."

As Brian was telling me this, Fernanda's words were ringing in my mind. The good life, the openness of the people, and the lasting friendships she had told me about were also echoed in what Brian was saying. There was definitely some sort of connection beyond religion between the Spanish and the Irish. I asked Brian what he thought it might be. "I think it's fair to say that both Ireland and Extremadura share a history characterized by long periods of economic stagnation, and there is an element of make the most of whatever fun presents itself while you can, because tomorrow will look after itself. Whether we are similar people or not, I know the overwhelming feeling from Irish people who have come to visit Cáceres is that the Spanish and the Irish get on fantastically well."

One thing was passing through a place and experiencing it from a tourist's perspective, but another was to settle down and see both the sunny and rainy days. I asked Brian about how his perspective evolved as he spent more time here. "I suppose my impressions were really my second impressions as I had been to the city briefly in 1996. In 2000, it was different as it quickly became apparent I was going to stay and try to find a job rather than just come for a holiday. I was amazed by the warmth of welcome from Carolina's family. I was never made to feel anything less than totally at home. For a city with a similar population to Limerick, where I had lived in Ireland, I was struck by how much more compact Cáceres is. In Ireland, blocks of apartments were the exception, not the norm, and whereas I could walk across Cáceres in twenty-five minutes, to do the same in Limerick would have taken three times longer. I was also very pleasantly surprised at the gentle pace of everyday life. For a city, it felt more like a village."

I was curious and asked him where he lived when he finally settled here. "I rented an apartment in the Calle Godoy, near the Iglesia de Santiago, an area that, as you know, we would come back to later to renovate an old house. It was not an area with many foreigners, so within a week the people who ran the local *multi-tienda* (corner store) and *panadería* (bakery) knew me. It was a great place to start. In the mornings I had to negotiate the daily routine of the city, trying out my faltering Spanish during interactions at the local shop, with the immigration section of the police, the town hall, the tax office. Then, in the afternoons, I had Carolina to support and encourage me and laugh off the misadventures of the morning!" He let go his inimitable laugh and said, "I recall one day early on when
I had arrived home without my keys. While waiting for the landlord to turn up with a spare set, I went into one of the local bars for a beer. The *panadero* (baker) spotted me and treated me to lunch. It was a small gesture for him, but it absolutely summed up my feelings about the *barrio* at the time. It was impossible for me to imagine the same thing happening in Limerick with the owners of the local convenience store. Here I was being accepted and welcomed into a community that looked after its own."

The Spanish job market can be remarkably inflexible, so I wondered what his first experiences were like.

"Later that summer I received my first job offer, teaching at a summer camp run by the university. I was offered that and subsequent teaching jobs by virtue of being a native speaker of English rather than any teacher training, and while I enjoyed aspects of these assignments, it was debatable who was teaching who. One virtuous side effect was that by the end of the summer I couldn't walk the streets of Cáceres without being saluted by the parents of the kids I had been teaching. It seemed to me I had more acquaintances in Cáceres after six months than I had in Limerick after twelve years."

While Brian had had to travel somewhat farther than Juanma and Fernanda to find a place that felt like home, they all shared a common sentiment I have always felt here. It's a feeling of belonging, no matter how far you may have roamed. It's a sense of generalized acceptance, and while you may never lose the sobriquet of being *el guiri*, *el irlandés*, or *el canadiense*, it is always meant as a term of endearment. Neither of us was under any illusions that if we had been from countries farther to the south that our reception would have been the same, but we could only speak from our own experience. We both felt welcomed and this made our desire to integrate ourselves into the fabric of our community even stronger. As that integration ran deeper, both of us felt it also came with a responsibility to become involved in the community. Those of us from abroad may not be able to vote and have our say in national elections, but if there is a reciprocal agreement in place with the country you are from, you can vote and be active, at least at the local level. Brian was a good example of this active participation. He had jumped in head first and had been elected to the school board, as well as being very active in the neighbourhood association.

We walked past the line of bars across the street from our kids' school with a constant stream of people slipping out of them after having grabbed a quick coffee and a second breakfast before heading back to work. Brian looked up at them, smiled, and said, "One thing for sure, my diet changed drastically. On arrival in Spain, new flavours were added— things like these *tortillas*, *embutidos*, or cured meats containing *pimentón de la Vera*. Olive oil replaced Irish butter, fresh seasonal fruit and vegetables abounded, and my diet became richer and more varied. I realized food is the real religion that truly unites all Spaniards. Carolina and her extended family introduced me to a broad spectrum of the gastronomic delights of Extremadura, and trips to Jerte, Madrid, and Cádiz in those early months just expanded that further. Fish took on a much more important role than it had in Ireland, a country that, despite being surrounded by water, has not developed a fish-eating culture." He stopped for a moment as we both waited to see if our kids would stop at the traffic light ahead and then said, "In general, the cost of produce was also much more reasonable than in Ireland. I remember the lady in the vegetable stall's surprise when I came asking for one red pepper, she, of course, assuming I wanted one kilo. At that time, nobody in Ireland went to the store for a kilo of red peppers! Then there are things like the first strawberries and the first cherries of the season that are cause for great gastronomic enjoyment. At that time, there was still a *panadería* in the Plaza de las

Canterías, and I used to get freshly baked bread, eggs, and milk in the mornings before breakfast. This all added up to a potent series of first impressions—I was completely bitten by the Spanish bug!"

Brian and his family were relative newcomers to the old town. I asked why they moved from the newer part of town. "It was always a strong wish of Carolina's and mine to live in or near the old part of town. We spent the best part of ten years searching for a place that would suit, and eventually settled on an old house that met most of the criteria we had and started the adventure of renovating it. That adventure is worth a book on its own, but suffice to say it was a more complex, drawn-out, and expensive process than we expected. We were extremely lucky to have a great architect and builder to see the project through, and to have had the help of a like-minded soul in the *ayuntamiento* (town hall) to get the building licence approved after a year of debate." Here he looked at me conspiringly, knowing I too had suffered some of these seemingly unending jouneys through red tape. He sighed and smiled. "There were some amazing discoveries, though. For example, when excavating the ground floor, they found a *lagar*, which is where grapes would have been pressed, and a *poceta*, which is where the juice would have gathered before being stored in *tinajas* (large clay jars). Through family connections we were told stories of the house being visited by children fifty years ago and used as a shortcut between Picadero and Villalobos streets. Also, through the residents' association history chats, we learned the Plaza de Picadero was so named because the animals being sold at the Plaza Mayor market would be stored there when waiting for the fair. If you look carefully at the walls outside our house, where the Calle Picadero reaches the Plaza de Santiago, you can still see the large hoops in the wall that served as hinges for large wooden gates."

I asked him how he felt once they finally got the keys to the house. "Our feeling after the process was that, given the large number of run-down houses in the old part of Cáceres, the town hall should be actively helping those interested in renovation for family homes to bring new people to this area. When we finally finished the renovation, we had the real pleasure of having the best Cáceres has to offer just a few minutes' walk from home: the old town, the Plaza Mayor, the Filmoteca, the Gran

Teatro, local convenience stores, the Iglesia de Santiago, a fantastic set of neighbours, and the reinvigorated residents' association, thanks to Juanma. We were welcomed from day one and have witnessed the positive development of this part of town. Our days are regimented by the bells of Santiago, a church that bears the scars of the great Lisbon earthquake of 1755, an earthquake whose wash created an island opposite where my parents live on the west coast of Clare over two thousand miles away—connections."

We crossed the street to the island that runs up the middle of the avenue and merged with others who were also accompanying their children to school. I asked him if they had any regrets about moving to the old town. Brian's eternal optimism wasn't blind. He confessed, "Of course, challenges remain. Things like parking and traffic are a constant source of conflict. We all know about the well-documented problems with the water supply. The pipes are way past their expiry date and are made of lead and need to be changed, but the question is who is going to foot the bill? Then there is the fact it has taken a long time to get good internet in the barrio, but this is improving, and we would not change our location within the city. Perhaps the most worrying thing is the prospect of an open-cast mine a short distance from the city. That is definitely a dark cloud on the horizon. I've lived in towns with mines much farther away and seen the decades-long saga of environmental damage they can leave, without a way to get proper recompense. I hope the powers that be in Extremadura think long and hard about the consequences before going down this route."

The schools in Cáceres were mostly designed and thought of before each and every family had one car, let alone two. There was no "drop-off" area available. For those unable or perhaps unwilling to walk their kids to school, every morning became a desperate dash to find an open slice of curbside where they could safely drop their kids off. Chatting groups of pedestrian parents spilled out onto the busy main street, making the scene slightly chaotic. "You know," Brian said, "as the years pass by, you gain different perspectives, and particularly when you have kids. Things like your circle of friends changes and you get to experience things in a different country from inside, things like the educational system and the model that society has for bringing up kids. There's a lot to debate there and you and I have long talked about it. But one thing I'm acutely aware of is that, as I haven't experienced that process in other countries, it's totally possible the perception I have of the advantages of the Irish system may be nostalgia getting the better of me. As you watch your kids grow, memories of your own experiences of childhood come to you frequently and you realize a lot of what you have in your head has been passed through a rose-tinted filter."

I knew exactly what he meant. I had lived abroad for more than half my life and I was no longer exactly sure where I was from. The places in between had begun to overlap and blend into each other. People often asked me about how certain things are done back in Canada. I then would have to make my way through the tangle of more than half a life's worth of memories to remember. Memories that were supposedly etched in stone, but in a language I had forgotten. Some things would be as clear as yesterday, while others acquired the patina of an aging photograph. A blurring that meant I often had to colour in the missing gaps in my memories. Jazz-like improvisations that might make for a better story, at least one that is more colourful, but a tainting that definitely calls their veracity into doubt.

We crossed the last street and when we reached the green gates of the school, our kids hoisted up their ridiculously heavy backpacks Brian and I had been carrying and ran off together. This was their place. This was their present, where they were growing up today. Not only was this place a world away from what both Brian and I had known, but it was also an entirely different era. While I could have only dreamed of running among Almohad castles when I was their age, the mobile phones that half of the parents around us stared down into would have seemed even more unrealistic or impossible to me. Back in our neighbourhood, we may be surrounded by monumental elements of the past, but here in the newer part of the city, the now, their now, is also very present. Brian saw my smile and, seemingly reading my mind, said, "The world our kids are growing up in is a million miles from the world we grew up in, in every aspect. I can remember my mum telling us about rural electrification in Ireland, and the fact that her aunt refused to install sockets in her house, choosing only light bulbs. After all, what would you want a socket for!? I have no doubt my kids have the same reaction when I explain there was just one channel on the TV in Ireland when I was a kid. Maybe all we can aspire to is to capture their imagination with our stories and ensure that some of the thread of experience and knowledge, and maybe a little wisdom that has been passed down to us, can be carried forward on their life journey to be passed forward to the next generations in time."

Adarve del Cristo in the old town of Cáceres near the Arco del Cristo Roman arch.

LEAPS OF FAITH

7

"OH MY! That is deeper than I had expected...considerably deeper." It looked like a surgical knife had been scraped down the exposed, scarred side of our house and made a sharp incision deep into the earth. The old house now seemingly teetered on a precipice. The trussed beam that spanned the gap was now its sole reprieve. I had just stepped into the street when I bumped into the chief archeologist who was overseeing the excavation next door. She smiled at my remark and quickly answered, "History around here runs deep."

We had been living in the house for years and the lot next door remained empty. Time passed and tiny hairline cracks raced just a little bit farther across our ceiling every year. We wondered if anyone was ever going to buy the vacant lot, build a house, and shore up our lonely wall. Every now and then we would hear the screech of the rusting blue iron door that was set in the temporary wall that had been built after the demolition. People would come, look at the property, dream of what they could do. They would then have their dreams smashed when they discovered that the red tape they would have to endure before laying the first brick was considerably longer than the arch that ran above the lot. If you consider that bureaucracy in Spain can at times be excessive, rebuilding a house in a protected UNESCO core is exponential in comparison. The screeching door would then slam shut once again, leaving the spray-painted "for sale" sign to continue fading under the Spanish sun.

There were times when the empty lot came in handy. One night, during a particularly strong storm, we were suddenly awoken by the sound of rushing water. In our sleepy fog, we slowly realized the water wasn't only falling outside our window but was cascading down from the ceiling above our bed. The message was clear: the patchwork repairs we had undertaken weren't enough. It was finally time to replace the ancient, undulating roof. That summer, the jinxed owners of the lot graciously gave us permission to use the space as a warehouse for all the material, while at the same time becoming an impromptu exploring ground for our young daughters in the nooks and crannies around the orange tree. A kind gesture that made it unnecessary to go through the hassle of asking for permission from the town hall to cut the road.

There was also another time the lot helped me save face, if not risk my neck. One day, as I rushed out the door, I heard it click behind me and immediately realized I had left my keys in the lock. Normally, this wouldn't be a problem, but our door can't be opened from the outside if the keys are in the lock on the inside. Worse yet, this wasn't the first time I had done this. The first time, which happened to be a rainy Christmas Eve, meant we had to call a rather expensive locksmith who ended up having to drill a hole through our treasured, handmade wooden door to let us, and Santa, in. A repeat performance of that disaster was definitely not what I was looking for.

As I was pacing in front of the house weighing up my options, my neighbour asked what was the matter. Our neighbour Manolo is a friendly grandfather who spends a lot of time outside his compact, ground-floor flat. Whether he's smoking or taking advantage of the open air and light, I often find him sitting on a stool in the street, using the defensive wall as a backrest while reading a book. I quickly told him what had happened while I unconsciously looked up at the three-metre enclosure wall that ran between Teresa's house and ours. Squinting up against the sun, Manolo asked, "Don't you have a patio that gives on to the lot?" I stopped going over the trouble I had got myself into just long enough to reply, "Yes we do, Manolo, but what are we going to do about that?" I pointed to the wall. "*Bueno*, we just need to get up there and then we're in, no problem!" Manolo enthusiastically replied. I thought about it for a moment and said, "Even if we can somehow get up the wall, what do we do once we're up there? It's more than a three-metre drop down onto a hard concrete slab." Manolo laughed and said, "That's no problem. I'm used to heights."

It was true. Despite his age, I had often seen Manolo up on the roof of the three-story block of flats he lives in, fixing the Arabic tiles. Once I had even seen him hoisting an air-conditioning unit up there with a make-shift pulley, all without any trace of safety gear. Just as I was about to answer, my neighbour on the corner Pablo walked up and asked what was going on. Pablo, a charming man with gentle manners who is a local building engineer who had helped me keep track of the advancing cracks in our ceiling, is the kind of neighbour you can always count on. If you run out of milk or need someone to water your plants while you're on holiday, he's your man. I explained what had happened and asked him if he had any ideas. "Manolo's right. If we can get over the wall, we should be able to access your patio if I remember correctly." At this, Manolo assured us, "I'm telling you, it's not a problem. After all, it's not the fall that is so important. It's all about how you land!" At this, he jumped up and simulated a hard landing, crouching down and rolling to mitigate the impact, all the while holding his cigarette tightly in his mouth. Impressive as it was, I wasn't convinced. Not only was I dreading admitting to my wife I had done it again, I couldn't even imagine what she would say if we let a man twenty years my senior plummet down from a three-metre wall in a botched attempt to fix my mistake.

We had to think about how we were going to get over the wall that mirrored the Almohad defensive wall just opposite it. "I have a ladder in the garage," Pablo said, "but I don't think it's going to be high enough." With that, Pablo walked over to his garage and brought out the step-ladder he had and, sure enough, it only reached about halfway up the wall. "We need to boost it up with something," Manolo assured us. While it didn't sound like the safest plan of action, he was right. "I think I have an old table in the garage," Pablo said. "It just might work." He emerged from his garage once again, this time with an end table that was around a metre high, just about the height we needed, even if it was somewhat wobbly. We set the table next to the wall, then placed the ladder on top of it. It looked like it would just about reach the upper reaches of the wall. Manolo got ready to hop up on the table when I said, "But wait, even if we get up there, how are we going to get down on the other side? And then there's the drop down into our patio. That also has to be at least three metres." At that, Pablo remembered, "Hang on, I've got that thick rope we've used before." I recalled the rope he was talking about. His house on the corner, like ours, has seen many generations of different families. The twists and turns that have evolved over the years make it difficult to move large pieces of furniture from one place to another, not to mention in and out of the house. On more than one occasion, we had hoisted large pieces of furniture in and out of his balcony window from the street below. If the rope could handle huge chests of drawers, it could probably hold my increasing middle-aged girth. While Pablo went to get the rope, I explained to Manolo that I couldn't, in good conscience, let him go up the ladder. This was my problem and I needed to fix it, and besides, we needed someone to steady the unsteady table and ladder. That and get help if something were to go wrong.

Rope in hand, I still wasn't sure how we were going to get down the other side. Pablo had made it clear he was coming with me no matter what, but I thought, even if we could find somewhere to secure the rope and then lower ourselves down, what would we do then? We needed the rope to get down into my patio too. We discussed the various options and decided we would go over the wall and, once on the other side, pile up the rubble that had been left in the lot high enough to reach the rope and untie. And if that didn't work, we'd have to admit defeat, which would mean going back up the rope and calling the locksmith.

With Manolo holding the shaky table and ladder, I climbed up the wall and thought about how all this would look if someone were to come along. Here were two solidly middle-aged men climbing up a ladder set atop a rickety table, with a retired man holding it all together below. The perfect heist it certainly wasn't. I could see the tabloid headline: "Foreign Man Suffers Fatal Fall while Breaking into His Own House." But I knew we weren't doing anything wrong—at least not technically. The owners of the property had given me permission to enter the lot and even encouraged me to have a look around every once in a while to make sure things were okay. The problem was the key they had given me to the blue door was with my set hanging on the other side of my locked door.

Once on top of the wall, I found some rebar sticking out of the makeshift wall and used my best fishing-line knot to secure it. I then awkwardly rappelled down the wall onto a pile of dirt that was conveniently piled halfway up the other side. Once Pablo had done the same, we began looking around the lot to see what we could use to pile up to untie the rope. Just as we began searching, a silver head popped over the top of the wall. It was Manolo. "Don't think I'm going to let you both have all the fun! Here, let me untie the rope." And with that he threw the rope down to us.

There were some stairs next to the orange tree that led up to a kind of storage room that gives on to the wall that separates the lot from our patio. It's a set of rooms that is embedded into the lofty wall of the monastery that overlooks our properties. I climbed up the stairs and up onto the sixty-centimetre-thick wall and looked down into my patio. In all the excitement, there was one last thing I hadn't thought of. What if the patio door was also locked? It really depended on who was the last to close it. While I usually leave it open, my wife almost always locks it. Even if I managed to get down into the patio safe and sound, a locked door would mean having to break the window and therefore negate the savings of not calling the locksmith. The entire mission would have been for nothing.

The drop was farther than the previous one, and the landing was littered with plant pots and other odds and ends that would make a fall even more dangerous. Pablo suggested lowering me down, as Sancho had lowered Don Quixote into Montesinos's cave, but I knew there was no nook in the wall to rest in on the way down. He was partly right, though— this was my Monte de Sinos (Mount of Fate) and I resolved to rappel down as before. There are some iron bars encrusted into the wall that barricade our bedroom window, and I secured the rope to them. I had always hated them and didn't mind the thought of ripping them out of the wall. That said, I didn't exactly relish any ensuing consequences were that to happen. As I slipped over the side, I kept repeating Manolo's words to myself like a mantra: "It's not the fall that really matters, it's all about how you land."

After what seemed like an eternity, with the rope burning my hands, I felt my foot strike hard ground amid the pots. I had made it. I looked up at Pablo and he shouted, "Now don't fall asleep like Don Quixote!" I walked over to the patio door and hesitantly placed my hand on the door handle and pushed down. It clicked; the door was open. Manolo had been right all along, no problem.

| I cautiously approached the fluttering red and white tape that ran between the two houses that flanked the hole. In front of me was an approximately 120-square-metre (four-hundred-square-feet) excavation site, complete with people in PPE so as not to contaminate any potential find. I got closer to the edge and looked down onto the series of trenches cut beside our house. "How deep did you dig down?" I nervously asked the architect as I envisioned fine cracks running across our ceiling widening into something much larger and more serious. "Oh, just over three metres," she nonchalantly replied. "Just down to where the Roman period begins." And there, down below in the reddish clay, I could clearly make out perfectly formed quadriform stone walls that would have once made up different rooms. From above, it looked like the outline of a miniature city. "Have you found anything interesting?" I asked. "Well, it depends on your definition of interesting, I suppose. If you mean any major discovery, no. But it's not every day we get the chance to have a look under the hood of buildings in inhabited UNESCO cores. This was a rare opportunity to shed a bit more light on what life was like over the centuries next to the defensive wall. If you look closely, you can easily see the three dividing lines as you travel up the stones. There at the bottom are the Roman foundations, then as you go farther up you can see the Islamic period, and as you get closer to ground level you can see the Middle Ages begin."

Even to my very untrained eye, you could see a perceptible change in the style the higher you went. These uncovered stones told the layers of the stories of the people who have lived here. I also understood what she meant by getting a unique chance to "look under the hood" of these homes. I had often heard taxi-driver tales about people in cities like

Toledo or nearby Mérida, the ancient Roman capital of the peninsula just eighty kilometres away. Stories of people who were undertaking some minor renovations in their homes only to lift up some flooring and to their surprise uncover a Roman mosaic or an Islamic burial ground underneath their feet. Rather than go through the potentially long process that having these excavated would entail, or worse yet, perhaps even having their property expropriated, many choose to quietly retile the floor and pretend nothing ever happened. What happened underfoot stays underfoot.

"So what happens next?" I enquired, still thinking about those cracks in my ceiling. "Well, we need to finish up the dig, but that shouldn't take much longer. We have basically excavated the whole area between your house and your neighbour Teresa's. We'll take pictures and catalogue everything, then if nothing extraordinary turns up, we will fill in the site with gravel and the story ends there. Well, not exactly," she chuckled as she lowered herself back down into the site. "The stories you can imagine down here don't stop at your wall. Just imagine what lies beneath your house."

Someone had finally bought the lot under the metals bars jutting out from our house. The street was going to regain its natural appearance. The wall would once again have its contiguous opposite. No matter how long and inconvenient the process, the wound was at last going to heal. "And that's when the odyssey started," Puri, my new neighbour, confessed as she gathered her thoughts, looking past me and out the large windows overlooking the wall and valley beyond. "The odyssey with the town hall, I mean until it finally granted us the licence to build. The whole process, from buying the empty lot, to getting permission, to completing the archeological survey, to actually building the house took over three years."

Puri, her partner Rafa, and I were sitting in their open-plan living room that opens out onto an ultra-modern kitchen that now stands on the first floor of the house they built. I was curious to hear their tale and what had brought them to the old city. Puri continued, "It cost us more than our share of tears." Rafa jumped in, "It was indeed a process, a traumatic process, really. Because first of all, it's the owner, it's you who has to pay for the archeologist and the work carried out by the team." I laughed and told Rafa about my encounter with the archeologist as we looked down into the pit. He seemed reassured by my story and continued, "It's the archeologists who determine when the excavation and work is complete. It's as if you sign a blank cheque because the archeologists' work can take a week, a month, three months, or a year. Then, if they find something important, of course everything stops *sine die*. All of this at the owner's expense, not the city council's."

Puri took up her former thought. "Tears...and prayers. Prayers that they didn't find anything! Honestly, it was difficult for us. Keep in mind there are so many layers of civilizations beneath us to go through. Then, to top it all off, when they initially gave us the licence to start, they 'forgot' to tell us we needed to do an archeological survey before starting construction." It was hard to believe that after having to wait so long such an important detail had been overlooked. Spanish bureaucracy can indeed be slow, but it tends to be thorough, exceedingly so in many cases. Apparently, not this time. "Anyways," Puri said, "as we hadn't been properly informed, we began the construction, and it really seemed to start off well until, someone, we don't know who, either said something to the town hall or directly filed a complaint against us." At this, Rafa exclaimed, "It was even in the paper! Something about construction starting in the Adarve, but really without much detail." Puri went on. "So then the archeologist from the town hall came by and told us he would oversee the necessary excavation but warned that, if anything turned up, we would then have to hire our own archeologist. And turn up, things did.

"Obviously, it depends on your criteria of 'remains.' These remains were, at least in the words of the man leading the construction, minor. I remember him saying, 'We find things like this every day up in my village of Ceclavín. I can't tell you how many bowls and stuff like this we have thrown away. Don't you worry. If we find something, when the archeologist is looking the other way, I'll get rid of it.' Andrea, the archeologist we hired and who you met, was good at her job and was very meticulous, but it took a long time. Then, in December, it started to rain and we had to put everything on pause once again. Reinforcements had to be raised so your house and Teresa's wouldn't be affected. It was an odyssey I tell you, an authentic odyssey."

As Andrea had told me when we looked down into the excavation, their stories were indeed our stories. We shared what lie dormant beneath our houses. I asked, "What did they find in the end?" Puri looked relieved. "Well, there was some polychromatic painting, shards of pottery, coins, and things like that, but thankfully nothing major." Rafa added, "Underneath where we are sitting, there were houses inhabited over generations, in richer times and poorer times, sometimes a single family, or sometimes multi-families occupying the same space. I imagine the way people lived depended on what the economic situation was at the time. There was one thing I really liked, though. A kind of arch that appeared during the excavation. It was a brick arch that must have come from some kind of cellar or cistern, but you couldn't really tell. It was completely destroyed and all covered by dirt. Then, next to the wall leading towards the street, they found what seemed to be the remains of a stairway that led downwards. You couldn't distinguish exactly what it was, but you could see a red colour and a blue colour, as if it had been painted with something. If you continued excavating in the street, something that would correspond to the town hall, you'd probably get a better idea of what it was. The town hall even admitted to us that when it had last done work in the street, it didn't do an archeological survey. Which means it has two different criteria. One for when it is paying, and a completely different one when it isn't." Puri smiled and drew a line in the air with her hand. "The archeologists told us this paint probably belonged to an aristocratic home that ran from Pablo's house on the corner, past yours, and all the way up to the nun's garage where the street turns left. They knew this from the colour of the paint, which was apparently used by a painter who must have been famous and who painted the houses of patricians down in Mérida, capital of the peninsula during Roman times."

Rafa had the situation quite clear in his mind. "You have to think that living within the defensive walls demonstrates a certain economic level for a Roman or someone during medieval times. During times of uncertainty or war, it would have been a good place to be. The more towards the centre you were, that is, the more towards the centre of the old area, the more protected you were. Up higher, where the palaces were, was a sign of wealth. As you got closer to the Adarve and the defensive wall, let's say the poorer you were. It's like saying, well, it was all luxury urbanization, but there were richer and poorer people, and here along the wall were surely the poorest of the rich. Then there were those who were on the outside; people at the mercy of any conquest or any assault of that type."

Despite the impediments, their lovely home now attests to their perseverance. But what was the source of this determination when faced with so many obstacles? Puri was the first to reply: "Rafa and I have known each other for over twenty years. We come from two different cities and two different worlds." To which Rafa quickly added, "We're both very distinct, like two contradictions together. I'm from Madrid, and I work in commercial engineering, which gives me a certain advantage. My job allows me a lot of freedom. That is, I don't have a set schedule. I have to adjust to certain objectives at given times, together with trips and meetings, but outside of that I can organize my life wherever and however I want." Puri then shared her story. "I was born in Ávila, and when I was two our family moved to Valladolid, where I was raised. I studied medicine and also did my specialty there. Now I'm a clinical microbiologist. My first placement was up in the northwestern corner of Extremadura in Coria, where I lived and worked for ten years. Then I was transferred to Cáceres in 2005."

Her story was like that of all the civil servants in the country. Human driftwood floating on the whimsical current of the public administration that could spit you out just about anywhere, often with very little warning. You could get lucky and end up in a place you wanted to be or that you liked, but the opposite was equally possible. Like teachers, every public servant, from judges and prosecutors, to police officers, veterinarians, and especially health care workers like Puri, has no real say in determining where their future lies. Their lives depend entirely on how high they score on the list of available jobs. Their position on this list is determined by an alchemistic scale that evaluates each candidate on just about everything—minus skill and actual know-how.

"Ever since we moved to Cáceres, we have lived in the old town," Rafa said. "It always struck me as such an interesting place. Before this house, we lived in the Plaza de la Audiencia, but even though that is the old

town, it is outside the walls and I had always wanted to live inside them."
Here Rafa laughed. "As I mentioned, I'm from Madrid, but if you go back
to my grandparents, they were from the Logrosán area here in
Extremadura. My father told stories of spending summers there as a boy,
but that bond broke long ago. So we ended up here because of work, precisely Puri's work, and I followed. Puri's two conditions for a house were:
1) that it had a patio, and 2) that it was inside the wall. Even though I followed
along in her wake, perhaps because she tried to look for the advantages of
the situation, I have since become aware of them too."

He picked up the various papers and documents they had collected
about buying the house and set them down again and said, "At first look,
it seems like somewhat of an uncomfortable place because you don't have
the facilities of a modern urbanization with wide avenues where you can
park wherever you want. But for me, there is this kind of sensation,
better yet two sensations I feel here. Whenever I come back from Madrid
or from Portugal, where we also have a house, the first thing I feel is the
sensation of eternity, and the second is of isolation. It seems that, even if
the news tells us things are going wrong in Madrid, about politics, or if
the Catalans are causing troubles, it seems as if we are in a bubble here
where nothing can happen to us. Of course, something can happen to us,
but it is just a sensation, a feeling I get here."

Rafa stopped for a second to collect his thoughts. Like Puri, he also
gazed out the window across to the sanctuary. "When the COVID lockdown began here in Spain, or actually just before it, I remember I was in
Madrid. The government hadn't announced it yet, but I saw it was going
to close down the country. I'm talking around March 10, 11, or 12, in 2020,
I can't remember exactly. My automatic reaction was to grab all the essen-
tials I was going to need, without knowing how long it was going to last,
jump in the car, and come here. That was it; my survival instinct took
over and brought me home." He shrugged his shoulders. "Now that I
think about it, it was definitely that, survival. It was a search for a refuge
that took me here. Of course, Puri was also here, but it wasn't only her.
There was something like that bubble sensation, that sensation that, as
Puri has said, so many civilizations have lived behind these walls. The old
town of Cáceres has been here for what, two thousand or more years? It

has continued to last. But then I think of a residential area in Madrid that was built fourteen years ago. Sure, it's full of cute little chalets, but that doesn't mean they will last. Maybe that's why I unconsciously made the decision to come here."

I could tell Puri appreciated what Rafa was saying. She said, "One of the biggest reasons we are here is because of Teresa, our neighbour. Like you, while I was looking for a place, I used to walk around until I finally came across the empty lot. The first time I arranged to see it, I came with a friend who happens to be an artist, a painter. She really liked it and was convinced we would have so much space and light. She was also sure the views would be spectacular. But the thing is, down on the street you could only imagine what you would be able to see. Teresa, as you know, sees everything that goes on in the street and came down to help me decide. She invited my friend and me up to her place so we could have a look. It might seem silly, but I like little details. Details, and of course that spectacular view."

It was getting late and it was time to go, but before I left I asked them both if they would do it all over again. Puri didn't hesitate. "If I'm able to forget all the incidences and grief we went through, yes. As I was saying before, you feel like you are transported to another time, or that many civilizations have passed through here, and you always have this in mind. But also here you live like you are in a small town but which is, in fact, within a city. You do things you would in a town, like say 'good morning' to people as you walk by. Then there is the fact you can simply walk everywhere. Advantages definitely outweigh the inconveniences." Rafa was equally quick to answer. "I have discovered things I wasn't expecting to find, and I really like that. When the lockdown happened, I could have chosen elsewhere and didn't. That is, in a situation of almost extreme survival, so to speak, I didn't think twice. Let me tell you a story. One time while we were building the house, we were over across the valley walking up the mountain. I don't know if you've been there, but there is this bench where it claims you have the best views of the city. To tell you the truth, the views of the city from over there are much more beautiful than the ones we have here of the mountain, because it is a view of a UNESCO city. Granted, from here we see the mountain and it is beautiful, but the houses built up on the other side are a bit chaotic. Anyways, while we were sitting, I turned to Puri and said maybe we had made a mistake. Maybe we should have bought a house on this side of the valley. She came back straight away and asked, 'Who would you rather be? The one who's beautiful, or the one who might get a chance to see her?'"

The Concatedral de Santa María in the Plaza de Santa María
in the old town of Cáceres.

LEAVE THE
LIGHTS ON

8

I AWOKE ONE MORNING IN MID-JULY to something out of place. It was an anomalous silence. The birds that had made their home in the bushy bougainvillea that crept up the monastery wall behind the house were hushed. The pre-dawn scandal they had been raising since they began building their nests was now noticeably absent. But it wasn't only the silence; there was something else. Under the spinning blades of the ceiling fan, I became aware of something altogether different as I lay on the sparse summer bed sheets. It was the smell of moisture. It wasn't the petrichor that comes off the steppe that surrounds the city as storms approach in the fall, but after weeks of consecutive temperatures in the high thirties, the slightly damp air felt like a cool shower. I looked out the window and was surprised to see a blanket of fog blotting out the sanctuary that topped the mountain across the valley. It was a scene that is often repeated during the winter months but not one you'd expect mid-summer. Judging by the generalized silence, everything else was also enjoying this momentary respite from the heat over the long summer months. The bell from Santa María up the hill broke the spell. It was nine o'clock and today I was meeting someone who knew the story of the city inside and out. Someone who had been welcoming travellers to the region for the past twenty-plus years. Someone who could do so in six different languages.

I met Marco Mangut at his beautifully renovated old home on the very edge of the protected area of what is considered the old city. Just one street over, lines of cyborg-like homes take over that look like a 3D printer spit them out. Functional, practical, and soulless. He led me up to the terrace, literally cut out of the roof, that looks out across the summer-burnt, undulating steppe that hides the Tamuja and Almonte rivers in its folds. In the far distance, the high mountains of the Sierra de Gredos added a deep blue to the background of the scene. The morning's haze had long ago burned off and the afternoon was now warm but bearable. I asked Marco what had made him decide to move to the area. "Look, I've always lived in Pinilla, which is the neighbourhood right next door. In fact, the Iglesia de San Blás, right next to my house, is where my parents got married, where they baptized me, where I made my first communion, and where the funerals of a good part of my family have been. My family had all always lived in that neighbourhood, but when I was ten years old in '85 my father decided to buy a place in Moctezuma." He slid his chair back to get out of the sun and looked over the cookie-cutter homes and said, "Back then, Moctezuma was a neighbourhood on the very edge of the other side of the city. When I turned twenty-five, if I'm not mistaken, in the year 2000, I decided to move out and live on my own. I had started working. Then I had money to buy a house and bought a small apartment in Nuevo Cáceres. That was even farther from the centre at that time, and I stayed there for something like five years. Then, in 2005, we moved again due to the work of my partner at the time."

Marco finished the last of his water and reached over to the jug to refill our glasses. "He was an English teacher, and he taught at home. Keep in mind, we lived in an apartment with one room and a living room...and, of course, while he was teaching either I would have to go to the kitchen, the bedroom, or sometimes even sit on the toilet bowl or leave the house. So, seeing we needed space, we started looking for a house. I have always liked the centre and the monumental area. Here, in fact, is the last line of houses of the special plan of the UNESCO zone. From here down is the 'normal' Cáceres, let's put it like that. Then I found this house that had been renovated by a young couple with two children and I fell in love with it."

I asked him if he had put much work into the place. "So I bought it in 2005, but the house was not as you see it now. It was only on the ground floor. Then, in 2017, we had to do serious renovations. The roof was collapsing and we had to replace it. Well, it wasn't exactly collapsing, but it had started to seriously sink and it started springing leaks. It also didn't have any insulation, so we died of heat in summer and then from the cold in winter."

A stork glided overhead, returning from its foraging out on the steppe. We both watched it disappear into the old town. Marco continued, "We got started on the project that was supposed to last four months that ended up being nine. During that time we had to empty the house. Of course, if you raise the roof, everything would have been left in the open and exposed to the elements. So we temporarily moved to a flat here, opposite the hermitage of Saint Blaise, to be close to the site. The truth is it is a house built to receive company. We wanted large spaces because there are always guests. Yesterday, just where you are sitting, there were people having lunch. The day before yesterday, another five people, and the day before that, eight. So you see what I mean, it's almost like a hotel."

Marco, like Juanma, Fernanda, Brian, Rafa, and Puri had all made an active choice to move to the area, even if their respective reasons differed slightly. I asked him what advantages he found living there. "Well, of course, I'm five minutes from work. I like old houses more than modern ones. I can't say exactly why, but I'm attracted to them. Then I saw this house. I saw flats in the modern area as well, but I don't know, when I saw this house...I liked it. And that's it, really. I fell in love with it and bought it."

When VIPs come to visit the city, Marco is often the first person they contact to show them the city, not only for his facility with languages but for his enthusiasm for his work and how well-versed he is in its history. I asked him how he got his start in the business. "Well, I wouldn't say it was by chance, because it really is something I have always liked, but perhaps the biggest reason is my father was a guide before me. Ever since I can remember, I recall walking with my father on tours through the monumental city. It's something I have internalized since I was very little. I tagged along with my father on visits because I loved them. I liked listening to him, but another thing was I also got to know the people who came on visits."

The sun had shifted and once again he moved his chair to escape its afternoon rays. He smiled. "Imagine, a provincial kid back in the 1980s, meeting people from places like Argentina, or from Costa Rica, or from France. For me it was very exotic. I enjoyed being with people, talking to them, and really that's where it all began. Because of my love of this profession, I decided to study geography and history, half in Cáceres and the other half in Scotland. I finished my degree in June 1999, and in July that same year exams were held to get certified in Extremadura to become a guide. I had about a month to prepare for the test and it was great. I got my guide card on my first try. To be honest, it didn't seem extremely difficult to me either, but, of course, I had been listening to my father my whole life."

Between his time accompanying his father and his own professional life, Marco had witnessed first-hand the growth of the tourism industry in the area over the past forty years. His testimony to the changes that had taken place over the years was unmediated and personal. Tourism and travellers of any type have a direct effect on the places they move through. Since Ibn Battuta witnessed the crumbling of the Islamic empire here in Spain, to the influx of the bikini-clad Scandinavians that brought about deep social changes down on the Spanish *costas*, travellers have always left a mark. For better or for Magaluf-all-inclusive-worse.

I was curious about how Marco perceived the evolution of the tourism industry over these past four decades. "My father started in the late 1960s or early 1970s, and he was one of the first guides in the city. He had studied French at the official language school in Madrid, because there was no language school here at that time, and, well, having a powerful second language enabled you to become, as what was called before, an information and tourism guide. For him it was not really his main career as it is mine. For him it was a complement to his main job, which was first as a teacher and then as a sports announcer on the radio." It made sense. Marco's smooth, powerful voice reminded me of my own father, who was also a DJ on the radio back in Canada. I told him, "I understand why he must have migrated to the radio, if his voice is anything like yours. It's a perfect fit." Marco nodded his head and said, "Well, they say my voice is very similar to my father's. In fact, callers still confuse us on the phone. Anyways, he started by doing radio shows, playing music, and finally he ended up on the popular radio station belonging to the COPE chain. He was a sportscaster for the rest of his life until he retired. All of this helped me to travel. I travelled with my father and the local basketball team on the bus from Cáceres in the '80s. I remember when the team was in the third division and played in towns all over Extremadura."

I now knew his father's story, but I wanted to know more about the changes in the profiles of the tourists Marco had seen over the years. I wanted to know who visited the city in the past and who was coming now and what their motives were. "It's hard for me to say about my father's time," Marco said. "Remember, for me, it was just all very exotic. If I remember well, they were groups with a lot of money. These were the people who could afford to travel back then. My father worked with a company—I remember it was called Pullmantur—and it arranged tours for people with a lot of spending power. Guiding for my father was an incredible bonus. I believe even if tourism was temporary and not his 'main' job, it's possible he earned more guiding than he earned working on the radio. This is because the rates were quite high at that time and tourism was much more exclusive than now." He shook his head at the thought and added, "Tourism simply wasn't as widespread as it is today; it wasn't so easy to travel. If it's difficult to get to Cáceres now, imagine what it was like back then!" With this exclamation, he raised both his hands to his head to stress and underline how frustrated he was with the situation.

"I do remember when I first started out, tourism here was a very weekend or long weekend kind of tourism. I'm talking about 1999, 2000, 2001. During the week, there was practically nothing, but ever since then growth has been exponential. Now, from around February 28, which is the day of Andalusia, which is like the official start of the annual tourist campaign, until the December long weekend, we are busy. Now tourism is much more generalized. There is much more foreign tourism than before, but that said, it doesn't even make up 20 per cent of the total. The great majority of our visitors are nationals, and, curiously, both the 2007 crisis and the COVID crisis have favoured us. Firstly, because it hasn't been possible to travel outside of Spain, and, secondly, we don't depend so much on the English or the Germans as they do down on the Mediterranean or out on the islands. In other words, the crises here have been good times for tourism here. Paradoxical, isn't it?"

It was that 20 per cent that aroused my curiosity. National tourists are at least somewhat familiar with Cáceres and Extremadura after having seen them listed on the national weather forecasts their whole lives. But who made up this 20 per cent, and what brought them so far off the well-beaten *paella* path that runs along the coasts? "Tell me more about the foreigners that make it out here, Marco. After all, you speak six languages, Spanish, Portuguese, English, French, Italian, and German, right? You must deal with your fair share?" He laughed. "Look, one of the most curious profiles of foreign tourists I have are foreigners who have a second residence in Spain. Those who live on the Costa del Sol or on the coast of Alicante or out on Mallorca. People who maybe twenty years ago spent six months in England and six months in Torrevieja or Torremolinos, and that was their vacation. Now they are keen on getting to know the interior of Spain and are increasingly interested in leaving the coast. And during their months in Spain, they are interested in learning about the interior as much or more than the rest of the tourists who come directly from abroad."

I often see Marco with different groups in the old town, speaking his Tower of Babel of languages, and asked him to describe the traveller that made it out this far.

"The cultural level of these visitors is very high. Imagine someone who comes here from Holland, from Sweden, from California, or from Argentina. This is someone who has travelled a lot. I mean, obviously you have to be realistic. The person who makes it out to Extremadura is not your first-time traveller. Recreational travellers rarely explore beyond the Madrid, Barcelona, Seville, Córdoba, Granada, and Toledo circuit. It's the same as those who go to the United States. They visit New York, Miami, and Los Angeles and skip the fly-over states. Or what about your home, Canada? A city like Edmonton? How many tourists go beyond Toronto, Montreal, Quebec, Vancouver, and maybe the Rockies?

"So these travellers, especially the European tourists, tend to be people who are very attracted to culture and gastronomy, which I think is one of our strongest points. Then there is the nature issue. We have more and more tourists interested in parks and ornithology who come specifically for Monfragüe National Park." He gestured out towards the mountains in the distance. "Then there are many who want to combine both, culture with nature."

I pass by these groups every day as I go about my day-to-day business and always try to listen in to what they are saying as they tour the city. In fact, I often come across Marco with groups and have always admired his ability to improvise. I remember one evening coming home from work and hearing him say, "The monumental city is actually a very quiet place and not many people live here." Then, as I passed by, he quickly added, "Except, of course, for Canadians like him." Needless to say, it drew a laugh from the group.

"What do your groups find most surprising about their visit to the city?"

"The truth is the surprise factor is less and less because there is a lot of access to information and people tend to arrive somewhat informed. But I remember, not so many years ago, when we would enter the monumental city and stop in the middle of Santa María square, how the people were literally shocked. The typical phrase I would hear was, 'I was not expecting this.' But this would happen even among Spaniards, though as I say, with today's access to information it happens less. But even still, it does happen and among foreigners more so."

When Marco said this, something came to me. In an age when the internet is awash with beautiful yet empty-feeling pictures of places on sites like Instagram, there was more and more reason to actually go out and talk to people, to hear the voices and stories of those who live among those gorgeous, filtered photographs. I told Marco one of my aims was to give a voice-over to what people were seeing, to somehow caption them with people's day-to-day life. I apologized for interrupting and Marco continued, "It's a very typical Spanish city, so different from the places where they come from. We are talking about countries where the main constructions are all made of wood. Seeing so many solid, robust stone buildings...the truth is they like what we have to offer, and they like it very much. There are areas in Spain that have lost that essence and authenticity due to mass tourism. For this reason, when many say they wish more and more tourists would come, I sometimes think twice and tell them the day that more tourists come, possibly Cáceres will cease to have the charm it has today."

What could not be ignored is the region has been almost criminally neglected over the past century or two. After the land grabs made by the northern nobility during the Reconquista, or Christian "reconquest," in the thirteenth century, a latifundia region was created that has since been marked by deep inequalities. The dominant, noble class leading the reconquest had been given sole access to the main economic resource of the time (land), and this wealth was augmented by the masses of peasant workers from the north, many of whom were forcibly relocated. These migrants either worked on the land or transferred rents and products back to the noble families. Few were able to succeed, as Juanma's parents had, and break this cycle.

Back around the turn of the twentieth century, on his travels through the region, Miguel de Unamuno wrote that this form of extensive live-stock farming and latifundia was to blame for the depopulation of the region. His idea was that cattle, sheep, and pigs were spreading at the expense of people, and that the local society was polarized into rich and poor because of the great inequality in the distribution of land owner-ship: powerful landowners, tenant farmers, and dependent agricultural workers all bore the archaic traits of shepherd villages. Instead of diversi-fying its activities when the first clear steps towards industrialization and the establishment of a national market were being taken in Spain, the economic system of Extremadura not only maintained an agrarian model but also basically rejected industrialism and deepened its agricul-tural roots. Rather than investing their capital in industry, the aristocracy and high bourgeoisie used their fortunes to acquire even more land, rein-forcing the exclusive economic focus on agriculture and livestock in the region.

These factors set the precedent for the situation that existed until only recently. Once the reconquest ended with the fall of the Nazarí empire in

Granada, many soldiers of fortune made their way to the New World and back. But once the great influx of wealth from the Americas ran dry, the area fell into a long decadent decay. As relatively recently as 1850, Extremadura made up around 4.7 per cent of the population of the country and contributed about 5.2 per cent of its GDP. Now it makes up only around 1.8 per cent. A decline many claim began with the industrialization of the country when the regions of Catalonia and the Basque Country were favoured over other regions. Sometime around the second half of the nineteenth century, the state began its unbalanced support towards Catalonia during this industrialization process. Partly due to its location next to France, the region was granted a monopoly over the textile industry through protectionist tariffs that made the rest of Spain its captive market. With this comparative advantage granted by the state to the Catalans, the rest of the country was left behind. Similar favour was also given to the Basques, after they declared their iron and steel industries to be of national interest. Both regions left the rest lagging behind. These events led to mass emigration and the ensuing demographic disaster Marcelo had told me about, leaving the region outstripped, outpaced, and increasingly outdistanced. If anything, land is perhaps the only thing the people of Extremadura have in excess, but without fair access to it, the people were forced to leave their homes and move away to the furthest reaches of the country.

This point was never made clearer to me than while sitting in a remote village in northwestern Ethiopia years ago. My wife and I had been speaking Spanish and a Catalan couple overheard us and approached, happy to share a common language and culture in such foreign surroundings. We ducked into a *tej bet* (honey wine) house, set among round mud huts in a residential compound to escape the ever-present dust and bruising sun. As we introduced ourselves, the couple told us they were from Barcelona and had been backpacking around the country for several weeks. We told them we lived in neighbouring Sana'a, Yemen, but had come over for a few weeks on a break. They asked where I was from and I told them. Then when they asked my wife, their reaction has stayed with me ever since. "I'm from Extremadura, from Cáceres, actually," my wife answered. "Extremadura! Wow, we've always wanted to visit but have never got around to it. It's just so...lost, so far away!" they replied after a very pregnant pause, obviously oblivious to the irony of what they were saying as we sat drinking our neon-orange honey wine, twenty-four hours from just about anywhere in the horn of Africa.

Ironic or not, there was some truth behind their reaction. The region has long been on the backside of forgotten. The masses of emigrants Marcelo spoke of often wanted to forget the pain of having to leave their roots to better integrate. The second generation was often even worse, wanting to completely erase their perceived "backwards" roots. The near-feudalistic loyalty the people of the region have given to PSOE has also been a double-edged sword. When the opposition party has been in power in Madrid, it has paid little attention to the area, knowing it would probably never win here. Whenever the reverse happened and the socialists were in power, the party felt confident enough that it could pass over the region, knowing it would remain the most voted party no matter what it did, or more precisely, didn't do. Other regions had got around this by creating regionalist parties that offer their votes in congress to the highest bidder, demanding something concrete in exchange for their loyalty. Attempts at creating regionalist parties in Extremadura, however, have never gained a foothold due to the ingrained servility towards the entrenched power sources that have ruled the region for so long.

One of the most glaring aspects of this neglect is the lack of infrastructure Marco had alluded to in his frustration. Glaring neglect that has left the people of the region living as what amounts to second-class citizens. If you look at a map of Spain, Extremadura is the only region that, to date, doesn't have any electrified rail service. Leaving it and the people who live here cut off from the rest of the country, unable to compete with the other regions on equal footing. Every year I have meetings in Madrid with colleagues from around the country and I am the only one who has to come to the capital the evening before and stay overnight simply because it is impossible for me to get to the capital in time for the meeting using public transport. Colleagues from far-flung places such as the Balearic Islands, or even the Canaries out in the middle of the Atlantic, can wake up early, hop on a flight, and be in Madrid in time for a 9 a.m. meeting.

The only option available to those who live out here is to drive or stay the night.

With this in mind, I asked Marco how he saw the future of travel here. "I believe there is going to be a very big change the moment in which, from next year, the rail connection improves. From what they seem to be promising, in the near future a connection will place us just two and a half hours from Madrid. This means an hour less than the fastest train we have now. This is exactly how long it currently takes to get to Madrid by car without traffic. The moment you have a means of transport equal to or better than a car, people will start to go by train. Especially those from countries with a well-established train culture, like France, Belgium, or Germany."

After a life of guiding people around Cáceres, I wanted to know what Marco's favourite place in the city was. I asked him, "Where do you go when you want to see something beautiful here in the city?" Marco took a moment and reflected, "The truth is the one place I really love, especially now that very few cars are ever parked there, is the corner where the Sande Tower is. For me, it's when you climb up the Cuesta de la Compañía and turn right and suddenly around the corner you find a tower with vines climbing up it that eventually completely cover it. It's beautiful, especially in autumn when the vines turn a burgundy red. It's one of the most beautiful sights in the city. I also really like the Ulloa Garden, especially in the winter. And then there is the sanctuary of the Virgin of the Mountain... It's difficult to choose one place. Then I think of the Plaza del Conde de Canilleros, and of course there is the Palacio de Moctezuma. I also really like that place. There are just so many. The truth is it's a city with so many fantastic hidden corners. Some few ever notice, not even the people that live here. Little things, tiny details like the abbreviation of the word cemetery ["*cemtiro*" instead of *cementerio*] engraved on the facade of the Casa del Sol, which you can perfectly see there. There's another in the Carvajal Palace, but that one isn't as easy to spot. These show us where the church cemeteries were." With that, Marco finished his water and got up to get us some more.

Things like decent infrastructure were out of the hands of the locals, especially if they kept on gifting their votes to the major parties for nothing in return. I asked Marco what he thought could be done at the local level to improve tourism. "The truth is my relationship with tourism councillors is a love-hate one, probably because I'm a bit of a pain in their necks. Especially when you consider that, before people come to power, they are very receptive and listen to you a lot, but when they come into power many deify themselves. Well, I have met few tourism councillors whom I can honestly say have been effective in their job." Marco stopped for a moment and gave an ironic smile, and after a pause went on. "What I can tell you is this current city council seems more receptive than the previous one, objectively speaking. Today, this afternoon in fact, I sent a message to Luis Salaya, the new mayor, directly on Instagram, and on the same afternoon we were given a meeting. I see this team closer, less distant than others. A good administrator needs to be humble and open-minded enough to see the good that was done before, as well as the bad. But what you can't do is to simply assume something that came from the opposite party is bad and needs to be changed. There are things that were well done in the past, like some of the projects that were started through the monumental city consortium. Just to toss them aside after so much work went into it simply because a different political party gave birth to it doesn't make sense."

It was getting late. The sun had slipped behind the surrounding buildings and Marco's small dog was getting more and more impatient to be let out. I knew I didn't have much more time left, so I had to start wrapping things up as the mountains in the distance faded to a deeper blue. "If you can think of one quick and relatively simple thing that can be done to improve tourism here, what would it be?" Marco didn't need much time to think. "To improve? That's easy. I think what Cáceres lacks, above all, is a varied and continuous cultural program throughout the entire year. As it stands, things are concentrated at certain times of the year and the city would be better served if these were spread out over the whole year."

It was time to go. Marco's dog, Myko, had had enough. "Before we go, Marco, can you think of one of the anecdotes or stories you tell during your tours that seems to resonate most with people?" Here his face changed a bit, and his engaging smile vanished for a moment. "One of the stories that seems to resound most with people is about a bombing during the civil war in Cáceres, which happened mostly in the Plaza de Santa María. You can still see the impact of the shrapnel everywhere in the square. I talk about what happened during the bombing. About little things like how the bishop, who was in the Episcopal Palace opposite, ran across the bomb site to read the people in the church their last rights as they bled out from the shrapnel. The palace that you see in front, which now belongs to a bank, belonged to the grandmother of my best child-hood friend, and she told me that on the first floor of the house, as it was the home of a noble family, they had a huge ballroom. The impact of one of the bombs was such that part of the piano in there ended up on the roof of the *concatedral* opposite the square. Workers only found it years later when they were renovating the roof of the church in the 1940s or '50s. Incredible but true, all the way up there!"

He left off for a moment and before standing up to go said, "But per-haps the closest story comes from a personal anecdote my grandmother told me that had happened to her mother. The bombing obviously caused a great panic in the main square, and my great-grandmother happened to be there. During the confusion, she lost one of the earrings her mother had given her on the day of her first communion and she never found it. There in the main square, what is now the Foro de los Balbos, there were some grocery stands. A friend of my grandmother's was so frightened she jumped into one of the huge clay jars, not realizing it was full of oil. And there she remained, drowned in oil. My grandmother was so traumatized from that bombing because Cáceres was left without electricity. Airplanes continuously passed over, and the people didn't know if the planes were Russian and were going to bomb them again, or if they were from [Franco's] Nationalist side. The Cervera aerodrome, where the fairgrounds are cur-rently located, was the one the Germans, who were allies of the Nationalists, used, which is why they continued to fly planes over the city. The trauma remained with my grandmother. She wasn't able to go to sleep with the light off until she passed away at the age of ninety-nine."

Avenida de San Blás just before it splits into the Calle Sande on the left and the Calle Peñas on the right leading up to the old town of Cáceres.

BARREN SQUARES

9

I STEPPED OUT INTO THE ROAD and turned up the Calle Sande, one of
a pair of streets that weave up into the old town from the neighbourhood
of San Blás. The sun had sunk low and the terraced housing along both
sides cast irregular shadows over the cobblestone street. The tables of the
street-level bars were beginning to fill up as neighbours came out to enjoy
the cooling evening air and do one of the things the Spanish do best:
socialize. The street then forks around one of those tasteless, inexplicable
four-story outgrowths that juts out from the solid, more or less homogen-
ous, stretch of multi-story homes that line the rest of the way. Crude,
coarse graffiti splatters the walls as the street veers off into what is perhaps the most heavily populated part of the old town that lies beyond the
defensive wall. Beyond the snaking electrical cables and mishmash of
generations of TV antennas, the steeple of the Iglesia de Santiago stood
out from the lines of homes as it turned a warm orange in the weakening
light of the setting sun. I was glad to be walking because I couldn't shake
Marco's flying piano story from my mind.

Each facade along the way had a slightly different look and feel. Most
were painted in varying shades of crunchy whitewash, with a brown or
grey band that ran along the street level, vain attempts to cover up the
abstract stains the rising damp leaves as it dries out. Some of the homes
had been recently renovated and had opted for an adobe-like plaster

facing, while others crumbled in abandoned decay. The homes I had visited in this street tended to lead away from the frequent rumble of the cars crossing the cobblestones. Those on the left were cavernous and often opened out into surprisingly large patios, some complete with small orchards and even spring-fed swimming pools.

The wrought-iron bars that guard every street-level window have at times led visiting travel writers to romanticize about dungeon window grills. However, in reality, they simply represent the widely held Spanish belief it is the owner's responsibility to keep outsiders out, rather than trusting outsiders not to come in. Behind each of these grills were stories like those Marco had told me. Generations of tales, memoirs, and urban myths that have built up over the years. You needn't go back to the times of the Romans but simply peel back a few fine layers of a lifetime or two ago and be amazed at the amount of life and of living that has taken place in these streets that grow quieter each year as people migrate to the suburbs. A street that eighty years ago would have had an overpowering smell of frying oil when a Cáceres institution was born along it. Patatas Fritas el Gallo, some of the best-tasting potato chips in the world, got its start in this street The company may not make these simple yet exquisite chips here in this street anymore, but its methods have never changed. A family celebration in the city is almost unthinkable without Patatas Fritas el Gallo on the table, and it's often a deciding factor whether you return to a bar or not, as much hinges on which brand of chips they set out to accompany your *tapa*. This chip shop wouldn't have been the only business on the streets. Supermarkets were rare or even nonexistent not so long ago; home-front shops were where you did your shopping. Now the last remnant of this neighbourhood life is Guadalupe's corner shop in Plaza de Santiago.

I continued climbing, occasionally hugging the walls when wider delivery trucks flew up the hill, and came out into the now quiet square next to Guadalupe's shop. Just a few months ago, a clacking stork would have claimed every spire of the large, bunker-looking medieval church dominating the square, but since the chicks have flown the nest, so too have mom and pop. To my right stood the vacant sixteenth-century palace of Francisco Godoy, a powerful symbol of what the movement of people and investment capital can bring about. Godoy accompanied Francisco Pizarro in the conquest of Cuzco, capital of the Incan empire, and later became governor of the city of Los Reyes. On his return to Spain, he married Leonor de Ulloa and had this palace built with the riches he had made in the newly discovered world, at least for this wave of Europeans. It now stood as a symbol for Juanma and the neighbourhood association's fight against the privatization of public spaces and served as an emblem of what *vecinificación* is not. The palace, belonging to the regional government, had been used for just about everything, the last being the headquarters of the Territorial Service of the regional Ministry of Education and Youth in 2012. But it had since been long abandoned and had seriously deteriorated. It was now the haunt of squatters and the homeless.

Several proposals had been made over the years by different branches of the administration to convert the building into either the home of the Official Language School, the Music Conservatory, or a multi-use community centre. All of these would revitalize the area and bring new life into a neighbourhood that had seen better times. Each of which were summarily shot down. In a strange twist of ironic fate, news emerged that the regional government had decided to not hand over the building to the people for public use but instead to an investment capital group based in, of all places, Lima, Peru. A somewhat shady Spanish businessman who wanted to convert the building into an exclusive five-star hotel for an investment fund had captained the deal. The cynicism expressed by the regional president about this public building, only metres away from the square where he presented his team of outsiders, was impressive as he gushed that the "capital" the Junta de Extremadura would be contributing was the building itself so it could be rehabilitated and (re)opened to the public and thus "provide a service to citizens." Been to a five-star hotel lately? Would the national and local police be persuaded to "clean up" the area so the less-than-desirable types that often drink in the neighbouring square wouldn't disturb the exclusive guests? Or would that service be taken care of by a private security firm, or maybe robots like those beginning to patrol the streets of Singapore?

The area seems to be a magnet for these types of back room deals, for just a bit farther ahead, past reams of graffiti and a few more abandoned homes, or even squats, I came out from the Calle Zapatería and found myself once again in the Plazuela del Socorro. The same square where I had first heard that word *"fuera"* bounce off the stones. During our conversation, Marco and I had spoken about the provincial archive up the hill that was partially screened by the enormous ombú tree that presided under the Torre de los Espaderos, placing it in a sort of purdah behind its evergreen leaves. He had reminded me of the philosophy currently held among architects that "newer" buildings or additions to older structures should always be made visible, like the different-coloured sand used when repairing sections of the Almohad wall in front of my house. He also believed the very granite used to build the archive would bake into that golden stone of the surrounding buildings after a century of summers. All the same, it still looked like a menacing penitentiary.

Night was falling and I was reminded of my wife's wise advice about your first visit to the city. "If possible, your first stroll through the old town should be done at night, thus allowing your imagination to create images that, even if they vanish with the cold, revealing light of day, will stay with you in some way." I decided to walk around the old city and reflect some more on the talks I'd had with people so far and their stories. I turned right along the Calle Adarve Obispo Álvarez, named after a bishop who was brutally murdered by French troops. This needless reprisal happened during Napoleon's retreat in the War of Spanish Independence back in 1809 for Álvarez's "crime" of exhorting his countrymen to unite against the French invader.

The great local journalist Sergio Lorenzo once wrote about it and tells the tale better than anyone. Apparently, the story goes that in April 1809 the seriously infirm Álvarez welcomed the Bishop of Tuy, who was also fleeing from the French, into his summer home in Hoyos, which is located in the Sierra de Gata in the northwestern corner of the province. The two bishops then had to escape to the nearby village of Valverde del Fresno and from there to Villanueva de la Sierra, where they holed up for three months. When the situation had seemingly calmed down, each bishop returned to his place of residence. Álvarez, the Bishop of Coria and therefore of the province, became even more ill than before. He was now bedridden, almost blind, unable to move, and awaiting his last battle. Very early on the morning of August 29, 1809, soldiers under the command of Marshal Soult entered the village of Hoyos. It was the fifth time they had sieged and entered the village. They quickly located the bishop's palace, killed the bishop's caregiver, and prepared to seek their cruel revenge on their victim, who was then eighty-five years old. They pulled him out of bed, stripped off his clothes, and threw him on his back on the floor. They shot him twice. The first was to his testicles and, after letting him suffer in agony, they delivered the mortal blow and fired the second in his mouth. A man who is remembered now by little more than a narrow street choked with cars of local residents.

From the bishop's parapet walk, or *adarve*, as the streets that run parallel to the wall are called, I came to one of Marco's favourite corners, the Plaza del Conde de Canilleros in front of the Palacio de Moctezuma. The square itself has recently been remodelled and is an oasis of calm that few visitors ever seem to find. My daughters and I have baptized it our "secret way" when we want to shake things up during our commute en route to school on dreary winter mornings. For some reason, not even the local teenagers looking for dark corners use the square. They seem to prefer to shelter under the eyesore of the overhead passage that connects the palace to the prison-like cube of the archive. It's a square that belongs mostly to the singing birds up in another overgrown, bonsai-looking ombú tree and the feral cats that lounge below when not trying to make the birds their lunch. Native to the Pampas of South America, this tree's elephantine roots spill out over the square before digging deep down below the surface. This interrelation between the Old and New World throws its shade over the fortunate wanderer who finds this quiet corner.

Almost every traveller has heard of the dreaded Moctezuma's revenge and more than a few have suffered from it, but the reality of the white-domed palace off the square that shares its name is anything but vengeful. Its origins date back to the fourteenth and fifteenth centuries, though the main work was done during the sixteenth to seventeenth centuries by a grandson of an Aztec princess, Isabel de Moctezuma. A princess who was married to a captain from Cáceres, Juan Cano Saavedra, and who maintained her noble titles after the fall of the Aztec empire. Juan Cano Saavedra was a fortune seeker and travelled to the Americas where he ended up joining the ranks of Hernán Cortés.

When the conquest of the Aztecs was complete, Juan Cano was married to the daughter of the Aztec Emperor Moctezuma II. Her name was Tecuixpo Ixtlaxochitl, but he decided to rebaptize her Isabel de Moctezuma. Juan Cano's decision to marry was perhaps unwise, seeing as Isabel had already buried five husbands before him. He never did get to see the palace completed. The main renovations that can be seen today, like the ice-cream-cone-coloured brick tower at the top, were made at the end of the sixteenth and the beginning of the seventeenth centuries by Hernán's daughter, Mariana de Carvajal y Toledo, who was married to Juan de Toledo Moctezuma, a grandson of Juan Cano Saavedra. The coats of arms of Moctezuma, Carvajal, and Toledo, both on the facade and inside the palace, reflect this history of ownership. The remarkable paintings and murals inside attest to a different narrative of what is called the "conquest." These relate a lesser-known, less-publicized version of the story. The paintings exalt Aztec nobility and attempt to create parallels with the Roman Empire while at the same time aggrandizing Spain's own feat on the American continent. Where else could the grandson of a subjugated monarch have built a palace and been welcomed as a member of the local nobility? Take the example of the English colonizer John Smith. He may well have romanticized his relationship with Pocahontas in his book, with Disney later exaggerating the myth, but the idea of Anglo-Saxon society accepting her as one of their own, let alone as a princess, is completely unthinkable. You only have to look at the treatment of someone like Meghan Markle to see that, even today, commingling at this level is still a fantasy. If there's one way to stay wealthy, best keep it in the families.

Leaving the Plaza del Conde de Canilleros, you once again reach the Almohad defensive wall. Walk far enough in any direction and you'll always find it or at least memories of where it once ran. From this spot the sometimes-chimerical medieval city really begins. Tour guides can often be overheard touting the city as the third-largest intact medieval city in Europe, and there is certainly some truth to that claim. It's the word "intact" that is interwoven into the fantasies visitors create in their minds. The stones themselves can tell different stories, depending on how you interpret them. As you turn left, you pass the rear of the pockmarked bishop's palace. Just before the arch where my daughters and I encountered the Lannister army, you come to an impressive Renaissance doorway to the left. Two angel-like figures, more ethereal than divine, representing Fortitude and Justice, flank huge solid wooden doors. The two padded rows of molded stone that arch over and around the doorway add to its celestial allure. But then you think, why is this magnificent door hidden from view in this extremely narrow lane? Try as you might, it's impossible to gain a perspective that allows you to appreciate it in its entirety, let alone Instagram it. The wall in front of the palace predates it by over a millennium, so that couldn't be the reason. A clue to the mystery is revealed when you read the caption that runs overtop of it: "OBISPO CALRZA DIÓCESIS DE GORIA." Thinking back to the poor bishop who was assassinated by the French, you realize the diocese is Coria, not Goria, and start to see something is out of place. Namely, the door.

It and others like it throughout the old town are pastiches made up from pieces taken from other buildings. Fabrications that deceive the viewer into thinking what they are seeing has always been this way. The doorway is indeed real, but it wasn't born there. In this case, the doorway comes from the Galarza College-Seminary that was built in 1579 and that once stood at the end of the Calle de Parras. The seminary was a direct product of the Council of Trent and went on to disseminate the ideas of the Counter-Reformation. But times have changed and, like the majority of the seminaries across the country, it fell into obscurity and disuse. In 1963, rather than foot the enormous cost of renovating the building, the palace was demolished and its three Mannerist doorways, as well as its coats of arms, cornices, windows, and bars, were patched onto walls behind the wall in the old city. Today, at the end of the street where the seminary once stood, stands...a parking garage.

Recycling and reusing construction materials is nothing new. Fashions change, caves morph into pagan temples that turn into churches, then into mosques, back into churches, and then end up as parkades. What is somewhat surprising to see, especially when you consider these pastiches were done so relatively recently, are civil public buildings, like the palace of the provincial government in Santa María square, displaying episcopal coats of arms stapled onto their facades without any heraldic truth or historical reason other than "it looks medieval."

Continuing upwards along the wall in the shadow of the defensive towers just over the other side, you come across another of these confabulations. From a break in the wall to your right you are offered an incredible view of the crumbling Torre de la Yerba, the town hall, the main square, and once again the deep blue mountains beyond. Looking down along the wall you see a sixteenth-century fountain you would think would once have been a main source of water in the city. In fact, the fountain originally sat at the southeastern edge of the old city in an area called San Francisco that borders the stream that runs out of the karst area where the caves are. Historically, this was an important watering station for shepherds and cattle producers as they moved their livestock through the area, especially during the transhumance or seasonal migration that saw flocks moving to places as far away as La Rioja, five hundred kilometres away. By extirpating the fountain from its natural environment, where until recently it served a practical function, it becomes entirely decontextualized. In a way, doing so is a rejection of what it really is, its true nature, and at the same time, it is a denial of the essence of these lands. Today, all that remains in its original location are the lonely remains of a stone bridge in the middle of a roundabout.

Turning back inside the walled city, two large palaces circumscribe the Plaza de los Caldereros, or the more entertaining sounding Boilermakers Square. The lower part of the square is home to the Casa de los Ribera, which now serves as the rectorate of the University of Extremadura. While the inside of the building has been completely refurbished, the outside is made up of a mix of granite foundation and cornerstones filled in with slate masonry that binds it all together. The grand arched granite portal, combined with the iron bars covering the ground-floor windows, lends it a somewhat harsh penal appearance. One that would bring to mind thoughts of being sent to the dean's office after having done something wrong, only taken to an extreme. Perched slightly above the square is the somewhat grander Palacio de la Generala, with a curious semicircular machicolation above its entrance from which defenders would have unleashed arrows on any attacker or student coming to complain about their marks.

Like the Casa de los Ribera and most of the fortified palaces in the city, Palacio de la Generala shares the same mix of granite and slate masonry. The building also belongs to the university and is one of its main administrative centres. Step back and the view from the square is the postcard scene that most envision when they think of medieval cities. Solid stone buildings complete with elaborate granite entranceways that are guarded by imposing wooden doors, with embrasures above for the archers. But if their original owners were teleported through time, they wouldn't recognize their homes today. To them, they would look unfinished or under construction. The bare exposed stone that resounds so deeply in our cultural memory as medieval is a movie set fiction. These palaces, and essentially all of the palaces around them, would have been plastered over, not only to protect the building from damp and the elements but also to beautify and adorn them. The glowing stones I have come to love would have been covered with sand and lime and, depending on the budget, might have included decorative motifs and the use of trompe l'oeil. Also included might have been patterns used since Roman times, where the "real" granite foundation stones were blended in with rectangular figures cut into the plaster, making it look solid. Granite is much more expensive and difficult to source than the mix of stones that make up the more haphazard-looking masonry walls. Times change, though, and so do fashions. It's only a matter of time before wallpaper and the popcorn stucco we found in many of the homes while looking for our house come back into fashion.

The postcard-perfect picture is also a stark reminder of what was perhaps the city's gravest urbanistic blunder of the twentieth century. Unlike many historic Spanish capitals, Cáceres did not have a university until 1973, and at the time Extremadura was the only region in the country without one. When you consider the University of Seville to the south was founded in 1505, or that one of the oldest universities in the world began up in Salamanca to the north in 1218, there has always been much catching up to do. During their first years, the faculties of the University of Extremadura were peppered around the old town, including the faculty of law located in the Palacio de la Generala. But as the student body grew so did the need for space. Less than a decade after the university's founding, the fatal decision was made. Rather than making the albeit extraordinarily difficult, if not herculean, effort to find space among the buildings belonging to the regional government, the church, and noble families in the old town and its environs, a decision was made to banish the campus from the city. It was exiled to the sun-bleached, treeless steppe beyond the horizon where it now sits, forty-odd years later, isolated, detached, and with its back turned, both physically and metaphorically, to the city.

Halfway up the *adarve*, or parapet, you enter a small square flanked by the Palacio de los Condes de Adanero and the Palacio de los Golfines. With its soaring defensive tower complete with reconstructed battlements, the latter palace played an important role in the evolution of the country during the twentieth century. It was here, from a balcony on the other side of the palace, that Francisco Franco declared himself Caudillo of Spain, Head of State, and Generalissimo of the Three Armies, thus spawning an eternity of movies about bumbling Latin dictators and their much more insidiously efficient real-life counterparts. Back in the square, you see what is perhaps my favourite view from the city. During the winter, the white-capped mountains of the Sierra de Gredos frame Moctezuma's flaking, white-domed roof, while in the spring storks squat on every corner. At night, it has a torch-like, outmoded feel that contrasts sharply with the world beyond the defensive wall. After a trip somewhere, bumping along the cobblestone road in a taxi, this view always reminds me I am home.

After enjoying the scene, I usually turn back into the warren of the old city, along the passageways so narrow that not even the most distracted driver could enter, no matter what Google Maps claims. The tight Calle del Arco de Santa Ana leads on to the equally slim Cuesta de Aldana. Turn right and you come to Franco's self-coronation site. Turn left and you come to another of my preferred corners of the city. Here, next to the lovely Casa Mudéjar, which features some of the few remaining Mudéjar elements of the city that applied Islamic forms and style to medieval and Renaissance Christian art. I played some of my first gigs as a resident here. Both the "garage," as they used to call it, and the Aldana bar next

The view of the Palacio de Moctezuma looking down the Adarve de Santa Ana in the old town of Cáceres.

door used to host live music. As a travelling musician, I've gigged in just about every place possible. From jazz festival stages to the most remote juke joints and strip mall disasters, but there was something about playing under a spectacular wooden roof that was built in 1483, only minutes from home, that was special. The sound of music has since died, but there is still a restaurant and bar in the palace where live music used to ring.

Looking up above the garage you can see one of the more modest coats of arms that tattoo the facades of the palaces across the city. So many dot the walls of Cáceres that it has been called the city of a thousand and one shields. This rather understated yet elegant crest happens to represent the Ulloa family. Others, like the Golfines's crest up the street, the Mayoralgo family's back in the square of Santa María, those on the Palacio de Moctezuma, or the crests back on Godoy's soon-to-be five-star hotel all attest to the lineage that ruled the city. All of these hereditary stamps imprint the families' legacies on the buildings and remind us the persistent and growing inequality around us today is nothing new. It's not so much what you know or what you do but who you know and what family you were born into. It's not everything, of course, but it certainly does help to have one of those surnames.

Genealogists find beauty in the symbology engraved on these stones, and while many are intriguing, the one I love most can be found on the left-hand lateral side of the garage, just about halfway down. There, lightly etched in the granite stone, is a blank shield. Simple, small, engraved markings like these endure on the building stones across the old town. As the buildings were originally meant to be plastered over, these marks were probably made at the quarry to identify which palace the stone was going to and were never meant to be seen. This one was more than likely an unfinished piece that got lost along the way, but I like to think of it differently. For me, it represents the rest of us. The nameless, the anonymous, the mongrels who may not enjoy the fame and fortune for having crossed the sea, commanding regiments, or triumphing in the stock market, but who instead carried their swords and later golf clubs, who do their laundry, drive their cars, and teach their children. For me, this little hidden symbol is the coat of arms of the 99 per cent.

In the Calle Orellana opposite the Aldana Palace you can still see some of the remaining decorative plaster that once coated these buildings. Its future, though, is precarious as it crumbles away. Farther up the street I came to Marco's favourite tower, la Torre de Sande, though from the opposite direction he recommended. Its leafy coat could still be seen in the twilight and flashed as the evening breeze began to blow. To the left was the fifteenth-century Casa del Sol, so named for its coat of arms featuring a face-like sun whose rays are being bitten by eight serpent heads. But what struck me most, especially in this light, was the minaret that rose up in front of me. In the dusky light thrown by the street lamps, it wouldn't have seemed entirely out of place to hear the Isha evening Ādhān prayer coming from the square tower adjacent to the equally square building facing me. This illusion quickly disappeared once its details came into sharper focus. Saints Peter and Paul atop the main entrance let you know just who the building belongs to now, but it doesn't take much imagination to see that the building reflects and resembles many I have seen on the opposite side of the Mediterranean, even if little or nothing remains of the mosque that once stood here. This is the highest point of the old town, and it makes sense that the Muslims would have built their fortress and accompanying mosque in this place. In fact, during the controversial construction of the ultra-exclusive Atrio restaurant and hotel, which also abuts the square, the remains of several bodies buried in Islamic fashion were found underneath the very cobblestones that pave the square.

Cross the square east and you find what is perhaps the prototype for the fortified palaces you encounter in Cáceres, the Palacio de los Cáceres-Ovando and its uncircumcised Torre de las Cigüeñas tower. I say prototype because the family who built it was one of the first Catholic noble families to establish a power base in the newly Christianized city. Its tower, easily the tallest in the walled city, is the only one that wasn't snipped like the Torre de los Espaderos in the Plazuela del Socorro after Isabela's edict. This was thanks to the family's loyalty to Juana la Beltraneja in the battle for the throne of Castile. To the loyalists of the winners go the spoils. Its location, next to where the Muslim fortress once stood, suggests it was one of the first pieces of land to be doled out after the much-vaunted reconquest. Its position explains a lot about what you see in the city and how it subsequently developed.

This is not a home that was meant to entice, nor was it meant to appeal to the senses. This is a fortress whose purpose was to intimidate and terrorize those outside its ramparts. This is a military castle masquerading as a Renaissance palace with only crests and pretty stones to attest to the latter. Unnecessary adornments and ornamentation are almost completely absent. Somewhat ironically, the only embellishments are the Arabic-influenced alfiz molding around the arched doorway and the Umayyadan-looking, horseshoe-arched windows that look out from the top floor. These palaces were also homes that exclusively looked inwards, very much in the style of buildings found across the Islamic world. There is generally an entrance hall where "outsiders" were attended to, but the rest of the home was private. This custom is echoed in later, more humble constructions in Extremadura, with a separate *zaguán* or entryway guarding access to the rest of the house. Almost every palace is built around elaborate courtyards that centre on cisterns that not only provided water during times of relative peace but also helped the clan resist in times of siege.

The established narrative dictates that the founders of these palaces, Christian noble families from the northern reaches, united in battle against those perceived as heathens in order to re-Christianize the peninsula. A land that was most likely only nominally Christian before the arrival of the Moors in 711. With them, the Moors brought Islam, the second creed to be imported from the Middle East to the peninsula in less than four hundred years. Legends of Saint James proselytizing on his Spanish holiday aside, if you consider the Roman empire officially converted to Christianity in 312 CE, no matter its renowned efficiency, the likelihood the foreign belief was widespread and universally professed by the time of the arrival of the Moors seems to be more faith-based than the religions themselves. The crusaders' fervour and zeal smacked of ulterior motives beyond that of redemption. When Fernando III, son of Alfonso IX, the "liberator" of Cáceres, conquered Seville, estimates are that around 60 per cent of his forces were Muslims. A number that would strongly suggest these were battles between dynasties rather than crusades fuelled by devotion.

Whatever the case, this confabulated cohesion didn't last long. Only a short time after the "invaders" were expelled, the city grew into what was really a set of military encampments constantly waging hot and cold wars with each other as the clans jostled for power and influence. This enmity is evidenced by the bare spaces that lie between the fortresses. Unlike many other medieval cities across Europe, the squares of Cáceres are barren, empty spaces. They are swathes of no man's land between what were once continuously warring fiefdoms, devoid of things like fountains, parks, or art that would have invited those from different factions to gather, interact, and learn each other's stories first-hand.

Various Catholic Virgin Mary figures.

IDOL WORSHIP

10

TWO WHITE TOWERS RISE UP from the reddish Arabic roof tiles that cascade over the cubist ochre tangle of the old town. They aren't necessarily beautiful and are in no way ornate, but the baroque Iglesia de San Francisco Javier or, as it is more creepily known in English, the Church of the Precious Blood, is one of the most conspicuous landmarks in the UNESCO core. It's a man-made cairn that can help the lost (tourists) find their way among all the narrow streets. It presides over one of the only public squares that might invite socialization in the old town. This somewhat stodgy granite square is a space that seems to fit in with its surroundings, but, like the doorway behind the Palace of the Bishop, this too is a relatively recent invention meant to appear authentic. The square was completed in the mid-1960s, and the clans of old could not have met here to learn each other's stories even if they had wished to. Even though it may be inauthentic and rather brutalist, the square and the shaded garden that leads off of it is a good place to meet, sit, and contemplate the relative silence.

San Jorge square gets its name from a modest statue of Saint George slaying metaphorical dragons that is set in the middle of a bifurcated stairway. Inside the white church, you find a much less metaphorical representation of another of the apostles doing his work. Saint James stands out in the sixteenth-century altarpiece by the famous sculptor Alonso

Berruguete. Here in Spain, Saint James is also known as Santiago Matamoros, James the Moor-slayer. In this image there is a very seraphic, Jesus-looking James, with his sword drawn high, sitting astride his steed as it tramples the heads of prostrate Moors. It's a recurring image that has been used over the centuries to fortify national resentments and scapegoat outsiders and all things foreign as the root cause of the ills the country may have been suffering from at the time. It's a rallying cry meant to create and identify an adversary, an 'other.'

This cry has raised its head and experienced a resurgence today once again in Spain, echoing similar movements across Europe and beyond. The rise of the neo-fascist extreme right has been fast. In just a few short years since its excision from the traditional Partido Popular (People's Party), an extreme right-wing party now sits in parliament and rules as a minor coalition partner in some of the autonomous regions. It's a party that openly embraces many of the fascist traits Umberto Eco once laid out, such as the cult of tradition and Catholicism, fear of difference, the belief that disagreement is treasonous, contempt for the weak and underprivileged, selective populism, and manipulative appeals to social frustration. Curiously enough, while it refuses to denounce Franco's dictatorship and, in fact, often hails the traits it views as positive, it is quick to denounce and even sue journalists who dare call the party out for what it is. When the party came to power, one of its first moves was to attempt to whiteout the past by revoking the Historical Memory Law put in place to reveal the truths of life under the dictatorship.

Mirroring far-right movements across the world, the essence of its message revolves around the idea that "the enemies of Spain" are behind every ill, and in every talking point it includes this illusory spectre. However, unlike other radical right movements around the world, this party's base mainly emanates from the very structure it constantly rails against: the public administration. The party's core is mainly made up of aristocrats, judges, members of the national police force, the civil guard, and civil servants. Taking pages directly out of the Trump playbook, the head of the party portrays himself as a rebel and an outsider, and this seems to connect with a wide base of voters alienated from the status quo, especially within a certain sect of young people. This despite the cynical irony he has never worked a day in his life outside of politics. This modern 2.0 version is extremely media-savvy, though. He knows how to spin such contradictions—which would normally turn off working-class voters— into convoluted conspiracy theories with simplistic slogans that cover the party's fascist tracks. It consistently votes against economic measures designed to help the working class, including those adopted during the pandemic to palliate the economic struggles people were suffering, such as the temporary employment regulation that saved hundreds of thousands of jobs across the country.

There is another aspect that differentiates this modern version somewhat from the country's historical fascists. While many of the surnames belonging to the party might sound familiar from Franco's fascist regime, the brains behind this "neo" version are not afraid of incorporating modern methods into the way the party is run. Both the classical fascists and this neo-fascist nodule exalt the nation and an imagined Hispanic race above all else. Their zealotry often drives the party and its followers to falsify history by creating imaginary narratives. On commemorative dates, such as the fall of the Nasrid emirate in Granada, the last Islamic toehold on the peninsula, the party exalts the supposed return of the Hispanic "nation." A nation that didn't even exist before the arrival of the Moors in the eighth century. This also raises the question of what exactly its definition of "Spanish" is, or as Spain didn't even exist at the time, "Iberian"? The "expelled" ruler, Muhammad XII of Granada, was born in Granada, as was his father. In fact, many of the conquered Muslim rulers were born on the peninsula and knew no other home.

This jingoistic flag-waving is extremely contagious and seductive to those who feel lost among the sociocultural shifts taking place across the Western world. Its siren song can unfortunately lead the gullible to commit atrocious acts in the name of this misconceived fanaticism. Acts like the painting of an enormous Spanish flag over top a panel of prehistoric rock art dating back seven thousand years in la Garganta del Muerto in Solana del Pino in the neighbouring region of Castilla-La Mancha. Perhaps doing so in the belief the artists who had painted the figures were also "invaders."

But where this newer generation differs most from Franco is that, while the dictator was happy to accept the aid of like-minded dictatorships like

Nazi Germany and Mussolini's Italy, it seems this modern neo-wing is willing to go beyond limiting its partnerships with countries of a like mind. The ideologues behind the party have close links to far-right-wing transnational movements around the world, like Steve Bannon's organizations, and consistently demonstrate a soft spot for multinational companies that bilk the system and pay little or no taxes in the fatherland. The party justifies its stance against any attempt to make Spain's taxation system more progressive under the supposed aegis of not wanting to raise taxes. This is exemplified in actions like its negative position on the so-called Google tax. A tax that looked to exact tribute from companies engaged in activities with annual revenues of at least 750 million euros worldwide and with revenues exceeding three million euros in Spain, at the ridiculously low rate of 3 per cent. Ridiculous when you consider a normal citizen making around fifteen thousand euros a year pays almost ten times that in tax. It's a heady cocktail of neoliberalism, national Catholicism, and fascism that marks a betrayal the ultra-nationalist Franco would not have favoured.

Where they do come together is the modern version is a party that does not shy away from using these deeply ingrained images to further its cause, constantly stoking fear of the 'other.' The party moves to capture the underlying disenchantment with how the "future" has turned out and wraps it in antagonism towards immigrants and minority groups. In one of its promotional videos, the party's leader is also presented astride a horse while Wagnerian music plays in the background, portraying him as an austere saviour, the fatherland's only possible redeemer against the enemies at the gates. A leader whose name happens to be Santiago.

Seeing as Christianity was as equally alien to the peninsula as Islam, myths and legends were needed to naturalize this foreign credo and spin it into something, if not exactly homegrown at least somewhat more manifest, more tangible to the local population if it was going to take root. An ideology and hagiography had to be created that was palpable enough that people would be willing to fight for and even die for its cause. One of the main dilemmas of adopting a foreign faith is that it is just that, foreign. A quick look at a map of Cáceres can attest to this. Trace your finger to the entrance of the old town and you find a square dedicated to one of the writers of the four gospels, a man from Galilee, Saint John. Then you have the aforementioned Saint George, the Turkish martyr whose closest contact to Spain was a visit to Libya during his travails. Along with him, there is the roundabout with the bridge segment in the middle of it in the neighbourhood of San Francisco, named after the Italian saint from Assisi. Down towards Marco's place, you come across San Blás, named after the relatively unknown Saint Blaise from Sivas, Turkey.

Undiscovered, that is, until medieval hagiographers got hold of him and compiled the apocryphal version of him being fed by birds and other wild animals in his hermit's cave. Then he was discovered by the as-of-yet-Christianized Romans. He ended up being martyred for his skills by having his flesh ripped with iron combs and being beheaded. This happened not before he persuaded a wolf to return a pig to a widow and save a boy from choking on a fishbone. Good acts that would lead him to be made patron saint of wild animals, pigs, wool merchants, and of course, sore throats. All of these tales may have been somewhat convincing to the locals, but they were still distant and remote. There was definitely some saint envy at the time.

The re-Christianizing public relations campaign was ramped up in the ninth century up in the province of Galicia with tales of floating lights and burning bushes. Special effects that appear to have shaken the collective memory of the inhabitants as to the supposed burial place of the mortal remains of Saint James. Relics that, as legend has it, had been smuggled out of Judea on a boat made of stone some seven hundred years prior. Thus giving birth to the cathedral in Santiago de Compostela, terminus of the most important pilgrimage in the Christian world, the Camino de Santiago. A southern branch of the pilgrim trail cuts through Extremadura, leading pilgrims northwards. While the most well established myth finds the saint's remains in Galicia, according to the monk Justo Pérez de Urbel, the link between Santiago and the peninsula began to spread well before the second half of the seventh century in Hispania, during the period of the Visigoths. In his interpretation, a marble tombstone that was found in the Concatedral de Santa María de Mérida, just eighty kilometres to the south of Cáceres, shows this. This tombstone alludes to some of the relics that were held in the church at the time of its founding, and among them was a relic of Santiago. This was surprising, as the body of the Apostle Santiago would not yet appear to those in Galicia until several hundred years later.

These connections were only the beginning. Once the reconquest began, so did the local boy beatifications. As the renowned Spanish author and self-exile Juan Goytisolo once wrote, "The abolition of polytheism created an infinite distance between the individual and his Creator facilitating the appearance of charismatic mediators, enjoying celestial powers, in the community of the faithful." He was referring more to the Marabouts on the other side of the Mediterranean, but at the time both religions were creating heavenly intermediaries to help secure believers among the competing religions. Here the Christians seem to have been more successful than their Muslim counterparts in creating interlocutors with the divine. On this end of the inland sea, believers yearn for a more human-like divinity, while the Oriental Orthodox Churches and conventional Islam tend to stress the more divine side of their divinity. The draw of a deity who had never been tarnished by taking a mortal form is one of the many reasons Islam, with its pure God, initially found so many converts among Eastern Christians and is one of the reasons why it eventually lost ground in the West.

In the late twelfth century, the mystic Ibn 'Arabī, perhaps the greatest of all Islamic philosophers, detailed around seventy-one Andalusian Sufi saints, four of whom were women. These saints helped the faithful bridge the infinite distance between them and a god that, according to the precepts of Islam, is forbidden to be portrayed. This prohibition works the same for Ibn 'Arabī's prophet from distant Arabia: a place where the mere thought of these saints would be considered heretical. While substantial, this number of homegrown saints pales in comparison with the number of virgin idols that would be miraculously "rediscovered," buried in fields and hidden in caves around the country as the reconquest ploddingly advanced south over the ensuing seven centuries. These images have since become an integral part of Spanish identity.

Icons like the Lady of Pillar, who tradition dictates miraculously appeared to Saint James here in Spain and is now found in the northwestern city of

Saragossa. Others include the Lady of Covadonga in Asturias who supposedly assisted Don Pelayo to defeat the Muslims and halt their advance in a mythical battle that has helped forge the Spanish identity over the centuries. Mythical in the sense that the first mention of the battle doesn't even appear in Christian chronicles until more than a century after the battle supposedly took place. Stories that read as if they were copied directly from the Book of Exodus, adding more to their mythical status. Arab historians of the time fail to even mention it, further raising the question if the battle ever took place. Then there are others like the very-Arabic-sounding Virgin of Almudena who, legend holds, was carved by Nicodemus and painted by Saint Luke and was brought by the Apostle Saint James to Hispania when he came to preach the Gospel. According to tradition, the statue was hidden in the walls of Madrid while the Arabs besieged the city only to be rediscovered by the Christians in the eleventh century, when King Alfonso VI conquered Madrid, another miraculously convenient apparition.

Much closer to home, just over ninety kilometres from Cáceres as the stork flies and 125 kilometres as the twisting secondary highways wind, lies the town of Guadalupe and the tale of the Virgin who helped reconquer the peninsula and then conquer a continent. Back in the fourteenth century, a humble, lonely cow herder named Gil Cordero was herding his cattle across the vast stretches of Extremadura. They were pasturing near the Guadalupe River when he realized one was missing. After a three-day search through the jagged quartzite boulders that make up the Sierra de las Villuercas, he finally found the animal lying dead on the riverbank. He inspected the carcass and was surprised to find no sign of predators like wolves having killed it, nor the marks of any scavengers. He took out his knife and began to skin the animal through the breast in the manner of a cross and it suddenly came back to life. If that wasn't surprising enough, out of the mists appeared the figure of a woman wrapped in a gauzy light who identified herself as the Virgin. I imagine he was given some time to take this all in, but once he had, the vision went on to give him a rather detailed to-do list. He was told to take his cow back and tell the local clergy what he had seen. She went on to insist he bring the clergy back to the very spot where his cow had lain dead and dig under the stones. There, she prophesied, they would find an image, but they were not to move it. Instead, they were to build a church and expansive town on that spot. Not being one to ignore glowing women hanging around remote rivers, he did as he was told and, unsurprisingly, when he got back to Cáceres, everyone thought the intense sun had got to him and no one believed him.

Somewhat dejected, he traipsed home only to find his wife surrounded by neighbours and priests who brought him the terrible news his first-born son had died. With the miracle of the born-again cow fresh in his mind, he threw himself on his knees and commended to the Virgin to repeat her party trick and resuscitate the boy, and in doing so, maybe, just maybe, they would believe his tale about the reinvigorated cow and follow her instructions. As he prayed, Lazurus-like, the boy rose up and sang, "Take me to the river," and those around him changed their tune and marched off with Gil to the banks of the river Guadalupe. They dug in the very spot he indicated and came across a small marble tomb with a figure of the Virgin in it, along with some other relics. This idol was some-what different from the others as it came with identification papers—papers that told the icon's story of being whittled by Saint Luke himself and added the backstory that the figure had been buried with him in Greece.

Sometime in the fourth century, the remains of the apostle and the icon were moved to Constantinople. From there, in 582 CE, the image was taken to Rome, just in time for an outbreak of a plague that would kill the reigning pope of the time. His successor, Saint Gregory, had a flash and ordered the image to be taken in procession about town. As it was paraded around the streets of the eternal city, a rather morbid angel appeared in the sky, wiping blood from a sword and, voila, the plague was finished. A few years later, Pope Gregory sent several relics, including the icon, to the Archbishop of Seville. En route, the ship encountered a terrible storm and again the Virgin was put to work and her miraculous charm managed to calm the waves. The image then found peace in Seville until 711, when the Moors crossed the Strait of Gibraltar. Seeing the fall of the nascent Christendom imminent, some well-meaning priests escaped north until they reached the isolated spot in the mountains of Extremadura and buried the image for safekeeping. There it lay until Gil Cordero's unfortunate cow came along.

News of the miracle reached the ears of King Alfonso XI, who was busy waging war on the Moors. He decided to visit the humble hermitage built around the site that Gil Cordero's family had been left in charge of and ordered a magnificent temple to be built. The monastery's fame, and accompanying wealth, grew over the years to the point that even Christopher Columbus became one of her devotees. The explorer always took a replica of the icon with him on his voyages to America, and the "New World" was conquered under the benevolent guise of this Black Virgin's patronage. A conquered world where you now find virgins of Guadalupe in Mexico, Bolivia, Peru, Uruguay, El Salvador, and across the Pacific in the Philippines. Twenty-four hours a day, around the world, you will find someone praying to this figure that saw its birth, or perhaps rebirth, in the valleys of this tail of the Appalachian chain.

Marianist images like these serve as telephone operators for the faithful with a direct line to a more distant divine. These virgins are seen as interlocutors that intercede and relay people's prayers to God. They act as perceptible go-betweens with the Almighty while providing a convenient out when prayers aren't answered. In Spain, each and every village, town, and city in the country seems to have one and Cáceres is no different. Worship of La Virgen de la Montaña runs deep in the city. It's an integral part of much of the city's psychological makeup. So much so that many nonpractising Catholics and even self-professed atheists will declare themselves devout to the idol, reinforcing Goytisolo's reflection on the innate need many feel for charismatic mediators with the supernatural. This virgin's story, however, is somewhat different from the others in that it never actually "appeared" as the others are claimed to have done. In this case, the less than celestial fingerprints of humankind happen to be even more visible.

Sometime in the early seventeenth century a man named Francisco Paniagua from the nearby village of Casas de Millán was making the rounds of the area, looking to raise funds to build a sanctuary for a religious figure he always carried with him. Lacking the saccharine charisma of the American TV evangelists, sometime between 1621 and 1626 he gave up trying to find benefactors and finally decided to build himself a rudimentary hermitage around a cave near where today's sanctuary stands across the valley from my house. His piety and devotion didn't go unnoticed and the parish priest of the Iglesia de Santa María, Sancho de Figueroa y Ocano, befriended the hermit, officially blessing his DIY hermitage on March 24, 1624. The very next day, Sancho de Figueroa y Ocano gave the first Mass in the newly beatified hermitage. While she hadn't officially made an appearance, Cáceres could now claim a virgin of its own. Unfortunately for Francisco, it seems the figure he carried with him was equally as rustic as his hermitage. Around the same time he was building his sanctuary, another figure was commissioned from an unknown Andalusian artist and this second statue is the one that is adored today. So much for good intentions.

Every year, ten days before the first Sunday in May, the figure is carried down with great pomp and ceremony from its sanctuary across the valley and is presented with the baton of the city by the mayor of the city. It's a tradition dating back to the seventeenth century, both in times of peace and times of calamity, when drought, disease, and locusts threatened the city. The act is much less riotous than similar scenes that are seen during religious pilgrimages farther south in Andalusia in places like El Rocío. In the festivals farther south, children are actually thrown at the image as it passes by while mobs of young men jostle and climb on top of the crowds in order to touch the icon. Here the atmosphere is much more decorous and formal and the overall atmosphere is devout and intense. To the outsider, the shamanic fetishization of the ritual is as impenetrable as those that most likely accompanied the paintings on the cave walls back in the Maltravieso cave.

On that day, a who's who from the city, dressed in their Sunday best, crowd the area near one of the city's traditional fountains, Fuente Concejo, to welcome the statue of the Virgin. During the ceremony, young girls dressed in their pure white communion dresses nervously twitch beside their more solemnly dressed mothers, some wearing the unwieldy *peinetas*, ornamental combs that sustain their shawls behind their heads. It's an act where women seem to outnumber men by almost two to one in the pressing crowds. Many of the men that do attend shift from side to side in their pressed wedding suits, privately lamenting the fact this is one of the few areas of the city without a bar in sight.

The local press reports on the event as if it were a fashion show, recounting the smallest details of the dress the figure is dressed in and carefully mentioning each and every benefactor that donated gold, rubies, sapphires, emeralds, and elaborate gowns and dresses to the icon. Once the image reaches the bottom of the valley, the most festive part of the pilgrimage begins with the municipal band belting out regional *jotas* and the national anthem to heartfelt hollers of "Long live the Virgin, long live the patron of the city, long live the mother of God, long live la Cacereña *bonita!*" Military personnel in their dress uniforms, as well as active members of the Guardia Civil, escort the procession as it climbs up to one of the most renowned streets of the city, the Calle Caleros just below the Almohad wall.

From here the procession winds its way up the narrow street, crowded with devotees, into the main square where it is once again welcomed by the mayor in front of the town hall. The speeches that are given by the mayor, the bishop, and other local dignitaries border on the bizarre, as tribute after tribute are paid to the good deeds of what everyone present knows is in fact a wooden doll. The procession ends in the Concatedral de Santa María, where the image is put on display for nine days, where every day its dress is changed by an enormous crew of eager women. These nine days become the de facto opening of the spring season in the city when locals take to the streets with the return of the good weather. Their daily mission is to guess the colour of the Virgin's dress. Lineups can snake out past the Arco de la Estrella into the main square when the weather is particularly pleasant. Because if there is one uniting factor in the city, more than even football, it is definitely this icon.

Religious pilgrimages and processions in Spain are not only something to see but places to be seen. Being present is a public affirmation you belong to a particular sect and is a tacit ratification of the status quo, all the while claiming a status that is associated with belonging to a particular group and place. By latching on to these long-held local customs, the participants form part of a combination of social and place identity and either consciously or unconsciously create an "us versus them" mentality. It's a tender area where tradition trumps everything else. You either believe and belong, or you don't. Unlike other cities and towns around the country like Almería, Gijón, Benidorm, or the nearby towns of Navalmoral de la Mata, Mérida, or Almendralejo, the statue has never been bestowed with the status of "Perpetual Mayor" and is only given the baton of power for the nine days that it remains in the Iglesia de Santa María. But even if it doesn't perpetually form part of the local government, its powers, or at least the powers of those behind it, are undeniable. In the case of the Virgen de la Montaña, its powers to stop plagues and pandemics are undecided at best, but what is known is it once had the power to topple a local government.

| Spring in Extremadura is brief and violent. The weather takes a serious turn at the end of April/beginning of May and, depending on the amount of rain over the winter and early spring, the explosion of growth can be phenomenal with the sudden intense sun. For a few short weeks, an intense vibrant carpet of green covers just about every exposed patch of land before the incessant sun, like Rumpelstiltskin, transforms it all into false gold that ends up turning a burnt brown as the summer progresses. This is festival season in the city and around the same time as the procession of the Virgen de la Montaña, another important event also takes place.

Back in 1992, Peter Gabriel was looking to expand his World of Music, Arts and Dance (WOMAD) project and the organization ended up bringing the WOMAD festival to the city. Back then, the city was still a very sleepy, provincial capital and the sudden arrival of tens of thousands of music lovers, some with little more than the shirts on their backs, provoked a social tsunami. It was a sociological influence on local society akin to the arrival of bikini-clad Nordic tourists on Spanish beaches back in the '60s. Overnight the streets and parks filled up with people sleeping rough wherever they could find a place to rest their heads. Makeshift stands went up in squares around the city with vendors hawking just about everything. Suddenly, the well-pressed, early '90s Spanish streets that normally looked like a vignette out of a Ralph Lauren ad were contrasted with dreadlocks, piercings, ripped jeans, and the obligatory accessory mutt.

The celestial civil coup took place before my time here, so I asked someone who had reported on it first-hand. Sergio Lorenzo is a first-class reporter whose investigative reports help unveil a forgotten past and present to his devoted readers, but he's also much more. He plays a mean sax and is the kind of person known to gift under-the-radar books to friends out of the blue. He's also a fellow transplant from the northern region of Galicia, another who has been here so long his roots are now mixed. We met over a few *cañas* on the Alfonso IX hotel's patio to talk about what he recalled about the incident. The hotel's streetside tables are a great place to meet near the centre, but it can also be somewhat difficult to really get much done as half the city seems to walk by to stop and chat while you're there.

We ordered the first round and I asked him how long he had been working in Cáceres. He smiled and looked at me through his character-istic horn-rimmed glasses. "I've been working here as a journalist since 1986. The first three years were with *El Periódico Extremadura* and then I moved over to *Hoy*, where I've been ever since." Our beers arrived, accom-panied with a small *tapa* of stewed, slightly spicy pig's snout with some bread on the side to sop up the sauce. I told Sergio I had heard the Virgin had somehow interceded in an election back in the 1990s and asked him what he remembered of the time. Again he smiled and this time used his index finger to underline the important dates. "Back in the '90s there was no economic crisis and the city was culturally very diverse, with many people wanting to do things and put on different projects. Back then, there was a lot of public funding floating around, and the different levels of governmental administrations were willing to put up the money to get things done. Not only them, even some financial institutions opened their purse strings. In 1995, everybody had their space and within their space there were no problems. The problem in 1995 was that in the same space two very different worlds came together and clashed...and there was thunder and lightning as a result."

He was describing the Spain I had first encountered when I travelled through the country in the '90s. A place where, for the most part, there was a live-and-let-live atmosphere all the while the trough was full. EU money was still flooding in and government administrations saw themselves obliged to spend their entire budgets on whatever they could before the year was out or face not having them renewed the following year. Musicians working the cover band circuit could work 180–200 nights a year, and even jazz musicians had beepers. The mayor of Cáceres promoted the huge outdoor drinking parties, or *botellónes* Juanma had told me about, and they took place in the main square and were even considered a tourist attraction. Times changed, though, and as the technocrats and men in black moved behind the wheel, we now career from crisis to crisis. In Spain the people were told they had lived beyond their means. It was the people's fault for building airports to nowhere, artificial ski slopes where it never snows, enormous conference centres in towns without even a McDonald's, and entire streetcar systems to places no one goes. The flow of money slowed to the slightest trickle in order to save the banks. One event that hasn't seen such violent cutbacks is the WOMAD festival. With an annual budget of around half a million euros, it is by far the largest cultural event in the region, and political parties from either side consider it political suicide to dare cut back its funding. Its ethos, however, has changed considerably since its origins.

I asked Sergio how he remembered the first years of the festival. He answered at once with one word: "Freedom. Lots of freedom, great music, and no crowds. Peter Gabriel may have come up with WOMAD in 1989, but the first festival in Cáceres was in 1992. In the first editions, Peter Gabriel himself, Bod Geldof, the Immaculate Fools, the Chieftains, Juan Perro, Los Lobos, Raimundo Amador...so many incredible artists have played out here in this small provincial capital. The concerts were very good and had something magical about them. One that particularly stands out in my mind is one of a Romanian group in the Plaza de San Jorge playing at sunset that was simply sublime, with a violinist playing the music in the background before the spectacle of a stork going from palace to palace. It was amazing."

It's a sentiment I hear every year the festival takes place: "This is nothing like the WOMADs of old." It sounds like a sad lament for times past, but at the same time, even the hoariest of chestnuts holds grains of truth. What is certain is the festival's demographic has changed. True, the dreadlocks and accompanying mutt crew still make an appearance, but they no longer sleep rough and are now by far the minority. It's the one time a year the *botellón* is allowed to return. The one time a year the main square once again becomes a huge open-air BYOB bar. In recent years, measures have been put in place to prohibit glass from the area, but the migration is a sight to see. Rivers of people of all ages, some as young as twelve and thirteen, totter their way through the narrow streets that lead to the square carrying five- and eight-litre plastic bottles full of *calimoxo* (red wine and Coke) and other mixed drinks. The local police are present at every access point and check that no one is carrying glass but let the booze flow into the square. The problem isn't so much the alcohol. In general, your average drinker in Spain is nonviolent. It's that many couldn't care less who's playing. They arrange themselves in circles around their drinks and turn their backs to the artists, many of whom have travelled halfway around the world to play. That is where the truth in the lament lies. The essence of the festival, the music, is now peripheral. While the photo op of twenty thousand people in the main square might be irresistible to the politicians who fund the event, I can only wonder what artists like Elíades Ochoa or Salif Keita think when they look out on a heaving crowd and see half have their backs turned to the stage.

We ordered another round. This time our drinks came with some delicious meatballs in a wine sauce that worked very well with the El Gallo potato chips that came on the side. I could appreciate the changes that had taken place in the festival over the years, but I still couldn't quite see how an icon could bring down a government. So I asked Sergio what happened that year. "Well, the first thing you have to remember is the procession of the Virgin is a tradition and traditions here are...never better said... sacred. What is perhaps the most striking thing when the image of the Virgen de la Montaña is brought down to the city are the people who go to see the event, or 'receive' it as they say here. There are people you do not expect in the least to be there. There you can see just about everyone from the city, from modernists to progressives to atheists. They all attend the ceremony because it reminds them of their childhood when they were taken by their parents to watch the proceedings. I think that's the spirit that unites them with their loved ones."

Nostalgia is a powerful tool. I could understand the social and psychological weight it exerts on people, but I still couldn't see how an icon, which is in effect an inanimate object, could bring down a government. So I pressed him a little further. "It's actually more simple than you think," he chuckled, then said, "The day they were supposed to carry the image of the Virgin back up to its sanctuary, the faithful who accompanied it became extremely upset and angry. They were unhappy the procession had to pass through all the stalls and piled-up trash in the square. At that time PSOE was in power and the mayor was Carlos Sánchez Polo. The timing was critical as local elections were scheduled just a few weeks later. I went that morning to the Plaza de Santa María, next to the *concatedral*, and when José María Saponi appeared, who was the candidate of the conservative Partido Popular, people began to shout, 'Mayor! Mayor!' And he indeed came to be. Even though he had been trailing in the polls, a few weeks later he won, and Saponi was then mayor from June 1995 to 2007, for twelve years!"

Sergio has an exquisite sense of humour. He stopped to take a drink and laughed, "But the story gets more interesting. Every year when the image of the Virgin is brought down, the mayor gives it the baton of the city down in Fuente Concejo. Then, when it is returned to the sanctuary, the brotherhood returns the baton. Yet that year they refused to give it to the socialist councilman Marcelino Cardalliaguet, who was representing Mayor Sánchez Polo. Like I said, the believers were very angry. Carlos Sánchez Polo apologized a few hours later, but there was nothing he could do. Of course, ever since WOMAD has never coincided with the ascent of the image of the Virgin. Never again. We all learn from our mistakes."

Fountain in the main square in front of the Real Monasterio de Santa María de Guadalupe.

BENEVOLENT SPIRITS

11

FOUR HUNDRED MILLION YEARS AGO the world was a much more unified place, geologically speaking at least. Picture a chain rising up somewhere between Alabama and Georgia that then traces up through Pennsylvania, New York, and up to Maine before crossing the border into the Canadian Maritime provinces. This swathe of rock continues up towards Greenland and Iceland before careening down between Scotland and Northern Ireland. From there it runs under the English Channel into France, crosses into Spain, dives under the Strait of Gibraltar, and finally ends up in the High Atlas Mountains of Morocco on the fringes of the Sahara. It's a mountain chain resting on three separate continents that used to comprise just one.

These were the Central Pangean Mountains. It was a range that once ran along the supercontinent of Pangea before it broke up, with each land mass drifting its own way to form some of the continents we know today. These broken links of a once contiguous chain are now marooned on three different land masses. This means the Appalachians in western Virginia, the rock that makes up Ben Nevis in Scotland, the sharp peak of Pico La Villuerca in Spain, and the 4,167 metres of Jebel Toubkal in Morocco share the same stone.

Eons later, this mountain chain would provide another link between worlds, this time linguistically. In 1528, during one of the first European expeditions to explore the southern ranges of the North American continent, the Spanish explorer Álvar Núñez Cabeza de Vaca lent a name to this range. His expedition wrecked on the gulf coast of Florida and it soon encountered Indigenous Peoples who kindly led the despairing castaways to a place where they might find some food. Cabeza de Vaca explained in his book, *The Journey and Ordeal of Cabeza de Vaca*, that, while they were foraging, "we also found samples of gold. Through signs we asked the Indians where they had found those things. They indicated to us that very far from there was a province called Apalachee, in which there was much gold, and they gestured that it had a great quantity of everything we valued." There was gold in them there hills! Along the course of history, the word for this world-changing discovery was then transcribed as "Apalachen," which has since evolved to the Appalachians we know today.

This linguistic link would have never taken place if it hadn't been for another momentous event that occurred thirty-six years earlier in the very same mountainous folds, yet back on another continent. It was a venture that would once again bring together elements from the separated land masses and change the world as we know it.

"Right there...in the middle of the square," Carlos said, as he gestured to the fountain in the middle of the square with his iced coffee. "Or at least this is the legend that's been passed down to us over the years. Supposedly in that very same fountain, they baptized the first Indigenous People Columbus brought back with him after his initial voyage to the Americas. In some way, I guess you could say the ongoing nightmare began precisely at this spot."

My friend and guide through the Maltravieso cave, Carlos Blay, had once again invited me to tag along on an adventure and we were having breakfast before our visit to the town of Guadalupe. This time the goal was to document the different official sites of cultural interest in and around the town with the extremely talented Peruvian photographer Jorge Armestar. Neither of us had met him before, but in this small town it didn't take long to find him. Just after we arrived, we immediately spotted him in his short-sleeved, white *guayabera* shirt, measuring camera angles in the busy Wednesday street market. His varied tattoos, big curly hair, thick-framed auburn sunglasses, and tapered beard gave him a look like a character straight out of a '70s road movie. I knew at once we were going to have an interesting day. He later told me something similar. "I guess you both looked a little out of place in the market. It was clear from afar you weren't looking for tomatoes, watermelons, or dishtowels. You both have the faces of people who have lived deep things, of having lived adventures. I mean no offence, but you also looked like you were adventurers during the off season. All the same, adventurers always know where the action is." And here he laughed. "Like sailors who arrive in port after a long voyage and decide to stay in that port to rest for a while."

As he snapped pictures of the market, I quickly understood Jorge was a fellow wanderer. Someone like me, who had left one continent and chosen another. He's an emigrant who defines himself as a "Limeño." After spending half his life in Lima, Peru, and half in Extremadura, he felt as I did: a mix from different places at once. He told me, "The president of the Junta de Extremadura called me this one day while he was introducing me to the Chilean ambassador. And it's true; I'm a Limeño. I feel I am from both places at once. I can't forget my Peruvian roots, and I'm very proud of them. But I have now spent almost half of my life in Spain, and specifically in Extremadura. It's a land I love and where I have had the chance to develop my entire professional career."

It was a sentiment I couldn't help but share.

As we finished our coffees, Carlos continued, "Colombus's journey can also be said to have got its real start here too. He met with the Catholic Kings Ferdinand and Isabella in Guadalupe and they agreed upon the funding for his first voyage. Without the money raised in Extremadura, the so-called discovery of America would have never taken place."

The town of Guadalupe is one of the main municipalities found in the Villuercas-Ibores-Jara UNESCO Geopark. The park itself was created to recognize the natural, cultural, and above all geological heritage found in the area. It includes the site where Gil Cordero found his "holy cow." After the apparition of the Virgin, he built a humble hermitage on the spot where he had been told he would find the icon, but in 1330 King Alfonso XI got wind of the miraculous bovine and ordered the construction of a fortified monastery to be raised instead. This was completed in 1336 and four years later the king himself came to give thanks for his recent victory against an invading Marinid force from the Maghreb in the battle of Salado down in the province of Cádiz. To show his gratitude for the holy intervention in the battle, he had the monastery once again enlarged.

We were sitting at a terrace on the main square, planning the various sites to photograph, when the conversation took a grisly turn from the baptismal font to the recent horrendous discoveries uncovered in my native Canada. The hundreds of unmarked children's graves that were being unearthed across the country on the grounds of residential schools for Indigenous children had made the news in Spain. A country that is perhaps even further away from coming to terms with its own legacy of abuse stemming from the Church.

The Spanish Catholic Church was still in denial mode and doing all it could to obstruct investigations into the increasing number of cases of abuse constantly coming to light. The disappearances of so many children in Canada, however, could not be ignored, and the Spanish press had been cautiously reporting on the pope's long-sought-after, yet tepid, apology. A supposed sorry that judiciously avoided any reference to the institution's responsibility. For the pope and the right-wing press, the cultural genocide against Indigenous Peoples that had been undertaken by the Catholic Church, with the approval and funding of the Canadian government, was still being reduced to something committed by individual Christians. Despite the overwhelming evidence the abuse and disappearances had been systemic, the Church was still refusing to admit any institutional responsibility. Being Canadian, it was a topic that was hard to avoid, yet one I couldn't come close to explaining.

"This perceived omnipotence is nothing new with the Church unfortunately, and something that is regrettably going to stop us from getting the pictures of everything we need today," Carlos lamented. "I have been trying for some time now to get permission from the ecclesiastical authorities to grant us access to the monastery, but just this morning I got word from my boss they have refused." It seemed strange to me the regional government was unable to make something like this happen. Carlos read my puzzled look. He explained, "The town 'La Puebla de Guadalupe' simply can't be conceived of without the monastery. What I mean is that its origin and development can only be explained in the monastery's shadow. From its beginnings, it was a 'royal' foundation, and in fact its name is still the Real Monasterio de Santa María de Guadalupe. Which basically means it's under the patronage of the King of Castile, who appointed the priors and also granted them the civil lordship over the town and a large part of the surrounding territory."

Cervantes observed the same impotence more than four hundred years ago when Don Quixote reflected to Sancho *"con la iglesia hemos dado"* (or *"con la iglesia hemos topado"* as it has become more widely known), which means they had run into the stone wall of the church, both literally and figuratively. Something that could be understood given the time period he was writing in, but this ongoing, high-handed autarchy in a modern democratic state is utterly baffling.

As recently as 1998, the conservative government of José María Aznar made some changes to the mortgage laws that allowed the Church to register buildings and property in its name simply by presenting a certificate of good faith that they were owned by the institution. In many of these cases, it did so without providing a single supporting document. Religious and nonreligious buildings alike were appropriated, many of which had legally belonged to the state since 1931. Some estimate that the Church may have registered more than 4,500 properties in its name between 1998 and 2015 alone. This number could be ten times more if you include those that had been registered since Franco's 1946 Mortgage Law. A further anomaly is that, as many of these buildings, like the Great Mosque in Córdoba and the Giralda tower in Seville, are considered of cultural interest, various administrations are required to finance restoration and cover operating costs. The bitter irony worsens when you consider the enormous profits derived from their liturgical use and tourist exploitation go to one pocket: that of the Catholic Church. On top of this robbery, the profits are tax-free due to the multiple tax exemptions agreed upon between the Spanish state and the Holy See before the re-establishment of the democratic state. It seems that some miracles can exist and that they really can have their cake and eat it too.

Carlos leaned back on his chair and said, "Guadalupe itself was not even considered a municipality until 1820, and in a way this interdependence between the monastery and the town is still felt today. They need each other, so they can't really afford to get along badly, but there is no lack of tug-of-war between the public authorities and the religious, kind of in the manner of *The Pillars of the Earth*." He grinned and said, "I remember one tense discussion with the Brother Guardian, which is what the superior of the monastery has been called since the Franciscans got here. He was utterly convinced the building work he wanted to do did not have to be submitted to an urban planning licence by virtue of the Concordat with the Holy See. In plain terms, they were above the law...madness."

We settled up with the waiter and Carlos suggested, "While the monastery may be off limits to us, it looks like the church is open. Why don't we check that off our to-do list?" Jorge agreed and we struck off, tripod in arms, to start on documenting the sites.

The church and attached monastery that rose up in front of us dominated more than half the square. Seen from below, the imposing stone walls flanked by their massive buttresses make the structure seem more like a defensive castle than a religious edifice. Only the petrified mascara-wand-like pinnacled spires and pointed Gothic arches above the entrances hint towards it being a place of worship.

As we entered the church, I expected a guard, a priest, or even one of the faithful to stop us because of the tripod, but there was no one at the door. Inside, only two or three people sat in prayer before the enormous gate that fenced off the altarpiece. The thick wrought iron bars strongly suggested "Keep Out." Carlos whispered, "You've probably noticed the grilles that often separate the nave from the presbytery is somewhat of a peculiarity of Spanish churches. I'm not saying it only exists here, but let's just say it is much more frequent here than elsewhere. It's really an ancient reminiscence of the sanctum sanctorum of the Temple of Solomon, which separated the most sacred part of the temple, one that could only be accessed by the priest." We crossed over the aisle to get a different perspective and Carlos continued, "Somewhat later, in the Visigothic period, it appeared in the form of a stone gate. In fact, the Hispanic liturgy is believed to have been particularly influenced by the Jewish rituals. This barrier we see in front of us was intended to represent that what happened on the other side was a mystery. It was a sacred microcosm and was covered with cloths at certain moments of the rite to conceal the magic taking place. The same thing happened with the Byzantines and Copts. As far as I know, no curtains were ever placed on the grille of Guadalupe, but don't forget that, until the 1960s, until Vatican 2.0, Mass was pronounced in Latin and with their backs to the faithful."

There, in the middle of the altar, sumptuously swathed in embroidered and brocaded cloth, sat the Hispaniarum Regina, the Queen of the Spanish-speaking world. The figure's blackened face and hand were the only features visible among the golden embroidery. On its head sat a crown that granted it this royal title. A crown that had been placed there back in 1928 by Pope Pius XI's representative in the presence of the flesh and blood King Alfonso XIII. Carlos whispered again, "Pilgrims from all over the world come here. This morning it is rather quiet, but I suppose the busloads have yet to arrive."

Jorge set up his tripod in front of the gate and started taking long-exposure photographs while Carlos and I explored the rest of the church. Contrary to many large churches and cathedrals around the country, what lay outside the gated sacristy was quite sparse and almost empty. The bulk of the monastery's treasures were kept in the income-generating museum attached to the church. Apart from the pews that still had stickers with COVID restrictions on them, the only other noticeable thing were the confessional booths that lined the walls that looked like they had come from the set of a medieval movie. Carlos saw the slightly disturbed look on my face and told me, "Back in school we had to confess every week. You had to say something, so often we just made things up. But that's the thing; it's all about control. If you know someone's deepest secrets, you'll always have that power over them."

We stepped out from the relative cool of the church into the quickly warming morning. I asked Jorge if the Virgin of Guadalupe was as adored in Peru as it is in Mexico and other parts of Latin America. He shrugged his shoulders and said, "In the area where my mom is from, in northern Peru, yes. And in general, in Latin America the attachment to Catholicism is very present. The ancient Peruvian cultures worshipped the mountains, the sun, the moon, the elements...so when Catholicism arrived, they put a cross on the top of each sacred mountain so people would worship the cross of Christ in passing. What Catholicism does is appropriate situations or circumstances so it has more clients. Surely, the Virgin of Guadalupe to them must have been some goddess or divinity worshipped by pre-Hispanic cultures. The Virgin just gave it another form."

We went down the large stairway that leads up to the monastery and started up the hill towards the Villa Alta to take some pictures of the traditional streets and architecture that make Guadalupe one of the most beautiful towns in Spain. Carlos pointed out the Mudéjar building to the right and told us, "This used to be the Colegio de Infantes o de Gramática and the Antiguo Hospital de Hombres. It's now the Parador hotel, but back in the Middle Ages this used to be a very important centre for learning. Scholars from all over Europe came here to study. Due to its riches and the money it brought to the church's coffers, it was granted an exception by Pope Eugene IV in 1442 to practise autopsies and surgeries. Believe it or not, this was completely prohibited by religious authorities elsewhere in Europe at the time. Some records also hint towards advances like the use of Penicillium back then." Here Carlos laughed and added, "Doctor Fleming visited here many years ago and, who knows, he may have first come across its use on his visit."

Jorge was taking pictures of the hospital-turned-hotel when a woman dressed in a smart summer casual dress asked us in a marked Sevillian accent, "Are you part of the workshop?" Carlos's eyebrows rose in surprise. He asked, "Sorry, which workshop are you talking about?"

"Well, the photography workshop of course! The one we are holding inside the monastery in the cloister." Jorge instantly flashed his disarming smile and replied, "*Qué bueno!* But actually we're here to document the region's patrimony for the regional government, but this workshop sounds extremely interesting. Please do tell us about it. You say it's taking place inside the cloister?" Her smile mirrored Jorge's and she told us, "Yes, it's actually just one of a number of workshops this week. If you're interested, you're welcome to follow me and join us. The group that's hosting these events is extremely open and I'm sure it would love to hear an opinion from a professional like yourself."

There was no need to consult each other. Jorge agreed immediately and we started walking together. Jorge looked over and saw the woman was carrying a fan that was at least forty centimetres long. "You have to tell me about that fan," he said. Her smile from before grew as she unfurled the colourful Asian-themed fan and said, "It's been an heirloom in my family for years. It was made in Manila and dates back to the Manila galleons between the Philippines and Mexico. Of course, back then they were still Spanish. We've been using it as a prop for some of the photography classes, but in this heat its original purpose works best." With that, she expertly flicked her wrist and closed it once again.

We walked around the monastery to the hotel that forms part of the complex, the Hospedería del Real Monasterio. We flashed past the people working at reception, who obviously were familiar with our newfound guide, and made our way beyond a sign that said "No Entry" onto an elegant patio shaded by palm trees and the stone walls of the monastery itself. The sounds of a polyphonic singing class drifted out from behind the stones. Our guide, whose name we never caught, introduced us to the person in charge, Juan, a man who was also dressed in smart summer casual clothes. Over a wide, perfect smile and expertly trimmed beard, he reaffirmed our guide's invitation and told us we were welcome to observe some of the workshops while Jorge took pictures. He led us through another series of "No Entry" doors and we suddenly came out and saw the cloister in all its splendour from the floor above where the monitored tourist itinerary passes.

Carlos stayed talking with Juan, while Jorge began snapping away. I wandered down the colonnaded hall, entranced by the medieval fantasy fountain in the middle of the large open-air cloister. I had just made it to the end when, out of the corner of my eye, I saw Carlos shaking an elderly man's hand. Just as this happened, I saw Jorge put down his camera and quickly walk towards them. Something seemed off. I too made my way back and arrived in time to hear them introduce Jorge to the Hermano Guardían of the monastery, a stern-looking yet casually dressed elderly man who fixed an icy stare at Carlos from underneath his bushy white eyebrows. As I approached I heard the guardian state, "As I was saying, the reason why I couldn't grant you access to the monastery for your pictures was because of the tourists. If they see people up here, then they start breaking away from the conventional tourist route and begin asking to come up here. But as I see you are well accompanied with these fine people, I guess you can remain. All I ask is that you please keep your visit as discreet as possible." He half turned to walk away, then smirked and added with a snigger, "If you don't, I'll do my best to see you all excommunicated." We echoed his laugh and our guide smiled somewhat nervously but, thankfully, offered to continue the tour.

Carlos and I began to lag behind as I kept stopping and looking out at the cloister from different angles. The sculpted fountain rocketed up in the middle like some sort of missile made of lace. This was surrounded by the lush green of trees and blooming flowers that reminded me of Persian miniatures of courtyards of palaces in far off Shiraz. Yet at the same time some of the ornamentation and arches looked like something from a castle in Bruges. Carlos noticed my captivation and said, "Few places have such an amalgamation of styles. Remember I mentioned Guadalupe has always been a nexus, a meeting place between worlds? Well, this mixture shows up in the Mudéjar building tradition, very much alive and present in the area. Almost all the masons at the time were Muslim, or *al-banni*, which means builder. Then there was a very strong presence of artists from Flanders, architects, painters, sculptors, and their like during the times of the Catholic monarchs in the late fifteenth and early sixteenth centuries. Personally, I think their bits are the most striking." Carlos pointed to the upper reaches of the temple and said, "Here in the monastery you have towers with pinnacles that could top a palace in Ghent, yet they are glazed with tiles that wouldn't seem out of place in a madrasa in Fez, Morocco. Where else can you find Nazari latticework and flamboyant central European Gothic tracery fused in the same window? It's pure fantasy. I think the aesthetic impulse you feel here in the cloister of Guadalupe is almost identical to the feeling you get in places like the patios of the Alhambra."

After getting as many photographs as possible, we thanked our hosts and excused ourselves, saying we had to continue documenting the rest of the town. Just as we stepped out of the *hospedería*, the three of us let out a long sigh, took one look at each other, and started to laugh out loud.

Jorge smiled, looked down at his camera, and said, "*Qué bueno!* Sometimes you just have to go with the flow. It's amazing where events can take you by just floating along with the current." I smiled and asked Jorge if this was something he had learned along the way or something he had always been able to do. "Keep in mind," he said, "I grew up in Lima, a city of more than nine million people. In Lima, the night starts in one place and you never know where you might end up…" Here he stopped for a moment and then regained his train of thought. "I love surreal situations, and these often happen if you simply let yourself go. Intuition is also a determining factor." He stopped again and then his ideas deepened. "Here in Extremadura there aren't any really big cities, but in the villages you find many friendly people who open their hearts and memories to you if you show sincere interest and respect. This openness usually leads me to experience situations that seem to sometimes come straight out of magical realism. When things like this happen, when things go just right, I feel so very happy. Of course, I try to hold on to these memories. I treasure situations like this in my head much more than something so cold as historical facts and data."

We still had a few more sites to document, but before getting going Carlos said, "I need to pick up some *pan de pueblo*, the local bread. If I don't, my family will never believe I was here. I'd also like to pick up some of the local blood sausage, but I don't think it would survive the heat in the car all day." Jorge and I followed suit and picked up some bread and then asked Carlos where we were headed next. "Remember the fountain in front of the monastery? Well, we're going to the source, to where that water comes from. It's a fourteenth-century hydraulic system that brings water into town to this day, El Arca del Agua." Carlos then gave us a bit more backstory. "After the Roman Empire collapsed, much of its technology disappeared with it, at least in the areas of the peninsula that were not controlled by the Moors. They retained this knowledge and then went on to develop their own techniques. Skills like bringing water into towns over large distances vanished from the north, and that's what makes this system so important and underscores the importance of passing down knowledge. It took almost a millennium to recover this ability after the fall of the empire. It's just another example of the learning that was happening in Guadalupe at the time. It was so important that the monastery, which was a huge economic emporium, considered it its 'most precious asset.'" Here Carlos stopped for a moment and then said, "It also happens to be the oldest water supply system still in use today in the Iberian Peninsula."

We drove up to a point that overlooked the honeycombed town with the enormous monastery crowning the middle. At the top was a *humilladero* with views across the entire valley. I had never heard the word before and asked Carlos what it meant. "These are small places of prayer at the entrances and exits of towns and were destined for walkers who were grateful for having arrived safe and sound at their destination, that or where they prayed for a safe journey before setting out. Extremadura and really all of Spain are full of *humilladeros*. They can be images, simple crosses, or small hermitages like this one. I imagine you're translating it in your head as 'humiliating,' but the etymological root is more likely 'humus,' the earth. That is, it was a place to prostrate. As you know, submission is a central ingredient of any religion, at least the ones I know of. This one is in a very well chosen spot. It's a natural break on the main trail and from here pilgrims can contemplate the monastery for the first or last time. Legend has it that Miguel de Cervantes, like many others, offered up the chains of his captivity in Oran as an ex voto in this *humilladero*."

Legend or not, Cervantes did write about "Guadaloupe" in his last book, *The Trials of Persiles and Sigismunda*, which was published just four days before he passed away. In it he describes the pilgrims' phantasmagorical arrival.

> *Our pilgrims had scarcely set their feet in one of the two entries of the valley environing the high mountains of Guadaloupe, but at every step they made new subjects of admiration arose in their minds, which then came to their height when they saw the great and sumptuous monastery whose walls enclosed the holy image of the empress of heaven: the holy image which is the enlargement of prisoners, the file of their irons and ease of their passions; the health of the sick, the counsel of the afflicted and the mother of orphans. They entered into her temple and, instead of Tyrian purple,*

Syrian damask or satin embroidered with gold of Milan, which they
thought to find hanging on her walls, they found crutches, which such as
halted had left there; eyes and arms of wax, which the blind and lame had
hung up; and napkins taken from dead men, all afterward living, whole,
free and contented after extreme distress, through the mercy of the mother of
mercies. Our devout pilgrims were so possessed with an apprehension of
these miraculous ornaments that, turning their eyes to every side of the
temple, they thought they saw captives come flying in the air, wrapped in
their chains to hang them upon the holy walls; the diseased there to hang
their stilts, and the dead their winding-sheets, seeking new places where to
put them because there was no more room left in the temple.

The road to the right led up to the highest Appalachian point in the
range, the Pico La Villuerca at 1,603 metres, and then a dirt track split off
to the left. Carlos edged his car over the corrugated dusty track surrounded
by Spanish broom and rock rose as far as he dared go and we hiked the
rest of the way through the dense chestnut forest. A thick iron door
guarded the grotto, but when Carlos tried the keys the deputy mayor had
given him, he found it already open. The heavy door screeched as it listed
to the side and we were met by a gust of cool air and spider webs. There
must have been at least a fifteen-degree difference inside from the
intense summer heat. The hollow itself was about three metres high and
a bit more than half a metre wide. The medieval ceramic pipes had been
replaced and a modern PVC tube ran between our feet, but the rest was
just as it always had been. There were no security lights and ahead was
pitch black. Jorge led the way, using his phone as a flashlight, pausing
now and then to get some sort of complete perspective for a photograph.
We continued about fifty metres into the absolute darkness until he
finally said, "I think this is about the best we are going to get. Unless the
cave opens up into some sort of chamber ahead, but if you look closely,
this grotto has been hewn out of the living rock. It's amazing they were
able to make it as big as it is."

We traced back our steps, avoiding the occasional toad, and stepped
out of the relative cool and were once again brought face to face with the
fierce Spanish summer. Carlos led the way to the next site about fifteen

minutes farther down the trail, a path that followed the pipes just underground. Along the way, medieval chimneys with ceramic pipes stuck out of the ground at various intervals that were built to vent rising pressure when the water flow increased and allowed access to the pipes below if they became clogged. As the heat began to really bite, the buzzing from the cicadas grew louder and even the ample shade from the surrounding tangle of chestnut trees offered little respite. Here we found two different sites. The first was a squat structure whose roof was completely overgrown with vegetation. A low iron door opened on to an open pool that collected and then purified the water before sending it along its way towards Guadalupe. Next to this, a larger iron door was dug into the very side of the mountain. Once again the inside was markedly cooler than outside, but here there was an entrance with two icons set above a tunnel that had been reinforced with brick archways. A fifteenth-century plaque was also encrusted into the wall, and after reading its opening pomposities, we realized it was actually an instruction manual for if the system got plugged up. Here several different chambers had been excavated into the mountainside. While the previous cave had been carved out with the purpose of transporting water, here the builders had set ceramic pipes deep into the rock to channel the spring water that still emanated from both the innards of the mountain and the ground below.

Jorge took off down the tunnel to the left, happy at the prospect of finding more to photograph in these tunnels. I followed Carlos into the darkness to the right, guided by the flashlight from his mobile phone. It didn't take me long to recall his nimbleness in cramped situations like this and watched as the light from his phone got smaller and smaller ahead of me. Before entering, he had warned us to watch our step and try to walk along the sides of the ceramic tile that carried the water between our feet.

Suddenly, I realized I could no longer see where I was stepping. I braced myself on the damp, clammy walls, brushing away the invisible scurrying creatures I actually preferred not to see, and tried to advance forward in the darkness. After slipping several times into shallow pools of water, and cursing myself for always wearing flip-flops, I reached into my pocket for my mobile phone and switched on the flashlight. Above me were interlocking bricks that arched off down the cave and I saw the walls were no longer covered in plaster. They were now bare, chiselled rock squirming with insect life. Ahead I saw the tunnel split into two and took a few tentative steps forward when my mobile phone gave up its last breath, leaving me once again plunged into an inky blackness. I attuned my other senses and listened closely to the sounds around me. Water and its various sounds were all around, seeping out of the walls and dripping into pools while in other parts gurgling out from the ground below. These sounds echoed along these etched-out passageways that had been built more than half a millennium ago. I told myself I could either stumble on ahead or wait until they came looking for me. My mind momentarily wandered to stories I knew of people lost in caves, like Tom Sawyer and Becky Thatcher. I then contented myself with the thought these caves were man-made and could only go on for so long with a limited number of conduits. I scrambled forward in the dark for a while when I saw a speck of light coming towards me. "Where have you been?" I asked. Carlos chuckled. "Come on old man, I want to show you a spot where the water is really springing from the ground."

Jorge had set up his tripod and was doing his best to artfully capture the water as it bubbled up from the earth in the penumbra. Carlos told us, "This system was a big part of the reason why Guadalupe grew and became so powerful. This entire valley became irrigable thanks to it, something that really didn't exist elsewhere at the time in Spain." Jorge looked up and smiled. "So I guess in a certain way its due to these conduits that a Spaniard, a Canadian, and a Peruvian are crawling around together in the dark. Sounds like the beginning of a joke. Next time, though, remind us how cold the caves and the water are. We could have left some beers to cool at the entrance and had an air-conditioned picnic before braving the hike back to the car."

Back out in the blinding light, the cicadas seemed to have redoubled their efforts and had reached a manic pitch. After the coolness of the cave, the summer heat felt like it had somehow managed to pick up even more intensity. We still had another stop at the fourteenth-century palace, la Granja de Valdefuentes, one of the palaces the Catholic kings had used on their frequent trips to Guadalupe. Carlos told us it was now in private hands and the mayor had once again smoothed the way to get us permission to see the property, at least from the outside.

When we got back to the car, we realized it had been powdered by the fine dust we had raised coming in and we were now better camouflaged among the surrounding terrain. The once-white car was now the colour of a light coffee with milk. Carlos called the guard who watched the palace and let him know we were on our way. We crossed the valley and pulled off the main road and once again found ourselves off-roading in Carlos's low-riding car. The dirt road was surrounded by a well-kept *dehesa* (pasture) that spread out beyond the horizon. Out here, we were beyond the reach of Google Maps and Carlos had to call the guard twice to make sure we weren't lost.

Just when we were about to turn back, we spotted the retreat. Hidden behind a stand of cypress trees we could make out a series of ornamented archways that were half-covered by a bushy row of enormous hydrangeas. The flowers had wilted somewhat in the heat, but they still gave the entire scene the effect of a '70s postcard. As we drove up, an enormous mastiff lazily got up, stretched, and wandered towards the car, its head reaching up well over the hood. Carlos lowered his window just enough and called out, "Is he friendly?" Manuel, the guard, appeared from around the corner and laughed. "As long as I'm here and it isn't nighttime, he is. When the sun goes down, though, you don't want to be caught wandering around here." We stepped out and greeted the miniature horse while we introduced ourselves to Manuel, who was somewhere in his mid-sixties but who moved around the yard with ease. He quickly informed us, "You're welcome to take pictures of the outside and from the ground floor of the patio, but that's it. Even if I wanted to let you upstairs in the gallery, there are so many security cameras around here that the masters would know immediately."

With that, Manuel opened a set of wide wooden doors that opened on to a shaded Eden. From within flowed the soothing sound of running water and the scent of lemons. This peaceful scene was momentarily interrupted as we stepped inside the entranceway to the patio. The skulls and horns of at least twenty-five prized stags protruded from each wall like some sort of primitive burglar trap, ready at any moment to skewer unsuspecting thieves. Manuel saw me start and said, "The owners are very avid hunters. Every year in the autumn we host several *monterías*, large organized hunting parties." I asked him what they mostly hunted and Manuel grunted. "The owners don't have time for small game. The finca is huge, some six thousand hectares, and as you can see there is lots of big game to be had."

After taking a few turns around the patio, Carlos and I stepped out again into the heat to get a closer look at the medieval arches and columns that stood behind the fading flowers. Carlos mused, "I would like to think the situation of the '*guardeses*,' as we call the guards that live and work in these large fincas here in Extremadura, has improved. When I was growing up, I had several friends whose families owned huge estates, and the *guardes* and their families were kind of like serfs for anything and everything. It used to shock me when they would invite me over for weekends. It was a relationship that lasted a lifetime and was sometimes even inherited from generation to generation. True, there was mutual trust and affection, but within an ironclad and immovable classism: each one knew his place. For example, they would never ever share a table. It was really quite close to the portrait of continual humiliation and disdain Miguel Delibes so accurately portrays in his classic book, *Los Santos Inocentes* [The Holy Innocents]."

We turned the corner of the palace and Carlos sighed. "Now I think it is more common to hire immigrants from Latin America or Romania to do this kind of work. And I say 'hire' being somewhat optimistic. I guess they hire them for the absolute minimum wage, or at least the husband, but in the end the whole family ends up working. Manuel here certainly seemed to have had better luck. But as he talks, take note how he always refers to the owners. He never mentions their names, they are always 'el Señor,' 'la Señora,' or 'los Señoritos.'"

Jorge documented what he could from the ground floor and we were about to leave when Manuel asked if we could give him a lift back into town. Seeing as it was market day back in Guadalupe, he wanted to pick up some things. Jorge and I piled into the back while Manuel rode shotgun, and it was then we discovered Jorge had another hidden talent. His photography had led him to take a genuine interest in the people and things he was documenting. And he had an uncanny ability to get people he had only just met to open up to him, either verbally or before the camera. Even occupational hermits like Manuel who had spent the last quarter century in relative solitude.

Bouncing over yet another cattle gate, Jorge asked, "So Manuel, how did you end up with this job? Did you know the family before?" Manuel thought for a second and said, "No, I used to hunt on the fringes of the finca and got to know the family through hunting. At the time I was working construction but got hurt and was out of work. This job has its challenges, but back then I was working 10–11-hour days and getting paid something like eight hundred pesetas. So when they offered me this, I talked to my wife and said, 'Why not give it a try?' That was around twenty-five years ago, but I tell you this job isn't for everybody. Most of the time you're alone, except when my boss or some of her thirteen kids come to visit." Jorge whistled, "Wow, that's a big family. How do you get on with all of them?" Manuel slapped his thigh and said, "I've seen them all grow up and we get on just fine. But I'm retiring come December and I don't know who they're going to find to replace me. But that's not my problem! It's time for me to look after my own family and my garden."

Jorge laughed along with him and asked, "What's the most difficult part about the job then?" Manuel's answer came quickly. "That's easy, the loneliness. I guess it's better now that they have all these cameras and things, but it used to be just me and the dogs out here. True, they let you know if anyone is around for kilometres, but just that feeling of being completely isolated can get to you sometimes." Jorge made a few sympathetic clicks with his tongue and then changed track. "Well, if that's the worst part, what about the best? What's the best part of this job?" Manuel looked out across the sea of holm oak trees and answered, "That's easy too. The ghosts." Jorge seemed to be expecting an answer like this and didn't skip a beat and reassured him, "Of course, they would be." Manuel continued, "What I mean is they keep you company. Not that I have ever seen them, but you hear them all the time, their footsteps and such." Jorge pressed further and asked, "Do you have any idea who they are?" Manuel nodded his head and said, "I'm pretty sure one of them is the patriarch, my boss's husband. He was a great man, and in fact he's buried right under where you were standing in the palace's chapel. But there must be many more judging from the racket they sometimes make. After all, el Señor isn't the only one entombed there. There have to be lots of priests buried under the palace too. As I say, I've never seen them, but my granddaughter has." With that, he paused for a moment and then turned to look back at Jorge. "One day we were kicking a ball around and one time after I kicked it to her, I noticed she paused for some time. I waited for a moment, then asked her to kick the ball back over. I won't ever forget her answer. 'To who?' she asked. 'You or that man standing next to you?' And I swear to you...I was the only other person in the room."

We dropped Manuel off at the market just as the stall keepers were packing up and he quickly hustled off to get what he needed. I was still taken aback by the story he had told us in the car and was impressed with Jorge's empathy. I asked what had led him to question Manuel. Jorge shrugged his shoulders and said, "Well, when I first saw him I immediately thought of *Los Santos Inocentes*, the Miguel Delibes story that was later made into a film. The one about the family that lives on a finca and takes care of it for a wealthy family. Well, that was the first thing, but I never fall into prejudice, thank goodness. So I was just curious and wanted to know more about his life in that space. You know, about how he was treated, about his relationship with the owners, if he was treated well, if he was happy...Really, it was out of a genuine interest in his life. I asked and he answered. We were fortunate to meet someone with such an open heart who told us what he treasured."

"But you didn't react, you didn't even flinch when he started telling you about the ghosts. How were you able to continue without distracting him?" I asked in genuine admiration.

"If I had reacted in any other way, the story would have ended there, with the sounds in the palace. Manuel would have closed off and withdrawn and would not have shared the rest. I always try to think I am no one to judge the reality other people live. My beliefs are no better or worse than anyone else's. In fact, often the beliefs of others enrich my perception of the world. As I told you while we were in the darkness of the caves, ghost stories, supernatural experiences, and things like that make me respectful and curious, never afraid. If there is something I'm afraid of, it's things like taxes and my outrageous monthly social security payments as a freelancer!"

It was clear Jorge spoke to people as he photographed them with respect and curiosity. I thought about what he had said and asked, "Today you told me that, while you enjoy taking photos of monuments, what you love best is taking pictures of people. As you aren't from here, how do you perceive the relationship between these stones and the people that live behind them?"

"Respect for these stones and for material heritage, especially in a country with so much like Spain, is fundamental. But that's only one side of the story. On the other hand, the current stories of the people who live here are also essential when trying to understand their relationship with their heritage. Their stories tell you where their people have been and where they are going." He paused and then added, "But there's something else. There are also circumstances that belong to the intangible heritage of a place, such as the old taverns that preserve the living history of towns and cities. These places may not be historic or considered beautiful, but they, too, have and maintain stories. The pity is these types of businesses, like corner grocery stores, pastry shops, or old hairdressers, are being lost. They are on the way to becoming extinct. We really must be careful to pay more attention to this phenomenon. Every time one of these stores closes, a part of the town's history dies. And the pity I feel is this space is then usually occupied by some urbanistic whim or by a soulless franchise without a story to tell or a past worth exploring."

We were just about to say goodbye to Jorge when he lit up his smile and said, "You probably don't remember, but you passed me as I was driving here." I smiled and thought, it's true, Carlos drives with the same enthusiasm as he does when he scrambles through caves. Jorge said, "Even though we didn't know each other by sight, I somehow knew my liaison, Carlos, was in the car overtaking me and he was with someone else. Before we even met, I knew we were going to get along and have an adventure today. I have no idea why. I guess it was intuition."

Jorge had to get back to Mérida and we were headed in different directions, so we parted ways. Carlos and I got back into the *café con leche* car and he asked me if I was in a particular rush to get back home. "No, I can't think of anything I need to be home for right now," I replied. "Good," he said, "because we can make one last stop. I know of some rock art we can check out on our way home."

Another of the lesser-known surprises of the geopark are the numerous panels of rock art scattered throughout it. It is also a stop along the Council of Europe's Prehistoric Rock Art Trails. To date, at least forty-one sites have been catalogued, but there are certainly many more yet to be discovered. Just as we passed through the town of Cañamero, we pulled off the main highway and followed the Ruecas River that wound its way up a tightening gorge. The surroundings greened as the walls of striated rock closed in. Down below, people were wild swimming in the dammed-up swimming holes. Both Carlos and I began to regret not packing our swimsuits.

We pulled off to the side and climbed the short, well-marked distance to the overhanging grotto. The recess itself reminded me of the area on the Portuguese border where I had seen the paintings with my brother-in-law, albeit the climb was much easier. Once again, this was a vantage point from which you could see friend, foe, and game crossing the valley. The large dam to the left somewhat marred the view, which would have been otherwise unchanged since the paintings had been drawn, but the similarities were clear. I searched in vain and could only make out a few of the paintings highlighted on the informative boards below. These paintings were not as well preserved as the others I had seen before and I could only make out a few lines and what I imagined were anthropomorphic figures.

Then my eye was drawn to a reddish blotch down below. I looked closer and as my eyes adjusted, the splotch began to take form. And then it became a dragon. I excitedly called over to Carlos, "Look! Look! A dragon! They were painting dragons back then!" Carlos walked over, patted me on the shoulder, smiled, and said, "I think imaginations are getting quite creative today. Read the information board. It's been a long day and it's time to head home." I looked down and, sure enough, there it was, the myth of the red dragon. It was, in fact, just an example of naturally forming oxide. I hadn't been the first and surely wouldn't be the last to project my mistaken conclusion onto something I had been hoping to experience.

A *dehesa* scene.

IN THE SIERRA
OF THE CAT

12

THE LAND AHEAD WAS YELLOWISH GOLD, sparce, and intensely hot. The two-lane highway unravelled from the city like a lit detonation wire snapping over a bristly carpet of cut hay. In the distance small flocks of sheep huddled together in scrums, pointlessly using each other to shade from the brutal sun in the treeless steppe. The few man-made watering holes that branch off from the culverts running off from the highway and dry creek basins were completely parched and, now in summer, the small creeks that flow through the area were just a succession of muddy puddles. The little rain that had fallen the previous winter had long since given up its last hurrah and these desiccated areas were ominous auguries of drier summers to come. The glare off the land was biblical in its ferocity. To travel across the man-made steppe that surrounds the city is an exodus meant to teach the God-fearing and climate-change deniers their deity is indeed vengeful. Several times a year, my family and I make the pilgrimage north along these roads to the *quesería* La Frondosa in Villasbuenas de Gata in the Sierra de Gata to visit one of the people who had a lot to do with our settling in Cáceres, Jill Barrett.

Our friendship goes back to when my wife and I were looking into buying a house in the city and the Spanish economy was a freewheeling rollercoaster. At the time, the economy was like an escaped convict who had stolen a car and was determined to never go back, riding high and fast on the intoxicating fumes of an overinflated housing bubble. The crews of masons from all over the country making temporary fortunes that Manolo had mentioned were hard at work around the country at the time. Entire neighbourhoods appeared overnight, so quickly that many weren't even hooked up to the urban water grids and they never would be. Banks were doling out mortgages faster than customers could be served at a McDonald's drive-thru window. Minimum requirements were often over-looked and it seemed as though everyone was buying a second or third home down by the beach. I had taken a contract job with a British univer-sity to teach English in the Ministry of Tourism in Gaddafi's Libya. The university was happy to write me an "extendable" contract, and that was good enough for the bank. All things come to an end, though, and as it became clear the contract would do just that as autumn settled in, I sent off an optimistic email from an internet cafe in the old town of Tripoli to an English academy in Cáceres, hoping against hope it would have an opening in the middle of the academic year. Thankfully, it did.

The English teaching world is a notoriously fickle industry filled with people in transition or those who got stuck transitioning without a backup plan. Folks who are often either running away from something back home or towards a chimerical panacea they almost never find. These high-flying dreams quickly become grounded as these runners spend their days elu-cidating provincial tweens on the intricacies of the English verb system in an increasingly difficult attempt to keep their heads above water. Spain acts like a magnet for these dreamers and is perhaps second only to Southeast Asia for attracting such escapees. A quick look at English teaching job sites online almost always lists Spain at the top, with the most job offers available. Requirements are low and often nonexistent if you have the right passport, and even if you don't, often a "Nordic" appearance will be enough to get you through the door. A year in "sunny" Spain can seem awfully tempting to recent graduates sending unanswered resumes out into the digital void. It can be equally enticing to someone gazing out a dark office window at yet another day of sleet and greyness in northern Europe. They fondly look back on the sun and sand during their last hol-iday in Benidorm and start searching for teaching work.

Fast-forward a few months in the country and these dreamers quickly come to the realization Spain is not a tropical country—winters are cold. Then the promise they heard when they were hired of being "just" three hours from the beach gets further and further out of reach between having to plan classes and trying to get by on a dead-end salary. As my Irish neighbour Brian had discovered, teaching itself is not for everyone, and it certainly isn't just a case of standing up in front of a class and speaking your native language. The breaking point often comes when confronted by an irate parent demanding to know why their seven-year-old is incapable of reading and reciting Shakespeare after three months of sixty-minute classes twice a week. The question becomes even more pertinent when these migrants find out they could be earning the same or more working as housecleaners. A job that would offer them a lot less stress from demanding parents, not to mention being able to leave their job at work and not have to spend their late evenings and weekends planning classes.

The puzzling thing is this billion-euro industry continues to flourish. Spanish children start obligatory schooling when they are six years old, and when they do they start learning English. This means by the time they complete their cycle of compulsory education at sixteen, they will have been exposed to at least ten years of English classes. So why the need for so much extracurricular support? It's because after a decade of instruction, many students leave the system without even being able to communicate on a basic level. So why are Spanish children still struggling so much with English? Some commentators attribute this deficit to the fact Spain is a relatively big power in Europe that punches far above its weight, linguistically speaking, across the globe. There is definitely some truth to this. Spanish is one of the most spoken languages in the world and, unlike Chinese, is spoken in many different countries. Strong countries with strong languages are notoriously poor at learning second languages. This is because their need to be heard and understood abroad is reduced. A quick look at the US and the UK, with their dismal statistics in second-language learning, demonstrates this fact. But this explanation is only part of the picture.

The real elephant in the room is the same problem Brian and I had discussed on our walk. The rot stems from the lack of accountability in the overly rigid Spanish education system. Teachers are chosen not via their skills as teaching professionals but by sitting a medieval-style exam. An exam that focuses primarily on memorizing material rather than synthesizing information and demonstrating an understanding of what teaching really involves and the empathy it requires. Those who pass the test are then transformed into teachers for life who are never again observed. Any inspection that may happen is primarily administrative and there is no real control as to what happens in each class. The very same parents that complain to the academies that their children aren't fluent after three months of private classes are either unwilling or simply incapable to effect the changes needed in the education system that would ensure more effective learning. Imagine a primary teacher who was incapable of doing simple math equations, or one that was unable to spell simple words properly? Yet when it comes to language teaching it's not infrequent to find teachers with only a relatively basic grasp of the language, or worse yet, educators that have absolutely no idea how to help their learners acquire it and who reduce language acquisition to lists of single words to translate. These crucial elements are completely overshadowed by the life-changing importance placed on the public exam that secures them a teaching position in a very difficult, inflexible job market.

Whatever the case, the system's failings this time worked in my favour and the reply to my email from that internet cafe in Libya was positive. My email barrage of CVs had a hit. There just happened to be an opening at an academy in Cáceres with Echo Hill. The outgoing teacher could not adapt to the cultural differences and had returned to the United Kingdom. Jill's runner was my opening.

The thin secondary highway joins up with a pristine, north-south, four-lane motorway that slices through the scrub on the artificial steppe that appears once the city slips behind your rear-view mirror. Thin patches of green mark the horizon where the Tagus River and its affluent, the Almonte, cut through the harsh landscape like rough-cut bulldozer tracks. Once mighty rivers, they lost their mojo long ago and are now mere IV drips that feed the enormous José María Oriol hydroelectric reservoir. The dramatic ups and downs of the rivers violently scar their banks. These vicious fluctuations aren't necessarily due to the caprices of the weather but are more a result of the energy auction market the electrical companies in the country have managed to manipulate and monopolize. A system that uses the most expensive energy source at a particular time as the benchmark asking price, even if only a small percentage of the actual energy produced is done so by using that particularly expensive source at the time. When the asking price for power is high, they dump the stored water in the reservoirs to create cheap power, leaving farmers and entire villages dry, praying for rain in an increasingly drier climate. The practice seems cruelly criminal, but the past forty years of revolving door politics now sees several ex-ministers, and even ex-prime ministers, sitting on the advisory boards of these powerful companies. The result is an immoral yet quasi-legal practice that will continue to scar the countryside until the year the seasonal rains completely fail and entire areas literally die of thirst.

Cross the rivers and you come to the first low mountain pass. Stands of tinder-dry pines climb up from the steppe and scatter across the hillsides, jutting out from the growing hills like the spiky fade haircuts of teenage boys. Fire cuts and bald patches stain the rest of the range like an advancing topical skin affliction. Pretty it's not, but the deeper greens provide some solace to your eyes after the parched landscape of the lower lying steppe.

On the northern side of the mountain pass, a darker green spreads as the *dehesa* extends to the sierra on the horizon. Along this stretch of the EX-109, the harsher granite scrub that framed the motorway on the other side of the pass now flattens out into pastureland dotted with sheep, cattle, and the occasional team of Iberian pigs. Stands of gnarled holm oaks mixed with ancient-looking cork oaks make up the bulk of this distinctive, pattern-like Mediterranean woodland. Each tree seems to grow to the same invisible ceiling and then fattens out, casting out its welcome shade. It's a park-like ecosystem where the handprint of humans can be seen everywhere. It's made up of great swathes of grasslands dotted with scattered stands of trees. The original mixed forests have been deforested over time by means of fire or through the introduction of livestock, creating open spaces within a "forest-park" where cattle and other livestock can graze. By thinning the trees, more grass grows outside the shade of the trees. During the brief springs, a green blanket decorated with wildflowers rolls beneath these shade-bearing evergreen monuments, but that was while the fleeting rains fell. Now, at the beginning of summer, everything has already dried up and turned a savannah-like gold.

These sparse, meadowed groves are working landscapes and have made up the timber soul of Extremadura and the southwestern part of the Iberian Peninsula for millennia. Even today, as people increasingly abandon the countryside in favour of cities, these manicured ecosystems make up around 50 per cent of the usable agricultural land in Extremadura. The land was certainly much wilder and less trimmed when the first hand-prints appeared in the Maltravieso cave, but humans have been shaping this land for eons. Recent palynological studies have shown that, as far back as the Neolithic period, settlers in the area began to cultivate and shape the land. In order to find out more about its prehistoric origins, I contacted José Antonio López-Sáez, senior scientist at the Institute of History of the CSIC, the Spanish National Research Council in Madrid, after reading some of the studies he had been involved in. A busy man with many research irons in the fire, he was kind enough to answer some of my questions by email. I mentioned to him I was interested in the beginnings of the *dehesa* and asked him when he thought the transforma-tion of the land had begun. He replied, "Probably in the middle Neolithic period, with the sedentarization of the population and its accompanying livestock. All of which placed a greater stress on the ecosystems. These people had become fully sedentary, which undoubtedly left a very noticeable mark on the paleo-landscape. A place that was progressively deforested as livestock and agriculture became more important. These Neolithic peoples chose today's pasturelands to settle in because of their great eco-logical productivity. Things like the easy availability of fruits like acorns for livestock, the abundant wood sources for their own uses, the prox-imity of water sources and rivers, and the fact they were plains and meadows where the habitat was simple. This in sharp contrast to the Iberian mountain chains, which were generally occupied much later."

If this transformation of the land were happening in the Neolithic period, then this time frame would also coincide with a lot of the rock art found in the area. I asked him if he saw a connection between the two. "Although rock art is often thought of as a means of access into the cognitive, religious, and cultural realms of a social formation, what we believe is rock art can help us understand the long-term rhythms of landscapes. It is intertwined with its construction processes and its use along time. We view rock art as an extremely relevant type of archeological evidence for the understanding of landscapes, mainly because it allows us to observe a territory as a meaningful cultural or social spatial entity. Otherwise, it would be easy to only see a compound of fragmentary spaces. The correlation between the distribution of Neolithic paintings and the pastoral traditional landscape may be further interpreted as a continuum of the use of a series of very valuable economic resources in the Mediterranean uplands over several millennia. These are marked by archeological indicators pointing to its beginning and, if things continue as they are, its end. Life along this continuum is not easy to grasp archeologically otherwise."

I noticed a note of alarm in his response and asked him what he meant about its possible end. "The resilience of what is left of the traditional Mediterranean landscape is a product of a dependency that exists between human labour and 'nature,' so much so that the ability of the Mediterranean landscape to stay resilient is totally dependent on the amount of investment in the social work in the area. These traditional ways of life, or perhaps better said, ways of work, produce and sustain these particular 'working landscapes.' It follows that any real environmental degradation is a product of sociopolitical disturbance or change, as it produces a stop or forces a shift in all of this invested work. This is what has happened over the past last decades in the Spanish Mediterranean basin, especially in the lowlands. A dramatic change in land use has taken place, which is likely an important factor in its degradation. In the uplands, work has traditionally been less labour-intensive and therefore the risks produced by abandonment have also been less pressing, but traditional ways of life fade away generation after generation. The ecologically fine-tuned Mediterranean environment as we know it is increasingly under siege, and the prospects for its future management and preservation are doomed to fail. That is, as long as they are not accompanied by policies that keep people living and working in this unique landscape."

The concept of the *dehesa* as it is now known dates back to the Romans. They were the first to establish large estates in these marginal territories with poor soil and pockmarked with huge granite boulders. A single owner controlled these large managed areas, and this gave rise to the spread of such a unique ecosystem. Later, as the reconquest crept through the region, these large extensions of land were conceded to the nobles and military orders that resettled the area. Then in the Middle Ages the land was mainly used for free grazing, acting as winter pastures where the transhumant cattle and flocks of sheep migrated to in winter in the southwest of Spain, to the valleys of Extremadura and farther south towards Andalusia and the Guadalquivir River basin.

Past the village of Torrejoncillo, the road forks in two. To the left, olive groves and *dehesas* lead towards Portaje and the reservoirs that feed the area. To the right, shadeless, sunburnt grasslands stretch out to a horizon fringed with the stubs of blue mountains. Cattle huddle on the horizon around the few remaining dugout drinking holes with water still in them or that have had water trucked in. The highway continues north until it sharply drops down into the true artery of the Valle del Alagón, the river that gives the valley its name. Presaging what's to come, trees start to reappear. These are not the hardy, drought-resistant oaks from before but stands of willows, cypresses, elms, and plane trees. Just as your eyes become accustomed to the change from the more muted greens and biscuit browns of the summer *dehesa*, shocks of fluorescent green cornfields, high as an elephant's eye, line the way thanks to the irrigation supplied by the river. Large bushy stork nests balance atop the telephone poles along the road, looking like percussion mallets until the trees continue to thicken and announce the river. As the view opens, the imposing Gothic cathedral of Coria reigns over the lush, flat river valley from behind the protection of the Roman wall that runs along where the river used to flow. At its feet, a forsaken medieval bridge stands stranded in cornfields that once were covered in water. This is the true cathedral of the bishopric of Cáceres and was the bishop's only seat until 1957 when the diocese was split in two. The building is much more opulent than the *concatedral* back in the old town of Cáceres, even if it, too, suffers the scars from the passage of time. Although, in its case, the wounds were not man-made.

Early in the morning on November 1, 1755, the faithful were gathered in the cathedral to celebrate a special Mass for All Saints' Day. Then something happened that would literally shake Europe to its foundation and expand and extend the questioning that had begun with the optimism and rationalism of the Enlightenment. The ground began to tremble. A fissure split out in the Atlantic, three hundred kilometres off the coast of Portugal and Africa, sparking a powerful earthquake that has been estimated at around 8 on the Richter scale. The tremors, tsunami, and ensuing fires devastated Lisbon and greatly affected cities on the African coast like Rabat and Agadir farther down the coast. Its effects were felt as far afield as France, Switzerland, and, as Brian had mentioned during our walk to school, the coast of Ireland. Here in Coria, three hundred kilometres upstream from the delta of the Tagus River and its affluent the Alagón that flows past its Gothic walls, the cathedral began to collapse with the congregation inside. A cathedral that contained in its reliquary a footprint of the Virgin herself wasn't able to withstand the force of the earth's tremors. The bell tower collapsed and some twenty people lost their lives, more than those who perished in the more severely damaged city of Seville.

Natural tragedies like this have taken place since the beginning of time. The world of those who first made their handprints in the Maltravieso cave also shivered and shook. But in their world of so many uncertainties and unknowns, it may have come as just another surprise. The Age of Enlightenment, however, meant that different readings were possible. Alternate theories were being offered on matters. Rather than instinctively revert to the age-old explanation of a just, yet vengeful, God punishing the wicked, enlightened thinkers like Voltaire began to seriously question such infantile knee-jerk theological analysis. If indeed the people of Lisbon were being punished for their supposed wickedness, what about those in Paris where Voltaire wrote that "voluptuous joys abound"? Was there not less debauchery in London "where opulence luxurious holds her throne"? When the majority praised the Virgin Mary for saving some, reasoning voices asked why those were saved when thousands were swept up and down the Tagus when the four-story tsunami rushed back in. Were they any more pious? Lacking sin? Philosophers like Immanuel Kant focused his energies on the study of natural phenomena and produced one of the first systematic attempts to explain earthquakes in natural rather than supernatural terms. Out of tragedy, critical thinking and questioning of long-held dogmas flowered as the brothels remained standing and the cathedrals of Lisbon and around Europe shuddered.

Continuing north, you reach Moraleja, the last sizeable town between here and Ciudad Rodrigo, seventy kilomentres to the north in the region of Castilla y León. It's a place that gives the impression of a Spanish take on a frontier town. From the outside, everything it seems to have to offer falsely lies on display on the heavily speed-bumped main drag. But its real lifeblood, its schools, swimming holes, and best bars, lie hidden behind the entirely forgettable string of low-rise apartment blocks and shop-fronts that line the throughway. From Moraleja, you leave behind the last shock of vibrant, almost fake, green cornfields and the first folds of the sierra appear as you leave the corporate limits of the town. Just beyond the last garishly painted disco, the vibrancy of the artificial fertility is dialled back somewhat and the irrigated land gives way to thirstier hills spotted with rock rose and olive trees.

Perales del Puerto, as its name suggests, is the next village and is the gateway to the area. Here, orange trees shade the two-lane highway as it passes through the middle of the village lined with shops selling agricultural equipment. Once you bounce over the last of the somewhat extreme raised pedestrian crossings, you emerge from a row of whitewashed buildings and are greeted by a panoramic view of the sierra that rolls out before you. From here the road drops down to the first of many rivers and streams that tumble out of the mountains. These are often dammed in the summer to create wild swimming holes that are always accompanied by the ever so civilized Spanish *chiringuito*, the small bar that serves reasonably priced food and cold beer to combat the heat.

These dammed-up swimming holes also serve another more vital purpose. Just a little farther up the road, you start to see the lasting scars left by the most serious affliction that blights this mostly wild area: fire. Spanish summers are not only long and exceedingly hot, but they are also extremely dry. These hills can go months without seeing a drop of rain and every summer it's only a matter of time before the first plume of smoke goes up somewhere along the range. The swimming holes are then quickly turned into reservoirs for the helicopters to dip their buckets into when fighting the fires. These can be sparked by natural causes, but more often than not the dark hand of man is behind them. Driven by generalized unemployment, a desire to reclassify land, or sometimes just pure malice, these pyromaniacs create the most harrowing scenes of devastation that spread, literally, like wildfire.

Livelihoods aren't the only things that can go up in flames in the blink of an eye. In 2017, just across the border in Portugal, sixty-two people lost their lives in one particularly deadly disaster. The majority of the victims were trapped in their cars as they tried to flee the unstoppable wall of flames. An entire sub-economy has built up around these tragedies. The lack of job opportunities makes firefighting an attractive option during the long dry summers, but no fires means no work and this can also drive some of the more desperate to commit such atrocious acts whose consequences go much further than a few weeks of paydays. Those irregular stands of maritime pines that stick out like overgrown stalks of corn that you can see from the road act like Katyusha rocket launchers when flames sweep through. As the resin in the pines heats up, it shoots off burning embers and seed pods that can travel kilometres in the air, starting up new fronts behind the burn lines and fire cuts firefighters create in their attempts to halt the advancing wall of flame. These trees are much less fire-resistant than the autochthonous trees like the cork and holm oaks that have evolved over time in the area. The difficulty is these take decades longer to grow than the faster growing pines and are therefore nowhere near as profitable.

The real crossroads of the sierra lies just beyond one of the area's few gas stations as you come up the EX-109 from Cáceres. The Guardia Civil often sets up checkpoints here to control the flow of goods and other substances from north to south and east to west. A dividing line between villages to the west like Hoyos, Acebo, and the promontory perch of Trevejo, and those to the east like Villasbuenas de Gata, Gata, Santibáñez el Alto, and just before Extremadura turns into the wide open spaces of Castilla y León, the picturesque Robledillo de Gata.

Driving up the gravel road leading out from the rear of the village to Jill's home, all that seemed a million miles away, or at least much farther than the one hundred or so kilometres separting her home from ours. Tall Katyusha pines line the stone walls that run out past the town cemetery until you come to the partially camouflaged caravan Jill and her family used to live in, and then to the DIY goat pens that help fuel her enterprise. A little farther down the road and you get to the beautiful house they recently had built, which also houses Jill's artisanal organic cheese factory down below. It's all a world away from the intricacies of teaching the present perfect and the English academies she once owned. As you pull in, you are invariably greeted by a troop of friendly yet rather barky dogs that help scare off the wild boar that can terrorize the goats and rip up an entire garden overnight. Jill stepped out of her laboratory in full PPE gear and said in her ariose voice from the moors of North Yorkshire, "So sorry. Just finishing up a new batch of cheese. I'll be with you in a minute." The conversion from English teacher to cheese maker was definitely complete.

We had arranged to meet at her place before heading over to one of the nearby swimming holes. It was still before noon, but the sun was already strong. Bees buzzed among the flowering mint that bunched up beside the door and scented the air each time the dogs splashed through the bushes. Tentative grape vines, protected from both the goats and the wild boar, were beginning to take hold and wind their way up the newly placed beams that would soon support the arbour and shade the entrance. "I'm so glad you could make it up," Jill said as she re-emerged from her lab in her normal clothes. "The girls are going to absolutely love seeing the baby goats. Did you know that's how I got started making cheese? A friend gave us a baby goat and after feeding her from a bottle, I was hooked." Indeed, the girls were excited. Since we had told them Jill had some baby goats, they had spoken of little else since and had already gone through a long list of possible names for them, only to decide they needed to see them first before giving them their monikers. "Ever since I decided to reduce the herd, I have been able to focus a lot more of my time on actually making the cheese. But I must admit, I do miss having more baby goats around. These new ones are absolutely gorgeous."

We walked up the hill and ran into Jill's husband, Carlos, bearing refreshments for everyone. We set up on their terrace that looks out over the valley. Staircased vineyards ran down towards the valley floor and the creek that delimits their property below. Every year Carlos's wine gets more interesting, as it's a completely organic process devoid of added sulfites and leans more towards alchemy than pure science. Some years it's sweeter while others find it less like a claret and more full-bodied, running more towards a red. We settled into the view and a few minutes later Jill came out bearing two large trays of many kinds of cheeses for us to try. My girls excitedly followed her instructions as she pointed out what the different cheeses were. "Here you have some fresh cheese and over here some different varieties of spreadable cheeses. This one is natural without any seasoning, then this one has garlic and parsley. This one is flavoured with thyme we grow down on the terracing, and then this one is spiced with black pepper." As she moved onto the next tray, my girls were busy spreading the different cheeses on the bread and crackers she had also brought out. Jill laughed and said, "I think I'll have to bring some more of that out. But before I do, don't forget to try these before you fill up. On this tray we have younger cured cheeses and these are more mature, aged cheeses. I use two types of fermentation, enzymatic and lactic. Both are made with raw milk and cream cheese balls in oil."

The cheeses were sublime, each in their own way. So completely was I focused on the irregular patterned wheels I have to admit her informative explanations only superficially registered. The crumbly, almost nutty-flavoured aged cheeses morphed from a milky yellow in the centre to a mellow gold the closer you got to the rind. The sharp taste had personality, like you were tasting the terroir and sense of place of the cheese. The younger cheeses were almost white in the middle with irregular air holes that disappeared the closer you got to the roughly textured white rind. These were solid yet instantly creamy once you took a bite. Each cheese had its own distinct nature, familiar yet completely individual. I asked Jill how she managed to make each cheese so singular. "The thing with producing cheese like this is the process lends itself towards this individuality and distinctiveness. Each batch and even each wheel of cheese has its own personality. The milk I use comes from free-ranging goats that graze here in the Sierra de Gata. Recently, my main suppliers are José, Erika, and their three lovely children in Cadalso, and Manolo in Hernán-Pérez. Local milk is obviously fresher and animals produce different lactic bacteria in different areas depending on what they eat. The milk we get comes from animals grazing on what you see around us and that obviously changes with the seasons." Jill had barely finished her presentation when my eldest daughter whispered to me she was glad we had lots of room in Mom's car to take home all of the spreadable cheese with thyme. Blessed indeed are the cheese makers.

We piled back in the car with our fermented booty and my wife drove the few kilometres to the natural swimming hole in Torre de Don Miguel. Perhaps the least "natural" pool along the sierra, as it is in effect just a rectangular concrete structure, but my daughters had fond memories of hunting for "water walkers," as they called the bugs that glided across the water, and they wanted to repeat the adventure. The *chiringuito* just above was also run by a couple Jill knew, which meant we'd be among friends. That said, here in the sierra you are rarely more than two steps away from a personal connection with someone else. When you meet someone new, it's rare you don't know somebody who, somehow, knows them. We set up under one of the tiki-style umbrellas and went to dip our toes in the water. Even though it was late June, and the temperatures had been in the thirties for some time, the water was cold to the touch. It may not have been extremely cold, but the temperature differential made it seem more like a stream flowing off a glacier in the Rockies than a wild swimming hole in southwestern Spain.

All the same, we jumped in. The temperature soon forced us to migrate towards the shallow end where it came up to our knees and from where we could watch the girls hunt their prey. "Remind me what brought you down from Sheffield in the UK to Cáceres in the first place?" I asked. Jill ventured a bit deeper into the pool. "Well, it was back in 1986, and I heard there was a teaching job offer at the uni in Cáceres. A professor in my English language department back in the UK shared the same specialty as the most senior prof here in Cáceres and they somehow knew each other. It happened that way, really. Even though the job turned out sour, at least it brought me here. Actually, you know the man

I'm talking about perhaps better than I do. I think he was your boss once?" she said with a wry, sarcastic grin. "Anyways, you can imagine what it was like dealing with him. First, the contract was quite shady, quasi-legal really, and then there was the bullying and abuse that followed when I dared question anything. I stayed on at the uni in Cáceres until it came to an end." Unfortunately, I did know who she was talking about and wasn't surprised. I had a similar experience and, in my case, had successfully taken the university to court for breaching my contract and similar managerial abuses.

One of the more unfortunate aspects about Spain, and especially Extremadura, is the rigid labour laws make it difficult for people to change jobs. This makes them feel they have to hang on to positions no matter the abuse they often suffer. The static nature of the job market helps entrench and empower abusive predators like those Jill and I had dealt with. Not only do they maintain their jobs despite their incompetence, but they often rise to even higher positions and then manage others with the utmost mismanagement, malpractice, and genuine malice.

Jill took a deep, calming breath and continued, "But even his nastiness couldn't put me off the country. I had fallen in love with the place on the train journey in. You probably know what I mean. All of those umbrella trees as you pass through the *dehesas*, the light, the savannah-like landscape...I was in love with the place before I even stepped off the train." I asked, "So you made the decision to come and work here sight unseen?" Jill smiled. "Well, to be honest, my original plan had been to go to China to teach, so Spain wasn't such a big thing really." I admired her initiative and perseverance, even after such a difficult beginning with an abusive boss. I asked her what made her stay on. "Basically, it was the lifestyle. You know, the way the day is organized, with the long lunches and flexible nights. As a young woman it seemed the antithesis of the UK. Back then, the pubs in England had to close at 11 p.m. Just before then you had to make last order, you know, the bell ringing and all that. It was nice to find a different way of going about it all. It felt so much freer. Then there was the different approach to things like eating and drinking. With all the patios out on the streets, it was all just so social and so different from England."

Just then my girls ran up to show us all the water walkers they had captured and now planned to release back into the pool. Jill took a moment and then added, "But at the time Cáceres was a much more conservative place than it is now, very, very conservative. I remember being stared at as I walked down Cánovas, the main boulevard. The first thing I would do when I got to work was to go into the bathroom and look at myself in the mirror to see if I had something bizarre or strange on me, like a piece of toast stuck to the back of my head or something." She laughed. "I guess it's because I dressed in a different way and had a different haircut. These things were so standardized here back then. Whereas now, Spain and really the rest of Europe is much more globalized, isn't it?"

The ambient heat contrasting with the coolness of the water had us slowly moving into deeper water while keeping the conversation flowing. I asked, "So after twenty-odd years living in Cáceres, why did you make the decision to move up here to the sierra?" Jill raised her eyebrows and said, "Well, you had something to do with that. After years of camping up here, we knew we wanted to take the plunge, but until you agreed to look after the academy for that year, we didn't feel we could make the break. Then a friend's aunt had a place we started to rent, and after some time here, we knew it was where we wanted to be. Now that I think of it, I'm glad we landed in Villasbuenas, mostly because I like the climate here better than the other villages. In Villasbuenas, the climate is quite benign, whereas in the other villages it can be so much windier. Perhaps because they are higher up, I don't know, but I like it here." Jill waved her hand and splashed some water on her shoulders, then added, "That's not all, of course. I think the people here are also more inviting than in other places. That's perhaps due to politics. It depends on who governs the place. Here, it's traditionally been more open and progressive and that's reflected in how people view 'outsiders.'" Jill took a quick dive into the water and when she came up said, "Another thing I really love about the village is that in Cáceres I was always a foreigner, someone, you know, different. But in the village, anyone not from there is considered an outsider. So that put me on equal footing with Carlos and anyone else who wasn't from there. Which for me was so exciting; to be on the same footing as someone from Madrid, Cáceres, or wherever."

At that moment a large group of young people started cannonballing into the river, pushing us across to the rocks that lined the opposite bank. "We were also at a different stage in life, acclimatizing having kids and all of that. We weren't going out at night much and unless you've got friends who have kids around a similar age, well it's not easy. That and we just didn't really click with any of the parents from school, for example, or at least not enough to have them over to dinner. It was all 'hi, how are you?' and that's about it really."

My kids had switched over to their snorkel masks and were now swimming around us, artfully dodging the intermittent cannonballs that continued to rain down. They were in search of the elusive trout, which were harder to find in this pool than in some of the other pools around the sierra. "When we moved up here for good, it was much easier to go out for some reason. With the three or four bars in the village, and the people being so friendly, we got our social life back." My oldest daughter called us over to see some fish she had spotted when I noticed my youngest was shivering. It was time to get out of the water for a bit.

We got back to our towels, and Jill asked me how my teaching was going. I was honest and confessed I was struggling to adapt to the new hybrid world with some classes online and others face to face, but was doing okay. She made a sympathetic gesture and said, "When we initially came up, I opened another academy down in Moraleja, but I found my patience had just run out. The thing is, becoming a mother made things different and from that point on teaching became difficult. I was using up a lot of my reserves of patience at home and it just ran out. It was also a difficult time for me. My dad had died and then my mum, and with me being so far away...it was hard. When your last parent passes, something changes in you. You then know you are suddenly on your own. There were no more strings attached to the UK, and it shook me up a lot. That, combined with my ebbing patience, well, I just felt I didn't have anything more to give."

I reached over, opened the cooler, and pulled out a few cold beers and passed one to Jill. "Then we found our piece of land and it was very comforting for me to be in the country. I had been brought up in the countryside and the land here...well, it just so reminds me of where I lived in England. It was just really similar, except the house wasn't on the top of the hill. It was at the bottom. That and the pine trees, of course, but the stream and the greenness all reminded me of home." My kids came down with some ice cream they had bought up in the *chiringuito*, and it was then I realized just how many young people were at the pool. I asked Jill, "During the pandemic there was talk about a neo-rural movement, of people abandoning cities and moving back to villages. What are things like in Villasbuenas?" Jill nodded her head and said, "You'd be surprised. It's actually hard to find accommodation right now for people who do want to move here. You've always had retired people come back and resettle from wherever, but now there are also young people who are looking for something different. In some cases, maybe their parents had passed away and they were left with a house, but there are others who are coming here and setting up small businesses, like restaurants or small hotels." It was soon time for lunch, but before we went up I asked, "I once remember Carlos saying there was a difference between those who choose to stay in the village and those who never had the opportunity to leave." Jill thought for a moment, then said, "It's possible, but really that could be said about anywhere. If you have the luxury to choose to be somewhere or to do something, you are always going to be happier, I think. You know who you should talk to about that? Our band has a gig over in Trevejo next weekend and the man who is organizing it, Dani, is precisely someone like that. He's someone who chose to come back."

The ruined Castillo de Trevejo with the Iglesia de San Juan Bautista in the foreground.

A RETURN
TO ROOTS

13

IN THE FAR NORTHWESTERN CORNER of Extremadura, with the white hilltop village of Villamiel behind and the peak of Mount Jálama rising up beyond, a castle rises vertically out of a flashing sea of olive groves. A mountaintop lookout framed by two mountain ridges; one running east to the larger villages of Acebo and Hoyos and another west towards Valverde del Fresno, Eljas, and San Martín de Trevejo, with the white specks of Portuguese villages in the distance. While it isn't the highest point of the Sierra de Gata, it is one of the most strategic points from which friends and foes alike can be seen coming and going. An *atalaya*, or vantage point the Arabs purposely chose to control this important crossroads. And while it isn't technically the centre of the sierra that isn't necessarily named after cats, for me it has always felt like the nexus of the range.

As you turn off the EX-205 onto the much smaller CC-2.1, the abrupt change in the road portends the long, winding climb ahead. Low-lying stone walls flecked with the granite so abundant in the area enclose the modest olive groves that give the impression of one continuous flowing sea from afar. Every now and then, these groves are interspersed with small, family-sized vineyards that produce the pale claret the region has been known for over the centuries. A wine so zealous of its roots they say it spoils if you take it over the mountain passes and out of the sierra.

Overgrown blackberry bushes climb over the walls, giving the road an even narrower feel, but you rarely if ever lose sight of the prominent castle ascending to your right.

Just as you enter the village of Villamiel, you turn off onto the even smaller CC-V-143 that leads up to the *pedanía* or hamlet of Trevejo. Its toponym sheds light on its age—*tres-vejo*; *très vieux*—older than you'd care to be, but it has since fallen from grace and is now simply a borough of Villamiel. As the skirts of the sierra become more pronounced, the groves of olives turn into terraces, taking better advantage of the increasingly angled terrain. Stands of chestnuts blend in with the olive trees and throw their wider shade across the many switchbacks that mark this short but sinuous stretch of road. If you happen across an oncoming car, you can immediately differentiate between the locals and tourists by the speed with which they pass you by. While visitors nervously slow to an almost stop and pull off to the side, locals hug these well-known curves and fling around them as part of their day to day. As you reach the top of the stone isthmus that leads out to the castle from the surrounding ranges, the trees seem to thin out. Then, as you round another of the stomach-churning bends, there the castle appears, looking like a granite outgrowth from a rocky crag.

These mountains have a special meaning to my family. My wife's father's roots run deep in the nearby village of San Martín de Trevejo, a small village that lies just over the western ridge from here. Fifty per cent of my kids' DNA may come from my side's far-flung, wandering ancestors from places as disparate as the UK, Ukraine, Norway, and Germany, but twenty-five percent of their roots stem from these patchwork-green mountains tucked against the Portuguese border. My father-in-law may have left his village some seventy-odd years ago, but whenever he visits the place of his birth, he still speaks the singular language, la Fala or Mañego, that was frozen in time in that remote valley. Many of his relatives were forced to migrate to the Basque Country and beyond for the very reasons Manolo had explained, but he still has family that never left. He had long told me about legends that had been passed down through the generations in the sierra of buried Arab booty and hidden Templar treasure in this castle. Legends he had explored first-hand back in the late 1940s and early '50s that I was now tracing to see what was left. Jill's suggestion to meet up with her friend who lives in Trevejo presented the perfect opportunity. I wanted to see if anything remained of the stories my father-in-law had often told me over our midday *cañas*.

To access the castle, you walk along a narrow lane that cuts through the small adjacent village built up from the bones of the cadaver of the ruined castle. Rough-cut granite stones make up the low and grey mossy green homes that line the tight main street. These scavenged stones from the castle ruins give the impression the village is a continuous extension of the castle walls. A few smallish windows that peer out from the cave-like homes have been whitewashed, but the only other flash of colour comes from the reddish clay Arabic roofing tiles that crumble above. The rest is a monochromatic stretch of granite Lego blocks of stone. At the beginning of the millennium, the town had a population of over six hundred people. This has steadily dwindled and now just over ten remain. Decades ago, there were enough inhabitants to guard the remains of the fortress and scare off would-be treasure seekers that came under the cover of darkness to look for the mythical buried treasure. Now more cats than people look out the windows as you pass by, a postcard from empty Spain.

Once you pass through the village, the pinnacle of rock that makes up what is left of the castle's keep is about all that remains among the detritus of the once-proud fortress. The Templar castle was built on the ruins of a Moorish fort that controlled the roads that branched off from the north-south Silver Way that ran from Sevilla up to the northern coast. These valleys guarded the roads that linked up with it from the Atlantic coast some two hundred kilometres away to the west. Once the reconquest meandered through the area, the stronghold was given over to a succession of military orders like those of Santiago and Alcántara that also used this bastion of power to extend their influence in the area. These paramilitary religious orders may have had one foot in the celestial afterlife, but they also had the other firmly placed in the pocketbooks of those they controlled from the mountaintop. After acquiring piles of wealth from the booty they amassed from the Almohad territories they conquered, they turned their gaze back on the subjects they had vanquished. As their wealth grew, so did the legends of hidden gold. Like the invasive blackberry bushes that crowd the stone walls that line the road up to the village, the pervasive stories were impossible to wipe out.

The castle's current ruinous state is due to the threat the French army saw it posed as it retreated during the Napoleonic Wars in the early nineteenth century. Fearing the castle could become a stronghold for the local militias dogging the army as it retreated, it tried, somewhat unsuccessfully, to blow it up, leaving the shell you see today. A cripple whose ruinous state has only been exacerbated by years of would-be treasure hunters picking away at its innards.

I skirted the walls past the belfry of the smallish Iglesia de San Juan Bautista and came across a few of the anthropomorphic tombs that had been hollowed out of the rock, whose mystery only adds fuel to the generations of tales of ghostly treasure. I turned up towards the keep and picked my way over the fallen masonry, remembering what my father-in-law had told me. As a kid, he and his friends had also heard tales of buried treasure. One day, a friend of his mentioned he had found a dark vault under the castle and was sure that was where the treasure was hidden. He and his friends immediately came up with a plan to make their fortune and find the treasure. They took to the goat tracks that criss-crossed the sierra and climbed the range that separates San Martín de Trevejo from Villamiel and arrived at the castle armed with some rope, the makings of a torch, and a vague plan. I could only imagine the sense of adventure and excitement the young boys must have felt as they set off to look for buried treasure. As a child growing up in the western reaches of the prairies of Canada, the very idea of a castle was something I only dreamed of. Imagine exploring an actual Templar castle with visions of doubloons dancing in your head.

I jumped past some of the rubble-filled *aljibes*, or cisterns that would have supplied the castle with water, and came to the keep. This was made of carefully dressed stone, its smooth face broken by the only remaining crest that hadn't been stolen or repurposed in the walls of the homes in the village. From outside it looked impressive, but as you enter you see it has lost two of its walls and the remaining three are only tenuously standing. I was looking for an opening that could have been the vault my father-in-law spoke of, and then I remembered something he had told me. Some blocks of fallen stone had covered the vault his friend had found. A very dangerous looking wobbly plank of wood led the adventurous visitor to climb up higher into the keep, but I kept my eye on the ground until I noticed a sinkhole that led down to what looked like an entirely different floor of the castle. The access had been cleared since my father-in-law's adventure, but it still meant a drop of several metres down into an empty-looking room in relative darkness. Then I remembered the rope. One of the key ingredients to their plan was a rope, a rope strong enough to hold the weight of someone that could also be used to hoist up any treasure boxes found.

As I peered down into the semi-darkness, the words he had often told me came to mind: "You see me now, a man in his eighties who has lived just about long enough to be considered old. But when I was a youngster, there wasn't a tree I wouldn't climb, a bird's nest I wouldn't reach, a cliff I wouldn't jump off, nor a dare I wouldn't take. I've got the scars on my arms and legs to prove it." And he was right. While there weren't any signs warning of danger, the drop down was significant to say the least. He may have repeated his story on many occasions, but it never changed. "So we were sitting there, thinking my friend who had found the place was going to go down first, but as we got ready, he blanched and said there was no way he was going down that hole. Keep in mind, we had not only heard tales of treasure, but we had also heard more recent reports of people who had been crushed by falling debris as they tried to dig through the guts of the castle." A short discussion later and my father-in-law volunteered to be the first lowered down into the gloom. They tied the rope around his waist and he slipped over the edge, filled with the excitement that they were about to come across their fortune. "There I was, hanging in midair with the rope biting into my waist. I trusted my friends, but as I couldn't really see the bottom, it was definitely a leap of faith. As I got lower, the light began to disappear because the only light coming in was from the entrance we had cleared and my hanging body was blocking most of it. When I finally got to the bottom, I could see in the penumbra there were more rooms down there, but I couldn't really make much out in the darkness. I hesitantly explored a bit further, and then I saw something on the ground in the shadows. But I couldn't make out what it was.

"I shouted up to my friends to throw me down the torch so I could get a better look. We were all really excited; we were sure this was it. We were positive we had found what everyone had been looking for over the years. This was going to be where they had hidden the jewels. I kept looking up, but nothing was coming from them. Even if I wanted to put on a brave face for my friends, with time, the darkness seemed to be closing in and my mind started playing tricks on me. I called up somewhat impatiently to see what was taking them so long. After what seemed like an eternity, they finally shouted down that they didn't bring anything to light the torch with and couldn't find anything else. So here I was down in the hole with the treasure just beyond my reach in the blackness. I had gone this far and we couldn't give up. I had an idea and told them to move the stone that was covering the entrance to let more light in. The block that had covered the entrance was huge and there was one boy less up there now, but they got together and pushed and shoved as hard as they could. Every time it moved, small rocks and dirt cascaded down on me. I started to worry I was going to end up like Ali Baba, trapped in his cavern of riches, unable to get out. The more they moved the stone, the more debris fell, but also more light was able to shine in.

"I could now at least see my feet and I advanced a bit farther in and came to what I had first seen on the floor of the cave. I quickly shouted up for them to stop moving the rock. The cave was indeed like Ali Baba's and had played a trick before my visit, but this time there was no treasure. There before me was the skeleton of a dog that must have come in looking for something only to find no way out. My treasure-hunter days ended as fast as they had begun. I quickly got out before I ended up like that poor dog."

I tried to link the ruins I was seeing with the legends I had heard. I was certain generations of boys before and since my father-in-law's adventure had done the same. And it would make sense. Perhaps the castle is more remarkable for its romantic associations than for what actually remains, but it definitely has something about it. Overly reno-vated castles and palaces may offer more to see, and are definitely less dangerous to explore, but there is no doubt its ruined state invites the imagination to fill in the gaps and invent what is missing in our minds. It's this imagined picture all these people have been chasing. The legendary treasures may have been carted off long ago or may have never even existed, but while it stands, the castle of Trevejo and the recently resuscitated village growing out from it is an interesting example of an attempt to reverse the seemingly unstoppable trend of emptying Spain.

Later that evening there was going to be live music thanks to Jill's band Ahora o Nunca, as well as wine tasting, local product sampling, and guided star gazing. Trevejo Celeste, as the festival was called, was part of a series of ongoing special events that were being organized in the village in hopes of changing the tourism dynamic that had, until recently, mainly consisted of busloads of tourists passing through, disgorging their hold for a quick photocall in front of the castle, and then moving on to the next destination. Jill had put me in touch with Dani, and I had arranged to meet him at his bar, the only one remaining in the village, El Buen Avío. He was also the organizer of that evening's event and is very active in reviving the flickering flame of life in the village.

Dani's welcome was warm as we sat down in the carefully refurbished bar. When I complimented him on it, he smiled and said, "You know, this actually used to be the village school, at least until they had to build a bigger one. Then it became what we used to call a *teleclub*. No one had TVs back then and everyone came here to watch it. The bar belongs to the town hall. I've been renting it for five years now, and I have to say things have gone well." I asked Dani if he was one of those fourteen inhabitants who are left in the village and he laughed. "No, I live down in Villamiel. I've been trying to buy a house here, but no one wants to sell!" I asked him what had brought him to the village. "My roots run very deep here. You see, I've always had a great appreciation for what this place means and what it stands for. I was watching the village die from afar and decided to do something about it. That's one of the reasons we have been putting on events like the one tonight."

"How has the experience been?" I asked.

"Well, the truth is, in the five years we have been here, for one reason or another, houses have started to sell again. As I said, I haven't been able to get anyone to sell me one. Now people are fixing up houses for tourists who want to stay here. We've grown from five to nine tourist apartments over this period. But also, since we started, a friend moved here to live. He bought a beautiful house and has been living here in the village for four years now. There is also another couple that recently bought a little house they have fixed up. They come up on weekends and holidays. In fact, there are a lot of renovations going on. Slowly but surely the village is regaining some of the life it once had."

Even still, I couldn't imagine that fourteen people, including tourists, could support a family. So I asked, "Is the bar a full-time job for you or do you do other things?"

"That wine you are drinking is one thing. I don't make it, but I organize the grape collection and distribute it. It's a highland red wine, made from grapes from the area of Machacascos in Villamiel. It's what they call natural wine with no added sulfites, one in which the winemaker intervenes as little as possible." When he spoke, he did so with care and his passion was evident. "I help in the process, but this is a signature wine and the man who signs it is Jesús Recuero. Private owners, small landowners from Villamiel, own the vineyards we source our grapes from. In Villamiel there are only two vineyards of more than one hectare. The rest are owners with vineyards of less than one hectare, and we buy the grapes directly from them. It's a traditional process and sustainable, but it can't be certified as ecological. This is because this type of certification has to comply with EU law. For example, legally, a privately owned vineyard of less than one hectare can't be considered organic. If you think about it, a vineyard of less than one hectare is surely more organic than a two-hundred-hectare vineyard, but the law is the law I guess."

The fresh, young wine in front of me was a product of the landscape I had seen as we climbed up to the village, but it was markedly different from the pale clarets I was used to from the area. I was puzzled and asked, "So how is this different from the *pitarra* wines other producers make in the sierra?"

Here Dani became more serious. "It's about the process. With natural wine, it kind of makes itself. Our process is artisanal, but it is made under strict sanitary rules and regulations. That is, it is not a domestic wine. I prefer to call *pitarra* wines domestic wines, because that is what defines them. That is their most defining characteristic, because with *pitarra* wines you can find wines with defects, wines in which they have used, let's say, somewhat differing techniques that all come from that very characteristic of being made at home, of being made in domestic cellars. Every home is its own world and each has its own quirks, with some good things and some bad things. This is precisely due to the fact they are domestic and are made by nonprofessionals, including me. I make my own wine too, but that's not the one I sell. The wine you're drinking, Antier, is made differently."

I laughed as I recalled some of the more unconventional winemaking techniques in these mountains my father-in-law had told me about over the years. He always speaks of a certain chief commissioner for foreigners and borders, whose posting was in Madrid but was from the village. The wine he made was the best around, and my father-in-law swore he added entire *jamones* (cured ham legs) to the vats. Legends also abound here in the Sierra de Gata and neighbouring Las Hurdes about some who throw cats into the mix. But these sound more like invented tales, that or were born from someone who was trying to avoid sharing their wine with others and spread the tales so no one called by their bodega to glean a glass.

"As I was saying," Dani said, "for those of us who live and work here, Trevejo is a special place and we enjoy welcoming visitors who share our opinion. I am happy that in the five years I have been running the bar and organizing events, things have changed. The important thing is not that we have attracted more people but that the quality of the people who come to Trevejo and the reason why they come has changed. It used to be that busloads of fifty or so people would arrive, fill the village with beer cans and trash, and then up and leave, which was leading towards the absolute abandonment of the village." He gestured outside and said, "We took over the bar, I guess, to regain a little order, a little sanity, and give back a little prestige to the people who make their lives here. And it's working. Over the five years I've been here, people now come to the bar to have lunch or dinner. They don't just come to see the castle in ruins, throw out the picnic blanket, and then leave their trash behind. I mean, that's all fine and good to do out in the countryside, but it's just that, there's lots of open countryside around here where you can do that. People now come to consume and do so sensibly. We like that people come here to enjoy more than just what the castle has to offer. For example, to drink the wines here, which as you now know are very special, to eat wild mushrooms like the Boletus when they are in season and the honey from Villamiel, and, of course, our olive oil. You know, things from here."

Dani leaned back and continued, "I also represent the family-run Hacienda Nava del Rey olive oils. As I said, my roots here go back a long way. Back in 1900, my great-great-grandfather made the trip all the way to Paris to enter a competition, the Universal Exposition, and he took home the silver medal. It's all thanks to the process we use, the age of our trees, and the special variety of olives we have here. We use 100 per cent *manzanilla cacereña* olives. We only collect them with hand shakers and nets or by hand, and we only harvest at the very peak of ripening. They are then transferred to the oil press less than twelve hours after harvesting in order to maintain all the properties of the fruit. The olives are mechanically cold-pressed, with the temperature never exceeding 26°C. This whole process produces a unique, intense, fruity green oil. It has aromas of almond, banana, and apple, with back hints of grass, and when you taste it, it has a certain sweetness combined with a light bitterness. Between the bar, the olive oil, the wine, and the events, I keep pretty busy." I ordered another wine and apologized to Dani. "Sorry, I can't stay for tonight's event, but don't think I just came to the village to see the castle. My in-laws have roots near here and there's a story my father-in-law told me that I wanted to explore."

Dani laughed. "No problem, and even if you did just come to see the castle, you now know there are other things to see. Speaking of that, Jill mentioned to me you are interested in prehistoric rock art. On your way back I have something to show you that I think you'll like."

We drove back down the curves of the mountainside to the larger village of Villamiel and met in the square. "I want to show you some petroglyphs that are near the village. They are on private property, but I know the owner and he's okay with us going out there. Thing is, he'd rather not make their whereabouts public yet. At least not until they can be properly studied and protected." I grew excited. I knew there were many petroglyphs in the neighbouring range over in Las Hurdes. The art in Las Hurdes was all catalogued and formed part of the Council of Europe's Prehistoric Rock Art Trails, but these were new or at least new to me.

After a short walk, there it lay: a Rolling Stones tongue of greyish rock lolling out of the surrounding dry brush. As we got closer, I could see that, rather than having a plain line running down the middle like the Stones' logo, this prehistoric canvas had various lines descending down the rock, interspersed with what initially looked like cowrie shells. Something that would seem unlikely given that most cowry shells come from the coastal waters of the Indian and Pacific oceans. An even closer look showed some holes among the lines that had been bored into the rock that had been partially cleared of dirt. The insoluble enigma of the past once again was looking up at me. An indecipherable message from a time so remote its passing had softened and worn the edges of cuts in the hard granite. Time's wear had disfigured the images so what now remained were poorly developed prints of what they originally were. Like the Stones' logo, summary interpretations can prove misleading. Many assume the hot lips are a reference to Mick Jagger's own, when the logo's origins lie in the unfurled tongue of the Hindu goddess Kali. If the link between a bloodthirsty Hindu goddess and rock and roll is unclear at first glance, finding a clear understanding of these lines and circles engraved so long ago seems unfathomable.

Readable or not, their intention is clear: a message and, more likely than not, a story. These are not casual doodles made in the corner of a notebook while listening to a lecture. To some they appear to be seeds, to others vulvas, both would coincide with thinking the symbols have something to do with some sort of fertility meaning or rite. But even if they were meant to represent seeds, vulvas, or something else to do with fecundity, we may have correctly identified what they are but might be entirely missing what they meant for the artists. Others might think they could be some kind of map or even a calendar, but these interpretations are for no reason more or less valid than others. What can be certain is that whoever made these did so with a deliberate intention. The time and resources required to make such deep grooves in the living rock were considerable. The wear on the tools used would have had to be justifiable in some way and certainly intentional. Altering a medium to create some sort of symbol, be it realistic or concrete, that provokes thought or emotion in the viewer is the underlying intent of all artists, from these beginnings of time until now. Their specific purpose may be unclear but a purpose is there all the same.

The shadows along the grooves lengthened. The harsher colours of midday were softening on the landscape, but the sky to the west over Portugal was still bright. It was time for Dani to get back to his preparations for the evening's performances. I thanked him for showing me something so special. He smiled and said, "This sierra is full of secrets. You just need to make the time to see them." A red-tailed kite glided over us in the direction of the village. It circled for a moment as if it had spotted something, then changed its mind and turned east to the region I would be exploring next.

Making *aguardiente* next to the *alambique* or still.

MOUNTAIN
ALCHEMY

14

ON MAY 17, 1886, a boy was born king. Shortly after the newborn monarch's first cries were heard throughout the corridors of the royal palace in Madrid, he was literally and metaphorically placed on an elaborate silver platter and presented to the liberal Prime Minister Práxedes Mateo Sagasta. A gesture that symbolized the power the prime minister had been entrusted with since the premature death a few months earlier of the boy's father, Alfonso XII. This early demise would foreshadow Alfonso XIII's tumultuous rule and eventual exile. Just twelve years later, the boy king's empire, stretching from Madrid to Manila to the turquoise bay of Santiago de Cuba, collapsed. The first empire on which the sun never set came to an end after Spain's disastrous defeat in the Spanish–American War in 1898. This undoing would presage the eventual fall of the Bourbonic legacy in Spain and lead to the launch of the United States of America as a global superpower. The Bourbons then lay in wait until the monarchy and Bourbonic rule was resurrected at the moribund hand of the dictator, Francisco Franco.

The loss of its last overseas colonies had a profound psychological impact on the country. The Spanish had never considered, at least administratively, these overseas territories as colonies. They were regarded as integral parts of the state. Amid the political instability these sea changes brought on, the boy king assumed the throne in 1902 when he turned sixteen years old. Immediately afterwards, in an attempt to consolidate the monarchy and strengthen its image, the adolescent monarch began to tour around the country to try and connect with his subjects. These trips didn't start off exactly as planned. On one of his first trips as king, Alfonso XIII's train stopped in the city of Valladolid en route to San Sebastián in the north. Local newspaper reports from the time speak of large crowds gathering awaiting their new king to make an appearance. But when the deputy, José María Zorita, approached the carriage, he was told the king was asleep. Zorita's pleas to wake him so he could greet the waiting crowd fell on the deaf ears of the officials accompanying the king and the fiasco was tremendous. Prominent newspapers, including the influential *El Norte de Castilla*, gave a full account of the region's disappointment. Blame was quickly placed on the staff accompanying the monarch, but nevertheless it wasn't an auspicious start to the campaign to try and humanize the king.

Two years later, Alfonso was once again in the vast scrub-coloured lands of Castilla, this time in Salamanca. There the young regent demonstrated he had come to know what his role should be and had learned to give the people the monarch they were looking for. With practice, he had discovered how to play the role of an affable, good-natured king who was close to the people. This time the charm offensive turned out to be successful. Even Republican-inspired newspapers of the time commented on the proximity of the regent to the people and praised his proverbial folksiness.

During the visit, a young poet named José María Gabriel y Galán recited a poem for the king. The poem began by stating the poet wasn't a minstrel or a courtier there to please the monarch. His intention was to simply use the common voice of the people. He was there to speak the truth. Then the poem radically shifted gears as he pleaded:

> *Señor: en tierras hermanas*
> *de estas tierras castellanas,*
> *no viven vida de humanos*
> *nuestros míseros hermanos*
> *de las montañas jurdanas.*

Majesty: in sister lands
of these Castilian plains
our miserable brothers
do not live the life of humans
our miserable brothers
of the Hurdes mountains.

He was describing a place in Extremadura, less than eighty kilometres southeast from that royal reception. A place that had been called "a stain on the civilized map of Europe." A quote that comes from a magazine called *Las Hurdes* that had been expressly created to further the cause of the people who lived in this isolated valley. It began that month's edition by making a direct plea to the king about a community that "have not known the wonders of the twentieth century and civilized life."

The late nineteenth and early twentieth centuries saw the apex of Eurocentrism, the idea Europe was the peak of civilization. Concepts like France's *mission civilisatrice* presumed Europe was meant to civilize the world by expanding its influence and implementing its model through colonialization. This world view divided the globe into two spheres: civilized and savage. By the end of the nineteenth century, there was hardly an area left on Earth where Europeans had not exerted and then extended their economic influence and military power. Regions like Africa and the American West were seen as socially backward, primitive, and inferior. Out of context encounters with inhabitants from these lands only served to strengthen the prevailing idea that an 'otherness' existed between Christian Europeans and non-Christian nations. The prevailing belief was the former were somehow superior, at least those that lived in their urban cities.

It's within this turn-of-the-twentieth-century context that the king's visit to Salamanca takes on brutal irony. During the same visit, an event took place that echoed the European infatuation with non-European "savages" at the time. Shows like Buffalo Bill's Wild West exhibitions, Barnum and Bailey's circuses, and "displays" of African Peoples like the Pygmies were extremely popular with European nobility and were attracting huge crowds across the continent. With the poet's words about the plight of those nearby citizens that lived so miserably still hanging in the air, an act took place that paralleled the freak shows of the circuses that were playing to packed houses across the continent. Bishop of Plasencia Francisco Jarrín had a group of inhabitants from Las Hurdes paraded in front of the regent. But these weren't "savages" from across the seas. These were the king's very own subjects, subjects living in a misery of goiter, malaria, rickets, and cretinism. Maladies that had all been but eradicated elsewhere in Spain. The latter was said to have been a result of a lack of iodine in the region's diet but was also exacerbated by the close blood marriages brought on by the valley's isolation.

Around the same time, a group of well-meaning intellectuals began publishing a magazine whose stated mission was to bring "culture and civilization to the forty-two hamlets of Las Hurdes, submerged in the solitude of the mountains and in the saddest solitude of poverty and dishonor." The group's main priority was to provide the valley with churches, schools, and roads that would bring about the "moral and material improvement of the miserable region." Churches, schools, and roads were its motto and the leitmotiv that ran throughout the history of the magazine. In an article that appears in the magazine dated September 30, 1904, it states: "Tomorrow, before his majesty the King Alfonso XIII, some miserable inhabitants from Las Hurdes will appear. They will arrive in Salamanca dressed in their best clothes, if the washed rags of the poor deserve such a name. The Hurdanos will come to demonstrate their skills in the art of Terpsichore, bringing to Salamanca the most typical of their region, a kind of Indian dance admirable for its strange novelty."

Following the demeaning spectacle, the king remarked the Hurdanos seemed like primitive men dancing in a semi-wild way. After the well-meaning entreaties of the organizers to in some way help these people, the king went on to mention he enjoyed hunting very much and that he had heard there was an abundance of game in the valley and that he would like to visit the region soon. It was there his interest faded.

Eighteen years would pass before the king made good on his promise. However, it would be a trip undertaken under motives that weren't entirely focused on the locals. The country had once again suffered another terrible military disaster, this time on a neighbouring continent.

Estimates of between ten to twelve thousand Spanish troops had just lost their lives in a military debacle. Spain's short-lived colonialist ambitions in Northern Africa came to an ill-advised, macabre halt just eighteen kilometres across the Strait of Gibraltar in the Rif Mountains of what is today Morocco. The struggling king needed a PR boost.

Around the same time as this colonialist disaster, the esteemed physician Gregorio Marañón was heading a sanitary commission that had been established to study the poor health in Las Hurdes. The acclaimed endocrinologist convinced the troubled and increasingly unpopular monarch to visit the area and observe the situation for himself first-hand. Surely adding it would be a propaganda opportunity to try and boost his tarnished image among his subjects by demonstrating he cared for the well-being of some of his reign's least fortunate.

| "Why does that guy have such nice shiny boots while the other people are all barefoot?" my youngest daughter asked as we looked up at the black and white photographs. She then looked closer and said, "Oh, that guy has that little mustache. That's the king, right?" One hundred years after Gregorio Marañón convinced the king to take the trip, my family and I were standing in Tecuixpo Ixtlaxochitl's Moctezuma palace, under the very frescos exalting her Aztec nobility, visiting a photography exhibition by José Demaría Vázquez. Campúa, as he is better known, was the official photographer who accompanied the king on this interior colonialist adventure, and he captured some of its most intimate moments. My daughter's maternal grandfather was born just sixteen years after the pictures were taken, in a village fifty kilometres away as the crow flies, and the images couldn't seem more remote to her, both in time and distance. The exhibit was part of a wider pro-monarchist campaign to commemorate the journey and an awkward attempt to somehow put a positive spin on the event. A campaign that included a repeat journey by Alfonso's great-grandson, the current King Felipe VI, up to the sierra. This time, rather than making the journey on horseback, the present king used a combination of official cars and helicopters that are always at his disposal to travel up the valley.

Back in 1922, the king and his retinue set off from Coria on a scorching June morning. They had to do so on horseback as roads, along with most everything else from the newborn century, ended where the valley began. It would be an expedition that mirrored the country's recent colonialist ventures across the strait, an exploration into the beyond. To round out the royal retinue, his valet, Lieutenant Colonel Obregon, the Duke of Miranda, head of the royal household, and Vicente Pinies, minister of the interior, accompanied him. The expedition's main architect, Doctor Gregorio Marañón, and his colleague Ricardo Varela were also present, hoping to document the diseases suffered in the area. Santiago Pérez Argemí, a forestry engineer, was also at hand to investigate the land and suggest possible improvements that would help mitigate the effects of years of overlogging, charcoal extraction, overgrazing, and forest fires. To chronicle the journey and hopefully spin it into something positive, the official entourage included the journalist, José García Mora, writing for the newspaper *El Debate*, and the photographer José Demaría Vázquez.

The curated black and white photos showed an affable, smiling king who, at least in the photographs, can be seen engaging with the Hurdanos. There was nothing of the elitist petulance of a King Charles III waving away servants to move things around on his desk. Instead the stills brought to mind the frontier aspect of the photographs of Teddy Roosevelt exploring the Rockies at the turn of the twentieth century. In one of the pictures, the king is walking along in the bright sunshine, his clean, pressed clothes shining in the light, while in the shadows, an entire village looks on. Their begrimed, humble clothing blend in with the shade and the slate stone wall behind them. Almost all their faces are unreadable, impassive as the rocks piled one upon the other behind them. All except one older woman surrounded by what appears to be two people suffering from cretinism. Her face is frozen in despair and seems to be desperately crying out something. An outcry that is silenced by the medium, yet her anguish can be felt all the same.

In the clean contrast between the black and white, the squalor the magazines of the time detailed was somewhat shrouded by this chiaroscuro effect. A closer look at some of the other pictures revealed the adversity the Hurdanos faced and their resilience to it. It could be seen in the intensity of their countenance. The illness and disease brought on by the poverty they suffered was deeply etched into their profiles as they stared out from stunted doorways at the procession parading by. A shared nescience of each other's worlds imbues the scenes with an irreconcilable duality, one that would never be breached even if they did sit and talk together. The very figure of a king, with all the hereditary privileges the institution entails, enshrined this dichotomy. The haves and have-nots would persist, and if any concession that arose from the expedition was made to better their plight, it would be perceived as benevolence rather than duty. The duty of a head of state to bulldoze the twentieth century into these valleys.

In the next room of the exhibition there was a grainy black and white film being projected on the wall. While Campúa was the official photographer of the expedition, several other photographers tagged along behind the official entourage. The filmmaker Armando Pou was one of them, and his moving images were the only ones captured during the journey. In between vignettes, silent-movie-style captions provided some backstory for each scene or supplied some silent picture dialogue for select scenes. These images were less curated and much more raw. Any romance that might have existed in the still images quickly disappeared. The dismal nature of their homes became painfully clear as more context was added. In one scene, the rotund bishop ungainly balances on his horse as a woman approaches him. Rather than engage with her, he purposefully looks away while extending his hand the other way so she could kiss his ring. One of the captions reads, "As the King arrives, the locals bathe his hands in tears exclaiming, 'Now we'll have roads, medicines, everything...just like people!'"

| In the cool, diffuse morning light, framed between an ancient, desiccated Winnebago and a three-story monstrosity home, stood the Cerberus of Castillo. It looked like some sort of gargantuan fetish placed at the entrance to the village to warn off outsiders. We had just walked up the main street that leads into the innards of the village when this metre-high mastiff hove into view and planted itself squat in the middle of the street, almost

daring us to approach. We slowed our pace for a moment and looked around to see if there was another way to enter the tangle of narrow streets that make up the village of Castillo, but to no avail. We then scanned the deserted street, thinking the enormous beast's owner would soon amble by, walking stick in hand, but no one came. We were about to change our plans when we looked closer and saw what was hidden in the guardian's impressive shadow. Flitting in and out from between its massive paws was a kinder of mewing kittens. The hound of Las Hurdes was more interested in babysitting than terrifying strangers. We wouldn't need Hercules's strength, Orpheus's music, or Sybil's honey-cake in order to pass.

After seeing the exposition of Campúa's photographs, I got back in touch with Jorge Armestar to see if he was familiar with the photographs and what he thought of them. He told me he had seen a few of them but hadn't been able to go to the exposition, but that he had spent quite a bit of time in the villages of the area documenting the traditions he sadly knew were on the verge of extinction. I asked him if he wanted to accompany me on a trip up to Las Hurdes to see for ourselves the immense changes that had taken place since Alfonso XIII's retinue rode through. He told me he had a trip tentatively planned to head up in late October and see the Chicharrona, a fall festival that smacks openly of pagan roots but which has since been syncretized into the Catholic events calendar. He asked if I'd like to come along. The problem was the dates of the festival change every year and he would let me know as soon as they were announced. A few days later, he sent me a disheartening message. The dates had been set, but he wasn't available. When I checked my calendar, neither was I.

Las Hurdes was beginning to seem a distant chimera when I got a fortuitous message from Carlos Blay: "Are you still interested in visiting Las Hurdes? My dad just sent me a message and said that this weekend some of his friends are going to be making *aguardiente, eau de vie,* from the must that's left over from the wine they made this year. As an added bonus, some of the area's most interesting petroglyphs on the rock art trail are just a short hike from there. Unfortunately, I'm busy and can't go, but my dad has offered to put you up and show you around. My parents have a house up there where they spend a good part of the year." The message jumped off my phone like the serendipitous invitation to join the photography course in Guadalupe. I instantly sent a message to Jorge to see if he was free. His answer was immediate: "*Aguardiente*? A disappearing tradition? See you Friday."

The week seemed to drag on forever, but late Friday evening Jorge and I drove up through the winding mountain roads that seemed like an impenetrable tunnel under the inky dark sky. The steady depopulation of the area means there is very little light pollution beyond the two or three larger villages. Thanks to this, Las Hurdes was granted a Starlight Tourism Destination certificate: great for stargazers, but not so much for those who couldn't see a foot beyond their headlights. Just past the comparative metropolis of Pinofranqueado, we turned off onto the tiny CC-156, a road that made the previous two-lane highway look like a Los Angeles freeway in comparison. The well-paved goat track took us deeper into the mountains, but the only way we could tell we were climbing was by the ever-reducing reach of our lights into the gradient of the slope ahead. Through our open windows we could feel the dampness of a river to our left, but we had no idea if it was right next to us or one hundred metres down an abrupt chasm.

Thirteen kilometres later, our lights shone upon a little sign that read, "Las Erías," and we turned off to the left. Carlos had warned us these roads hadn't even been conceived of until the 1970s, and that we would have to park at the foot of the village and make our way up to his parents' place on foot. To add to the challenge, these *alquerías* or hamlets were under the administrative control of the town hall in Pinofranqueado, which means the little lanes that make up the villages are nameless.

Jorge got out of the car, stretched, and effused, "Fate has got us this far. I'm sure we'll find the place easily." I had to agree. From what Carlos had told us, around forty people lived in the village during its high season in summer and we could always ask someone. That is if we came across anyone to ask. We walked up a hill and under a lovely stone arch made from the slate that makes up this range. The soft orangish light from the lone street lamp gave the archway a cave-like air. That is until we could make out it was topped by a half-finished, three-story brick aberration. Just another of the horrors that mar the congruity of these hurriedly disappearing architectural wonders. The lane zigzagged farther up the hill until we saw a figure standing in the half-light of the moon. A closer look showed us a familiar face. It was a Carlos Blay look-alike, albeit with a whiter beard. "I've been expecting you and I heard some unfamiliar voices from outside the open window," José Carlos said. "Welcome, come on in."

He opened the door and we stepped directly into a kitchen with a low roof with thick wooden beams running across the whitewashed ceiling. "Due to the lack of constructible space, the homes here were often very vertical. This is where they used to keep the bigger animals like mules or donkeys," José Carlos laughed. "Now it's our kitchen and dining area." He led us up to the next floor, artfully arranged with mandalas and books, and said, "The goats were usually kept here on the second floor, and then the families lived on the third floor." We climbed the stairs and he pointed out the bathroom and the room where I'd be sleeping. "The heat generated by the animals below helped keep the families warm in the winter, but now we have a pellet stove that does the trick. The houses back then were really nothing more than a shelter where both man and beast only spent the night. The alcoves where the children slept were often less than two metres long and had no windows and corn husks were used as mattresses." Here he pointed at some recesses in the wall and then gestured towards the middle. "A curious thing about Las Hurdes is that the cooking fires were made in the middle of the common area, usually on a slab of slate. Which in itself isn't strange, but they usually didn't have chimneys. The smoke would rise among the wood to the last floor to smoke chestnuts, peppers, corn, and meats, and then escape between the slate that made up the roof. There was practically no furniture, at most a chair, a trunk, and maybe a shelf on a wall, hardly any crockery." Things had certainly changed. This old, traditional home had been repurposed and had taken on a new life.

After checking out the house, we went back downstairs to the ground floor to the kitchen. "Sit down, you must be hungry. I made a Spanish omelette and roasted some red peppers from my garden. I've also got some wine from Robledillo de Gata just over the mountain range you couldn't see coming up here over in the Sierra de Gata. And if you want something sweet, I have some *perrunillas*, cookies made with the same *eau de vie* we will hopefully see them make tomorrow morning." With that, we sat down to a long dinner filled with stories from the more than twenty years he had been coming to the village. Stories that were intertwined with anecdotes from his travels that ranged from adventures in Mali to encounters with snake venom salesmen on the Orinoco to visits with the Yanomami and Yaruro Peoples of the Venezualan Orinoco basin. As the oversized bottle from Robledillo wore down and the clock wound on, Jorge finally said, "While I could listen to these stories all night, didn't you say the tradition here is to start making the *aguardiente* very early in the morning? We should probably get some rest."

"You're right," José Carlos admitted. "Besides, I bet you are curious to know what your surroundings look like. I've had many guests arrive at our next-door bed and breakfast at night only to be surprised at what they see in the morning. Good night."

I woke to the smell of coffee just as the morning light began to trace the fringes of the treeless peaks of the mountains outside my window. Downstairs, José Carlos had already made a batch of coffee and was toasting large slices of bread that looked like they had been cut from a large round loaf. "Where did you find bread like that?" I asked in sleepy surprise. "Up across the line in La Alberca in the province of Salamanca. There used to be a bakery here in the village that made really good bread, but the woman passed away and there was no one to replace her."

I quickly realized my question was a result of my own prejudice. Eleven years after Alfonso XIII travelled through these valleys, the surrealist movie director Luis Buñuel produced a pseudo-documentary about Las Hurdes called *Tierra Sin Pan* (Land without Bread). It was meant as a critical response to the anthropological documentaries that were surfacing at the time from French filmmakers working in Northern and Sub-Saharan Africa. While Europeans of the time were collecting artifacts and anecdotes of underdevelopment afar, one of Buñuel's intentions was to show this was still very present and endemic within the confines of Europe. While his outcry may have been well intentioned, the consequences meant staining an entire region with a tarred legacy of poverty, hunger, and backwardness that persists to this day. The film's images were so damning that immediately after its screening in Madrid the Republican government banned it and defended its decision to an appeal launched by the director under the pretext it did not represent any of the regional dances.

I admitted my bias to José Carlos. He replied, "The people here obviously don't like talking about Alfonso's visit and they definitely are not keen on Buñuel's film. But while it certainly can't be considered a rigorous documentary, and some of the most shocking scenes were obviously staged and unreal, the general misery that is portrayed can't be denied." This was true. The film reflects the generalized abandonment of a land that wasn't found in some remote African or Asian mountain range but in Buñuel's own country. I drizzled some of the emerald green olive oil from the sierra over my toast and thought to myself that, these days, these scarcities are unimaginable, both economically and sociologically. But there was one way that these mountains could revert to being a land without bread, namely if there was no one left living here to make it. At that moment Jorge came down the stone stairs. When he saw the breakfast spread, he enthused, "*Qué bueno*! Nothing like a good breakfast before setting out on an adventure. That, and if we're offered to try some of the *aguardiente*, it'll be prudent to have something in our stomachs."

When we finished breakfast, José Carlos advised, "It's a lovely three-kilometre walk to Castillo along the Esperabán River, but that would take some time. If we want to get there to catch the entire process from start to finish we should probably drive." We stepped out of the house to a completely unexpected scene. A colony of around thirty cats of all sizes sat upright outside the door and they certainly weren't as surprised to see us as we were to see them. José Carlos explained, "There have always been feral cats here, but during the pandemic lockdown the people of the village started feeding them, thus interfering with natural selection and all that. Now we have a bit of a problem as you can see..."

We retraced our zigzagging steps from the night before and came once again face to face with the unfinished brick aberration atop the slate arch. In the morning light, it looked even more indecent. We mentioned to him our surprise last night at seeing this unbefitting gateway to the village and he sighed. "It's been like this since before we moved here, and that was twenty years ago. Unfortunately, it's not an isolated case. Look around; these incongruous behemoths are everywhere, like a communicable disease that is eating away at the traditional architecture of these villages. Look at that one over here." He motioned with his hand a little farther towards the river. "That huge house belongs to a local couple who emigrated from here to the Basque Country to live and work. They only come here during the summer months. Given the size of the house, you'd think the family was huge, but it's only the two of them."

Once again, there was that word I had heard back in Jarandilla with Marcelo, "emigration," but conceived of within national borders. José Carlos continued, "The Portuguese are way ahead of us in these matters. There's a stark difference when you cross the border. They have much stricter building and zoning regulations in rural areas that are aimed at maintaining some of the homogeneity of these jewels. But here, at least at the local level, it would be political suicide to try and implement something similar. By the time more tourists arrive, and arrive they will, the natural beauty will still be here, but I'm afraid the slate roofs and traditional homes will have long ago disappeared." One thing was to erroneously freeze an area in time, pointlessly trying to maintain it as a quaint portrait of times gone by, but another was to bulldoze and erase the past without any sincere attempt to preserve and adapt the patrimony that had been left behind. José Carlos's completely refurbished home was a fine example of this ethos.

The sun had yet to crest the mountains and while the night had been warm, heavy dew had fallen and the laden pomegranate trees that reached over the stone walls silently watered the streets. In the strengthening daylight we could see just how confined the valley actually was. Mountains rose up sharply from the riverbed on both sides, like heavily treed steep palisades. Closer to the river, terraces planted with single rows of olive trees had been cut from the rising wall of rock until the incline became too sharp to make it feasible. Winding our way down the river, José Carlos told us, "There just isn't much room for growing things here. There was maybe enough to keep a family from starvation, but certainly not enough to grow and expand. That was, of course, for the few who were fortunate enough to even have access to land." This problem of land use was one of the pretexts for Alfonso XIII's visit and the reason why a forestry engineer had accompanied him. Long before the king's time, the mountainsides had been deforested for things like shipbuilding and coal production. Yet it's a challenge that remains today. In many places, the mountainsides are now covered in impenetrable pine forests that could easily turn into deadly walls of fire. That in a valley with only one way in and one way out.

"There's only one bar left in this entire valley," José Carlos lamented. "The owner is a friend of mine and he's the one who has offered to show us how the *aguardiente* is made." This was saying something for Spain, a country with more bars per capital than any other in the world. Even after the pandemic so mercilessly castigated the industry, the National Institute of Statistics reported in 2020 that Spain still had 277,539 hospitality establishments. That's one for every 175 inhabitants. Curious, I asked José Carlos, "But isn't he afraid of the Guardia Civil? I have always heard it cracks down pretty hard on these types of activities." José Carlos smiled. "It's true; they used to be very hard on it. So much so that people had to go out into the woods to do it. But now it seems they are more inclined to turn a blind eye, especially if it's done, like this, on such a small, personal scale."

We pulled up to the last standing bar in the Esperabán valley and walked past the tables that lined the terrace that led into a grassy back-yard. That's when I first saw the *alambique*, or still, framed between the wooden outlines of a colourful outdoor swing set. It looked more like some sort of abstract piece of copper lawn furniture than a still designed to distill wineshine. An above-ground swimming pool filled with greening water sat behind and the entire scene had the feel of someone about to cut their lawn rather than take part in any sort of clandestine activity. José Carlos introduced Jorge and I to Poli, our alchemist for the morning. He was dressed in a tracksuit and looked like someone who might soon become a grandfather if he wasn't already. As we shook hands, his enormous mitts told another story. They were the thick, bone-crushing hands of someone who knew what it meant to work with them. He smiled, shrugged his shoulders, and said, "Well, this is it. I woke up really early so I decided to get a head start and got this first batch brewing. Don't worry, though, I have enough pomace for two more batches, so you'll be able to see the entire process if you want."

Jorge was already at work, snapping pictures of the copper boozing R2-D2 that gently steamed in the morning mist. Poli explained, "The process is pretty simple. Once you finish fermenting your wine, you take the pomace, the stuff that's left over, husks, stems, branches, and all, and fill up the bottom of the *alambique* with them. Once it's good and packed, you put on the hood where the condensation takes place. This big receptacle on top is filled with cool water, because for the evaporation to take place there needs to be a contrast, so it constantly needs replenishing. The alcohol rises, condenses under this bubble that is pushed up under the recipient, and then slides down this pipe and out into my waiting container. The most important thing is the temperature. Normally people heat the *alambique* on an open wood fire, but it's harder to control. If it gets too hot and the wine rises up, it can spoil the whole batch. That's why I use a butane burner." He took out a bucket and started to smear a paste around the seal between the bulbous bottom of the *alambique* and the top. "What's that for?" I asked. "It's to seal the two pieces," he said. "If you lose steam, you lose your *aguardiente*. I'm using a mash of chicken feed I had lying around, but traditionally people use mud. That said, bread paste is the best because it bakes on there and really makes a tight seal. Now we just have to wait for it to start streaming out."

"Where did you buy the *alambique*? Did you have it made?" I asked. Poli laughed. "No, I bought it at a market in Portugal. The damn thing cost me more than a thousand euros. There was a guy in Valverde del Fresno in the Sierra de Gata who was going to make me one, but he suddenly retired. The Guardia Civil busted up my old one, but that was back when it was actively policing this."

While we waited for the first drops to fall, José Carlos and Poli caught up on local gossip. I took advantage of the lull and slipped over to warn Jorge about something I had been cautioned against by my brother-in-law Rafa. He had experienced this process years ago in my father-in-law's village and forewarned that the first stream of *aguardiente* to appear is much more condensed than the rest that follows. If the combined end product came in at around 40 per cent, that first spurt was considerably higher.

As the village started to wake, neighbours started passing by, asking how things were going before stopping in the bar for their first or second breakfast, depending on if they had been working in their orchards or gardens or not. While Jorge was taking some close-ups, the first drops began to fall and then they turned into a stream. Poli stepped up and held a glass under the stream. He held it up to the light and admired its complete transparency and then handed it to Jorge, whose anxious eyes briefly met mine. "As my guest, here, take the first sip." Jorge thanked him for the honour, looked back at me, and then said, "Bottoms up!" The effect was immediate, his eyes bugged out for a moment and his lips puckered tight before he let out a long breath. "*Qué bueno!* But, wow, is that strong!" Poli proudly smiled and passed glasses to José Carlos and me. "Top of the morning to you," he said. "This will get the day moving." I timidly took my first sip and, even though I had prepared myself, I was shocked at how it scorched as it went down my throat. There was no real taste, yet in my nose I could sense the wine behind the burn. "This batch should make around fifteen litres. The last ones are less clear and I usually mix those with honey from my cousin's hives. You simply dip the combs into the *aguardiente* and they come out clean after a while," Poli explained. "Why don't you take a walk around the village? This is going to take a while."

On our way we passed Cerberus, who was still playing with the kittens, or better said, they were playing with him. Just before the lane that delved into a jumble of homes there was a sign with an upturned wheelbarrow underneath that read, "*prohibido aparcar en el volvedero.*" I had never seen the word "*volvedero*" before, but I could understand it from the context. The sign meant it was prohibited to park in the place where you turn around. We entered the older part of the village and, as José Carlos had mentioned, there was indeed a contrasting mix of architecture. Some of the traditional homes had been refurbished, proudly displaying their stone masonry. A few others had been converted into tourist apartments, while other traditional houses were on the verge of collapse. The traditional slate roofs that used to slink over the contiguous homes like the scales of a snake were definitely a minority now, and even the Arabic tiles had mostly been replaced by plasticky imitations atop square brick homes.

We came to a small square with flowers in the middle and I looked up and saw what looked like a church bell atop a building that had a rudimentary sign. This one read, "Asociación Juvenil," or youth association, but it clearly wasn't a church. "What's with that?" I asked José Carlos. "That can't be a church, can it?"

"No," José Carlos replied, "it's the town's PA system. They use a code with it I have never learned. The first time I heard it, I asked someone what it meant. It was autumn, like now but cooler, and the chestnuts had dropped from the trees. They told me the ringing meant the chestnuts were ready and that it was forbidden to range goats in the chestnut tree forests until they had been collected. It was then rung when the harvest had finished and pasturing was allowed once again." José Carlos looked up at the bell and continued, "In fact, believe it or not there is no functioning church in the village, nor in mine. There are fewer believers and even fewer priests these days. The churches they did have here are usually dreadful creations that were built in the '60s and '70s. I think there's only one working church left farther down the valley. There used to be a *romería*-like atmosphere every Sunday, with people parading down the valley to Mass. But now most people are either too old or simply have other things to do."

That reminded me of something else I had read about Alfonso XIII's voyage. One of the most common requests from the people was for more churches. This obviously pleased the bishop who also accompanied them for part of the journey. That is until they discovered the request was made not necessarily out of piety or religious zeal but for more practical, earthly reasons. Churches were mainly requested because of the restriction that people were only able to bury their dead in sanctified places. Having a church nearby would mean they wouldn't have to lay their loved ones to rest so far from their homes. Even today, only twenty-five properties appear in the catalogue registered by the Church between 1998 and 2015 under José María Aznar's conservative government. These are distributed throughout the different municipalities of Las Hurdes. Most of those registered are churches, temples, and hermitages, but they also include some annex buildings, a few towers, and the parish school in Nuñomoral. This catalogue includes the properties that, in the period between 1998 and

2015, the Church registered in its name with a simple declaration and without the need for other supporting documentation. When you contrast the twenty-five properties of the Church in Las Hurdes with the 982 registered in Extremadura and the thirty-five thousand in all of Spain, the disparity is striking. The Spanish Church had been actively evangelizing in the Canary Islands, Africa, Asia, and America since the fourteenth century, yet it still had relatively little presence in these valleys. When you consider that bread is equated with the body of Christ in Catholic rites, perhaps Buñuel's title had another reading, as a land lacking organized religion.

Passing through the square we were struck by the smell of woodsmoke. It wasn't the acrid smell of a burn pile but the sweeter scent of burning oak. Which was strange given it was already around twenty-three degrees and it was still early morning. We turned down the hill towards the river when Jorge stopped dead in his tracks. The smoke was drifting out from a driveway that led towards a man who was stoking a fire. Atop the blaze sat a much more soot-blackened, yet almost identical, R2-D2 unit. "Good morning," Jorge somewhat anxiously called out. "I see you've got some magic going on up there. We've just come from another alchemist who was also brewing up a potion at the entrance to the village, but with a slightly different approach." The slight, lithe-looking man turned and gave Jorge a wide-eyed, bright smile. "Then you've been with my *cuñado*! Yeah, you can definitely say he and I work differently." The word *"cuñado"* in Spanish is a term laden with deep cultural references. On the surface, it means brother-in-law, but, depending on the context, it can mean much more. Definitions range from a friendly yet intense rivalry between men, to a politically illiterate brute you rue having to invite for Christmas dinner. The word has so much baggage it has even become a noun: *cuñadismo*. This idea refers to someone who has the unfortunate tendency to express opinions on any subject, usually in a completely uninformed manner solely on the basis of individual experience or with the intention of lording their opinion over others. We would soon learn this potion master's definition was the first.

Jorge motioned with his camera and asked, "Would you mind if we come up and I take some pictures of the process?" The man beckoned, "Of course, come on up. The *aguardiente* hasn't started bubbling up yet, otherwise I'd offer you all a taste." This was more like the scene we had been expecting before we encountered the more sterile setting up at Poli's place. "I knew Poli was also making a few batches today. He uses that butane ring, but I guess I'm more traditional," our host conceded. "There's just something about using wood. Sure, it's a bit more work and more difficult to control the temperature, but it's like when you grill something over an open flame, the taste is just different." He stooped down to stoke the fire once again and added, "Of course, there's a lot more cleaning up to do afterwards this way, but to me it's worth it. That and with wood, I can get it hotter at the beginning so things go a bit quicker." He then picked up a bucket and with his sooted hands started to seal the ring between the two pieces of the *alambique*. "What are you using there?" I asked. "Just everyday mud," he said. "It gets the job done and tightens up the seal when it bakes on there like clay."

Jorge was snapping away when a woman came out of the barn-like garage with an old porcelain jug and a cheesecloth. She didn't seem surprised in the least that three strangers were standing around, mesmerized by the fire, and said, "Not too many people know how to do this anymore." She placed the jug below the long spigot coming out of the *alambique* and said, "Not even our kids do. It used to be my husband would go to work and then come home and go to work again here in the fields. But now our kids just want to work once. I guess you can't blame them, but when we're gone, who's going to remember how to do this?" She laid the cheesecloth on the mouth of the jar and started stacking up firewood within her husband's reach. "Where are you all from?" she asked. José Carlos moved closer and said, "I live up in Erías, but Jorge the photographer is from Lima and Troy here is from Canada." "Erías you say?" her curiosity seemed to grow. "How long have you lived there? Some of my people are from up there." And with that she gently began doing what the Spanish call *haciendo la ficha*, a subtle yet extensive form of questioning meant to uncover and establish common links between people, like an informal oral registry of marriages and property. As she spoke, she slipped between standard Spanish and the dialect spoken in these valleys. Her swapping *o*'s and *u*'s reflected the relatively recent isolation of the valley and harkened back to the Leonese language that was spoken when the valley was resettled after the reconquest. Once she was satisfied with José Carlos's replies, she turned to Jorge and said, "Want to come and see our pig? We only have one left. We slaughtered the piglet yesterday and roasted it over the fire after we finished making yesterday's batches of *aguardiente*. Normally, we'd also roast chestnuts over the coals, but this year they are late in falling. I guess it's been too hot and not enough rain."

We got back from visiting the pig just as the first drops began to fall. "You see, we put the cheesecloth over top to keep things like ashes from falling into the jar." He quickly picked up a glass and caught the first spurt of *aguardiente* as it started coming out. Jorge asked him to hold it up and pose in front of the *alambique* when he noticed the word "Kiko" stamped on the upper bowl. He motioned towards it and asked, "*Qué bueno!* Is it common to name *alambiques* here?" Our host laughed, shook his head, and said, "No, my son put that there several years ago. That's my name, Kiko. I've had this *alambique* for quite a while now. We bought it over in Portugal, but it wasn't easy to bring back. Back then the Guardia Civil was checking for these things when you crossed the border. I remember hiding it under a bunch of towels we had also bought over there." Kiko then deferred to José Carlos and offered him the first sip. When the glass came around to me, now knowing what to expect, I took just the smallest sip. Like Poli's, this burned the moment it hit your palate, but behind the burn there was the slightest hint of smoke. Whether or not it was worth the extra effort wasn't for me to say, but Kiko was right about one thing: the wood-burning fire did change the taste.

Once Jorge had finished documenting everything, he said to Kiko, "Thanks for being so generous with your time and knowledge. We'd love to stay longer, but we told your *cuñado* we'd be back to see him load another batch and we shouldn't keep him waiting." Kiko offered us another round and said, "No problem, just make sure you let Poli know whose tastes better!" With that, he laughed and once again stoked the fire. Just as we turned to go, his wife came out of the barn with more buckets of pomace for their next batch. She called out as we left, "Thanks for taking the pictures! As I told you, once we're gone, no one is going to remember how to do this. At least they'll have your photographs."

We walked back up the village and once again past the kitten keeper and arrived just in time to find Poli cleaning out the steaming pomace from the bottom of the *alambique*. We told him about Kiko's *cuñado* challenge and he smiled. "Well, he may be right. But this evening, while he's still trying to scrub off the soot from his *alambique*, I'll be sitting with my feet up watching the Real Madrid game. To each his own, even in a tiny village like this." He carried the steaming pomace up to his chicken coop and then came back down and showed us how he packed the bottom with another load of pomace and then added a bucket of water. As he set it back onto the butane burner he stopped for a moment and said, "Kiko may be right for another reason. I bought this butane tank yesterday and it cost me twenty-two euros. Just a week ago they were eighteen. If inflation keeps rising like it is, I, too, may go back to the old-fashioned way. If there's one thing that's plentiful around here, it's firewood."

We shared our last glass of *aguardiente*, said our thanks, and set off on the two-kilometre hike up the Esperabán River towards the petroglyphs. Just outside the village the trail cut through some dense pine cover that opened up as the valley narrowed. The trail itself was made up of chunks of flinty slate hemmed in by rock rose and broom, which at times dropped off to the right one hundred metres straight down to the riverbed. The mountainside above was patchy and irregular, with some stands of chestnut trees but mostly bunches of pine growing in different stages. All this was interspersed with the dark scars of fire. José Carlos pointed to some bushes and said, "One of the only resources they had here was to make charcoal for braziers from the heather that manages to grow among these rocks. In the times that Buñuel was filming, they would carry it up to the province of Salamanca and trade it for stale old bread."

The river below was low, but it wasn't just a series of ponds, it was flowing. A remarkable feat after the bone-dry summer the region had experienced. You could tell from the scarring on the banks it could flow with much more intensity, obviating any real flood plain where you could cultivate crops. Every square metre of irrigable soil had to be hacked and terraced from the mountainside. But even on these inhospitable slopes, low slate walls had been built to fence off the narrowest tracts of land, some planted with olive trees but most of it now unused and abandoned.

Across the valley ran the road Jorge and I had driven up on the night before. Jorge said, "Well, we knew the river was close last night and the road was curvy, but I never would have imagined this." José Carlos pointed to the flinty stone beneath our feet and said, "Imagine, the only way up and down this valley until around the 1980s was this goat track. That's why the Hurdanos are cagey in regard to promises that are never really kept. After Alfonso XIII rode through, some changes were made, but these roads didn't appear until the socialist government of Felipe González took power in the early '80s. Kings can come, like the recent visit from Felipe, and dictators can go, but they have heard the platitudes before. What they remember are deeds."

In the shadier parts of the trail, ferns grew alongside the mossy stone, contrasting sharply with the general aridity along the trail after the long summer. We came to a fork in the valley where the Zambrana Creek flowed into the Esperabán. A new bridge had been built and made the crossing easy. José Carlos said, "This trail is part of the Ruta de las Alquerías. You can descend this trail from up past the last village in this valley, Aldehuela, all the way down to Pinofranqueado. It used to be the main trade route through here and there was a lot of traffic. So much so the *alquerías* used to concession off parts of the trail where people would be granted the right to collect the manure that fell along the trail."

We climbed up to a plateau on the other side of the Zambrana. From this point you could commandeer the joining valleys, and it was here, carved in the flat slate beneath our feet, we saw the petroglyphs. José Carlos said, "Locally, these have always been known as the Moor's footprints. Basically, because anything deemed 'old' here is dated back to them, no matter how old they are. But these are not as old as you'd think and no where near as old as the paintings you saw with Carlos in Maltravieso." In the midday light it was hard to make the engravings out in the mottled stone. It took some time to adjust my eyes, but once I did, I could trace the two long knives or swords that gave the site its current name, Tesito de los Cuchillos, the Crest of the Knives. Given their subject matter, these had obviously been carved after the advent of metalworking. A rudimentary Latin inscription scrawled underneath that could be interpreted as "beware of my arms" or "protect my weapons" also helped date the incised engravings to the Roman era.

The shoed footprints or the other motifs were more difficult to date, but the vantage point this crest offered made it obvious why they had chosen this spot. This little hill had been used from time immemorial to observe the comings and goings along the valley. You could see everything, but more often than not there was probably nothing. Weary shepherds, listless centurions, and bored guards had seen countless kings and emperors come and go long before Alfonso and his hereditary successor travelled up the neighbouring valley. To pass the time and the tedium, they had shared a message with the future. One that can still be read and interpreted today.

The same couldn't be said for the accompanying information panel. Years under the blazing sun had been less kind to it and now only the title could be made out. José Carlos had a fine sense of irony, so when he saw me trying to decipher the information, he joked, "A few years ago, we met with the minister of tourism of the region. He was adamant we come up with new ideas and new ways to attract tourists; anything new was his obsession. And while I didn't necessarily disagree with him, I dared offer him some advice. From my humble position, I told him new ideas and such are all well and good, but before we start off on new initiatives, didn't he think we needed to maintain and keep up what had already been done first?"

Portrait of Manolo.

ALTERNATE NARRATIVES

15

"IT'S A PRETTY GOOD STORY... definitely better than the officially sanctioned version, but it's not what really happened." Manolo winked at me with an avuncular grin, all the while emphasizing his points with his still very agile hands. I had just told the story I'd heard from Carlos Blay about the son of one of the quarrymen, Joaquín, first realizing there were hands painted on the walls of the Maltravieso cave when Manolo's aged eyes lit up. He went on using his index finger as punctuation. "As you know, the official story that's been handed down is that Carlos Callejo first discovered the paintings, but it's not true. It's possible the boy could have discovered some of the other paintings, but the first people, or at least the first people in a very long time to enter that cave, were the Pérez Hurtado brothers from Seville, Rafael, Joaquín, Antonio, and...me."

Stories like this don't come easily, and when they do, there is always some sort of serendipity involved. This new twist drew my passage along the Rock Art Trails to a close. A few months earlier I had been investigating a new *alquerque* my daughters and I had discovered engraved in one of the stones behind Santa María church when one of my neighbours, Fátima, came up and asked what we were so engrossed in. We showed her the Arabic board game with its Union Jack-like cross in the stone and she mused, "Our neighbourhood is full of surprises like this. You only have to remember to keep looking." She would know, being the director of the

Escuela de Bellas Artes. I had known Fátima since I had taught her now grown children years before at Jill's academy and she was always friendly and inquisitive with my kids. She asked me what I was up to nowadays and when I told her about my work on a book that began in the Maltravieso cave she said a phrase that turned everything upside-down.

"Maltravieso? Really? Did you know my father was the first one to see the hands?"

With that, I knew I had to meet her father, but it took a few months to connect with the active eighty-seven-year-old. Manolo and his wife live happily out in the countryside, on a plot of land about twenty kilometres outside of the city. Close enough to be able to access anything you need from the city, but far enough away to not feel the urban weight surrounding you. If it wasn't him who was busy, it was me. But one day the planets aligned and Fátima sent me a message saying to come to her house. Her father was in Cáceres and was keen to talk. Fate would have it that Fátima lives just a few houses up from Juanma's place, so I immediately hurried up the hill to hear his tale.

"You see, at the time I was working at Correos, the Spanish post and telegraph company. I worked for Correos for more than thirty years, but in the afternoons I also picked up other jobs. I've been working since I was twelve or thirteen and must have worked more than thirty or forty different jobs. Back then, at seven o'clock in the morning I started at Correos and finished at three in the afternoon. Then at four I would be at my afternoon job." My eyes widened somewhat. Across Spain, you frequently find people who work split shifts, with a long break for lunch, and then they start back up at five or five thirty. Manolo looked back at his wife who was sitting behind him on the sofa nodding her head at what he was saying. "If it wasn't for my wife, our kids wouldn't have got the education they have. But even though I worked hard, I had some afternoons free. And when I did, what I liked to do was to head over and watch the excavations at the quarry." At this note of recognition, his wife's head nodded with a bit more vigour.

"As I was saying, on the afternoons I was free I would walk over to the quarry and watch them work. They used to make these thirty- or forty-centimetre holes just by using a hammer and a metal bar. Once they had made maybe fifteen or twenty holes in the rock face, that's when they would fill them with dynamite, and that's when things would really get exciting. Back then, the rock surrounding the cave reached out maybe thirty or forty metres from where the entrance of the cave stands now, about to where the interpretation centre is. Anyways, before they set off the charges, the Guardia Civil would make sure everyone evacuated the area. It even cut traffic back on the old highway that runs behind the quarry because of the flying rock.

"So one day we were standing on the highway when they set it off, and as it exploded a huge plume of dust rose up from the site, much more than was normal. We said to each other, 'Look what's coming out of there.' When the dust finally settled, we ran up to the site and that's when we saw it. There was a small opening that hadn't been there before, about one metre high and about sixty or seventy centimetres wide." This new detail changed everything. Manolo was suggesting either the cave's original entrance had been in a different location, or this entry had caved in sometime with the passage of time. Either option was entirely possible, as the area's underground water system had eaten through the karst stone and left it a honeycombed maze of rock. Manolo saw the look of surprise on my face and enthused, "Some say the cave reaches all the way to Aldea Moret, which is almost two kilometres away." Here his wife stopped nodding her head and exclaimed, "Back then they wouldn't even let you build in the area because they were afraid the ground would give way underneath the weight of the buildings." Manolo interrupted, "And it has! Remember when they were building the secondary school? A huge grotto opened up while they were building it and they had to fill it up with truckload after truckload of rock." He paused for a moment to collect his thoughts and then resumed. "At the time there were four or five mills in the area, each with their huge smokestack that turned the rock into lime."

"Okay, Manolo, so you were there when the cave first opened, but that still doesn't explain how you came to be the first person to go into the cave. Weren't you a bit nervous to go into a cave that had just been blown open and that so much smoke and dust had come out of?"

"Well, as I was saying, I've been working since I was about twelve years old. Over that time I have had so many different jobs. I started out helping out in shops and then rode around the province in delivery trucks. One of my first jobs was during a plague of locusts in the area and I was paid twenty-five pesetas to mix some sort of terrible insecticide they had back then with some feed. It was like you were mixing sand with lime to make cement, only we had no gloves or masks. Then, during the hottest hours of the day, we would go out to where the university now stands and spread it around as though we were seeding crops. Another of my first jobs was as a cleaner in a well when I was fourteen. Up in the Espíritu Santo area, towards the sanctuary of the Virgin, there was something like five wells that supplied the water for Cáceres. I would have to go down thirty-six metres to the bottom and help out the sweepers. Down there was a three hundred-horsepower electric water pump from England and it would pump the water out of the well so we wouldn't drown. I was hired as a general helper and would stay down there from ten o'clock to eight o'clock in the morning. One time there was a power cut and we had to get out of there right quick before it all filled up with water. I guess for this reason I wasn't really afraid of these things."

"But how did it come about that you actually went into the cave?"

"Well, I saw the opening and immediately asked Raphael for some coveralls. Everyone around started shouting 'Manolín! Manolín!' that's what they called me back then, 'You can't go in there, don't be crazy! There might be gas, who knows what is in there.' But as some of them saw I was determined, the brothers decided to join me. I can't remember if there were four or five of us. Now that I think of it, maybe there was another young guy whose father also had a piece of the quarry business, but he's passed away since." Here Manolo took out a manila folder and dumped some pictures out on the table before us. "Several years ago, a reunion was organized and an assistant of Antonio Casares, the discoverer of Atapuerca, came. In these pictures you can see several of us. The newspapers were there, along with groups of kids from different schools around Extremadura. During the reunion, we got to enter the cave again. Well, those of us who still could manage to crawl around. The other brothers' father was Telesforo. He was called 'el Frances,' the Frenchman, because he had worked in mining in France for many years. The poor man came back with silicosis and spent most of the day in bed. Anyway, it was a long time ago and whether there were four or five of us, I can't recall. We picked up a carbide lamp and we went in."

It's here where Manolo's story diverges from the accepted narratives. The stories that get heard are mostly told by the powerful. Their names are the ones that are remembered. Those without means, the nameless, get left behind and become forgotten. Since the times of the rock art painters, the narratives that have been passed down have been the official, accepted version of the tribe. That of the shaman or the tribal leader, whether they were their hunting exploits, their victories over other groups, or the discovery of new places. Magellan's name is the one remembered, not the eighteen crewmen who also survived to tell their now forgotten tales. The name Sacagawea may not sound familiar, but without her, Lewis and Clark's expedition would never have succeeded. The fabulously named Scotsman, Mungo Park, is remembered for being the first European to see the Niger River, but the guides, Johnson and Demba, who led him there are only remembered as being "local," even when Park himself stated their names in his book.

"I'm telling you, no one really wanted to go in. Although this one here in the picture called me on the telephone one time and said his brother Raphael was the first to enter the cave. I told him he was mistaken and that it was me. Whatever the case, as I said, the opening was small and we had to enter on our hands and knees. We got in and immediately past the entrance we saw on the right a room filled with water and then another with water too." I asked, "What else did you see, what was the ground like?" Manolo quickly replied, "Remember that there had just been an explosion and we weren't sure if there could be another, so we weren't in there very long. On the ground, there was just dirt and the rubble from the explosion. We looked around a bit more, and then up on the wall of the cave we saw it. There, we saw some scrawl and the outline of a hand painted in red."

Firsts are complicated to speak of in this context. As Carlos Blay had told me when I had visited the cave, the age of the handprints ranges across tens of thousands of years. Successive waves of people coming through the area had left their mark and had obviously seen those that preceded them. There could be no real "firsts," but Manolo's story did raise some questions. I asked, "So how did Carlos Callejo become involved then?"

"Well, as I told you, at the time I was working for Correos and he was my boss. And well…" There was a long pause before he started up again. "I was his secretary for around ten years. He was the kind of boss who would call you to come and move the brazier as he sat with his butterfly collection. Sometimes, when we had to go out and repair the telegraph lines, he would come out and supervise the work, and when we broke out our lunch, he would take his picnic basket and sit two hundred metres away from the rest of us. Different times, I suppose. During those years, more than once I remember saying to him, 'Don Carlos, you do know I was the first to enter the cave there in Maltravieso.' And no answer, nothing. As he was the one who had made it public, well…not a yes, not a no, just silence."

Manolo's face didn't read sadness, nor bitterness, just incomprehension. He shook his head and went on. "His son Alfonso also wrote a book about the cave. There was a big presentation at the Gran Teatro and there we were, expecting to hear something. But again, silence. He only spoke of his father."

Prehistoric rock art drawings in Parque Nacional de Monfragüe.

STONE
CARTOONS

16

"A PROMISE IS A PROMISE." Carlos was smiling as we left the city heading north along the EX-390, leaving behind the last remaining blocks of cookie-cutter townhouses that have sprouted up in the area. "It's true, it took us a while to get the timing right, but as I guaranteed to you when we left the cave, I have more to show you. Today, I want to show you some of the paintings we found years ago in Monfragüe." He patted the dashboard and looked up at the clear blue sky and continued, "It looks like today's going to be a beautiful day, especially if this little Ford of mine deals with some of the off-roading I have in mind."

It was January 7, the day after Epiphany or Three Kings Day. The day marking the official end of the marathon Christmas season in Spain. Just like other places around the world, here the holiday season begins earlier and earlier every year. Christmas carol creep now starts in late November and is in full swing by the time the mega long weekend the Spanish craft every year around December 6 and 8. It's a long weekend the Spanish use to travel because during the more traditional dates of the holidays, like Christmas and Epiphany, visits with family generally come first. Once New Year's Eve passes, the prospect of a New Year dawns, but you are then sucked back into holiday season madness, revisited as shoppers rush to buy food and presents for December 6, the big day for exchanging gifts. Some families have chosen to adapt the Santa model and give their children gifts on the twenty-fifth so they have more time to enjoy them before going back to school. But most kids get double the fun as almost all get something on the sixth as well. This definitive Spanish tradition of the three kings, whose bones supposedly lie in the golden sarcophagus in the imposing gothic cathedral in Cologne, Germany, has withstood the cultural onslaught of Saint Nick and his reindeer and remains strong.

The landscape on the northern fringes of the city is a vast, treeless steppe with sharp knobby knees of rock sticking out here and there from the rips in the bleached straw. These are the *llanos* of Cáceres, an arid savannah that, now in winter, boasts rare patches of different-coloured greens. These provisional wetlands burst into an allergy sufferer's nightmare during the brief violent spring only to be quickly burnt to parch by the sudden change to summer. The area has been designated a Special Protection Area under the EU Directive on the Conservation of Wild Birds, as well as a Special Area of Conservation under the EU Directive on the Conservation of Natural Habitats and of Wild Fauna and Flora. It's one of the largest reserves of steppe birds in Spain and an important wintering centre for a wide range of species that pass through these unpopulated, open spaces on their way to and from Africa. Depending on the season, you can find cranes, great bustards, partridges, shrikes, starlings, spotted cuckoos, black storks, Eurasian stone-curlews, lapwings, Montagu's harriers, black and red kites, little owls, lesser kestrels, and the punkish-looking Eurasian hoopoe. Look down from the sky and beyond the random team of cattle or flock of dusky sheep and you can find deer, hares, foxes, shrews, and timid otters that lurk from pool to pool as the creeks and streams dry up.

Flecks of green cling to the small watercourses that cut through the steppe and feed into the meandering Guadiloba River that runs off to the left of the highway. And then a glint on the horizon announces the newest fever to spread across the land. Carlos looked out over the fields and commented with a fair bit of irony in his voice, "Welcome to the newest gold rush of Extremadura." The glint I caught soon turned into more than a shine as the surrounding countryside morphed from brown to silver. Entire football fields of photovoltaic panels reverently looked up to the mihrab in the sky in lines so organized any mosque would look chaotic in comparison. Thousands of modules of solar panels quilted the country-side, lapping up the unstinting sunshine that now provides renewable energy for hundreds of thousands of homes.

Just over ten kilometres from the city, the return of the *dehesa* signals a change in the topography and the promise of a greater water source. A deep furrow sinks down from the steppe and marks the course of the Almonte River as it meets its affluent, the Tamuja, and flows into the overflow of the José María de Oriol reservoir. The two-lane highway winds its way through the dense vegetation and down the flank of the river valley and comes to a scene you often see spanning the rivers of the province, generations of bridges side by side. Sixteenth-century bridges lie in each branch, one stranded in the Almonte while the other flounders in the Tamuja. Each series of stone archways are connected by a small promontory that marks the point where the rivers meet. Depending on the level of the water in the reservoir, these disused bridges can be entirely covered and hidden from view by the waters, but after the electric company Iberdrola dumped a huge portion of the reservoir's reserves at the end of the summer, both bridges could clearly be seen. Farther down the scarred banks, the remains of an early-twentieth-century bridge were also exposed. It had been made useless and had to be destroyed after the waters rose above its deck when the reservoir was completed. The modern utilitarian bridge that now takes you across the fluctuating waters is entirely forgettable, but the stark contrast between the wooded valley and the ten-kilometre swath of steppe on each side of the river valley is definitely marked.

Downstream, huge black pipes run down the hillside and dip into the river like enormous drinking straws. This is from where the city of Cáceres drinks. Long ago, the city's reservoir out in the *llanos* became too small for the growing demand and now water needs to be pumped up from the river to keep the taps running. There's a running joke in Spain that likens the dictator Francisco Franco to a frog. An amphibian autocrat who hopped from reservoir to reservoir in his obsession to irrigate these dry lands and help convert Spain into the breadbasket and orchard of Europe that it has become. There is some truth to the joke, though, because no democratically elected government has since been able to undertake a public works project big enough to be able to guarantee the city's supply.

Farther up the road, with the reappearance of the *dehesa*, the sierra that serves as the backbone of the park we were headed to ridges the horizon. From here the hills look pale and rounded, like antediluvian beasts stretched across the horizon. These suddenly disappeared as we dropped into a thick fog and the knotted holm oak trees seemed to be levitating in the air. Carlos slowed up a bit and said, "You never know when you'll run into fog out here. Sometimes it lies like a blanket down by the rivers and streams, but today it looks like it runs all the way to the sierra and the Tagus River. The livestock is normally well fenced in, but it's the deer that can be dangerous. They easily jump the fences and can be just around any corner." These grazing lands, broken here and there by sparse stands of wood, were the perfect frames for the distant sierra when it peered out of the mist. In the early morning light, the cottony fog gave the hills in the distance an impressionistic look that sharpened as we approached.

The road narrowed again past the village of Torrejón el Rubio. The thickening scrub along the way took advantage of the inherent difficulty for livestock to graze in the increasingly rumpled and wrinkled landscape as we got closer to the sierra. This mountainous fold fans out over seventy kilometres, running up from the Villuercas mountain range to the east and then into the Alagón Valley and Sierra de Gata farther west. Our first stop was just below the remains of the Arabic castle that crowns the park, a national park that defines the very soul of the province. It is famous for its birding and well-preserved Mediterranean scrubland and forest, unfortunately some of the last remaining stands around the Mediterranean basin. But this area hasn't only been shaped by nature. Humans have long played an important role in its evolution and our footprint can be seen on the very rock that makes up the park.

The Romans, who were relative newcomers, knew the area as Mons Fragorum, a dense mountain woodland, and intense preservation efforts over the years have kept it so. But hominids were present in the area long before the Romans invaded the peninsula, and our genealogical ancestors have left a pictorial record of their lives painted on rock faces in over one hundred different sites throughout the park. Carlos was part of one of the first projects to catalogue these finds more than twenty years ago. Monfragüe National Park was my last of the five centres in the province of Cáceres that form part of the Prehistoric Rock Art Trails found across the continent, and I had heard the rock art here was the equivalent of the Sistine Chapel.

The park itself isn't necessarily close to any large urban centres, but several villages fall within its boundaries, which makes it somewhat unique when you consider the traditional view of national parks. The world's first official protected area was the Bogd Khan Uul Biosphere Reserve in Mongolia. It was officially sanctified and placed under protection in 1778 by the king and Khuree Minister Yundendorj. This was done more for spiritual reasons than purely conservationist ideals, mostly because the mountain was considered sacred and local people would not hunt in the area or collect firewood from its slopes. Just under a hundred years later, in 1872, Yellowstone National Park was established under US President Ulysses S. Grant. The underlying conservation ethos of the time saw natural places as pristine paradises that were supposedly untouched, willfully choosing to ignore the influence Indigenous Peoples had had on the land for millennia.

This back-to-Eden view that has influenced conservation ever since was made clear in one of the speeches President Teddy Roosevelt gave a few years later in 1903 on the edges of the Grand Canyon: "I want to ask you to keep this great wonder of nature as it now is. I hope you will not have a building of any kind, not a summer cottage, a hotel or anything else, to mar the wonderful grandeur, the sublimity, the great loneliness and beauty of the canyon. Leave it as it is. You cannot improve on it. The ages have been at work on it, and man can only mar it." The balance between preservation and public use was tipped in one definite direction while obviating the fact previous inhabitants and users of the land had recently been expelled, driven from the area by force by state-sanctioned militias.

The establishment of Yellowstone gave rise to subsequent national parks being created in Australia, Canada, New Zealand, and then just after the turn of the century Sweden created Europe's first national park, Sarek National Park, in 1909. While some of this conservationist thought played a part in the birth of Spain's first national park in 1918, its creation was also centred on national hagiography. The Spanish National Parks

Board wanted to commemorate the twelfth centenary of the greatly exaggerated, if not mythical, battle of Covadonga and did so by creating Montaña de Covadonga National Park, now called Picos de Europa National Park. The first article of its declaration made clear this hagiographic focus: "Covadonga will be subject to special protection on behalf of the State. All the monumental work carried out there, including the tombs for the remains of Pelayo and Alfonso I the Catholic, will be arranged by the Ministry of Public Instruction, by means of a proposal to the Royal Academy of Fine Arts of San Fernando. The projected works in Covadonga to solemnize the 12th centenary of the Reconquest will be finalized within the current year, in order to proceed then with their execution." It would take close to forty years for the next park to be created out in the Canaries in 1954, and Monfragüe was granted this distinction in 2007.

Before making the trip with Carlos, I spoke to someone who knew the area as well as just about anyone, Paco Castañares. An extremely amiable man whose CV is as long as the park is wide. He had served as the director of the environmental agency of the regional government of Extremadura and was a former deputy in the assembly of Extremadura (also in the provincial council of Cáceres). He was also the former mayor of his hometown, Serradilla, and is now president of the recently created Amigos de Monfragüe, an association whose main aim is to protect the interests of the park and those who live in it. He has had ample experience on both sides of the decision making process at administrative levels and I asked him about the complicated dance of combining the needs of a national park with those of the many villages, lives, and livelihoods found within it. His reply was clarifying and insightful.

"Monfragüe is the result of human interaction with the local environment for the past ten thousand years. Its first inhabitants were nomadic hunters who came looking for food. Here they found such an ample array of resources that the nomads became sedentary, cultivating the land and taking advantage of what the forest had to offer. They then began grazing their livestock through the dense forests and eventually founded the first permanently inhabited nuclei that later became villages. To ignore this is to ignore the fact the national park we now see and know is the result of ten millennia of human interaction in a privileged environment. One that has exemplarily maintained its natural values."

Paco paused for a moment to let that sink in and then said, "You see, the people of Monfragüe have always got along well with their environment. Throughout the ages, they have tended and modelled it with care, knowing full well only thus would they be able to obtain the best results from the land. The attacks on Monfragüe have always come from outside and were caused by the public administration." I was somewhat surprised someone who had worked so closely in the administration saw things this way. He then detailed some of the attacks. "Things like the construction of the dams that in effect castrated the then wild river, or the planting of eucalyptus that destroyed thousands of hectares of centenary holm and cork oaks that are native to the area. An exotic species from Australia never had a future here in the first place. One of our main objectives as an association is to see that the hydroelectric uses, that, in fact, Spanish law prohibits, cease forever. We also revindicate that this natural space should once again be reconciled with the people who still live in its environment, as it always was and as it should never have ceased to be."

Unlike many national parks around the world, you're never quite sure when you have actually entered Monfragüe. There are no ostentatious Smokey the Bear signs to welcome you, and there are no North American-style toll booths to charge you a fee and let you in. The *dehesa* just keeps falling past your window. We drove deeper into the park along the EX-208 and then veered off when we came to a sign that pointed us towards the Castillo de Monfragüe. As the road climbed up to the castle, the fog slipped away behind us and a jagged tentacle of rock rose up ahead. Earlier in the week, I had made a reservation with the tourism office in Torrejón el Rubio, and as we came to a little wooden booth below the rock face, we saw that Martín, our guide, was waiting for us.

Carlos stepped out of the car, adjusted his still-obligatory face mask, and looked up at the rock face and said, "Things have changed quite a bit over the years; none of the fencing or stairs were here." A mass of cubed grey granite stood before us with an oxidized red slash across the middle, opening onto what looked like a puncture wound. A kettle of fifty, sixty, maybe a hundred massive griffon vultures wheeled above. Even at such great heights, their enormous wingspan made sure they were clearly visible against the Mediterranean blue. Vultures are called *buitres* in Spanish and the poetic collective name for them is a *bandada*. The words a *bandada de buitres* rhyme together with the rhythmical purr of a Harley Davidson. The word, at least for someone like me who is a Spanish language learner, was new and when learning another language context is crucial. There in Monfragüe National Park, this was not a problem. The correct word might be a *bandada*, but in Monfragüe they can more accurately be described as an *inevitabilidad*. An inevitability of vultures. Imagine that.

The vultures you see here are not all from the area. The extensive livestock and wild ungulates that live in and around the park provide substantial numbers of carcasses as a result of the traditional cattle farming and rewilding processes. This carrion buffet acts as a magnet, and studies have shown that griffon vultures from as far afield as the Pyrenees and even southern France will make the eight-hundred-kilometre journey to feast in the area only to head back a few days later after stuffing themselves.

Periodically, one of the local carrion cleaners would audibly swoop down into the many nests hidden between the cubist stones above the opening while we were getting ready to climb up into the cave. A closer looked revealed many bald white heads sticking out from the crags in the rocks above. A committee of feathery thugs guarding the entrance to the lair, yet as Mark Twain once pointed out, although vultures may have the look of a professional assassin, they are a bird that commits no murder.

A chain-link fence was draped over the top three-quarters of the opening and a greenish metal staircase led up to a barred fence that blocked off the remaining part of the entrance to the semi-lateral-lying grotto. Martín opened up by saying, "Thanks for getting here as quickly as possible." He had sent me an SMS earlier that morning, asking if we could move up the visit. He wanted to clarify the situation and told us, "When my colleague scheduled the visit, I guess she had forgotten I had a doctor's appointment today. Living in a village like Torrejón has its advantages, but having to go all the way to Cáceres for a routine doctor's appointment isn't one of them."

While we quickly got to know each other, Carlos told Martín he had been involved in a project regarding the discovery of a large part of the park's prehistoric art, but he promised not to interrupt. He was more than happy to take a back seat and learn some more from someone local. Martín began, "Then, as you know Carlos, what you are about to see is what is perhaps the best set of rock art paintings in the whole park, which is saying something when you consider there are over one hundred different sites spread out throughout the park."

Carlos and I both smiled. If anyone knew about these different sites, it was him. While we were driving up from Cáceres, I had asked him about the project he had been involved in. "It was a very memorable experience for me. It was the first time I was really able to get down into the trenches. What I mean by that is it was my first real experience working with what had until then only been theoretical study." I asked when this project had taken place. "It was back in 1995," Carlos said, "just after finishing my second year of studies in Italy. When I came back, I found out by chance that the University of Extremadura was looking for volunteers for a project that planned to document the cultural heritage in the area of Monfragüe park. The project was going to be coordinated by an archeologist of the Junta de Extremadura, Hipólito Collado, and José Julio García Arranz, who was a professor of art history at the same university. I knew both had done previous research on schematic rock art in other parts of Extremadura, and this time they were focusing on Monfragüe." When I asked how big the project was, he responded, "The bulk of the team was made up of history and art history students from the Complutense University of Madrid and the University of Extremadura. The team was occasionally filled out with restorationists and topographers, but I guess in total we were about fifteen people. To be honest, it was a while ago and I don't remember the exact number. I do remember it was mainly carried out over four summer campaigns. These were intense. We worked from sun-up to sundown, conscientiously prospecting all the rocky outcrops, often in very difficult terrain."

It was hard to believe something this transcendental had remained uncatalogued until relatively recently, so I asked Carlos what he remembered about this: "We immediately knew we were in an area with an absolutely exceptional potential for schematic rock art. It was terribly exciting to wake up every morning knowing you were sure to discover something new, something that had remained unknown or at least ignored for thousands of years. It was the first time a large team had carried out such an exhaustive research project on rock art in Extremadura. That said, it is also true the technical means at our disposal, analog photography, totally manual topographies, etc., were very limited. Then there was the limited budget. As I said, we were volunteers. Nobody was paid, we slept in bunk beds and ate sandwiches, but we knew we were part of something remarkable and that's what mattered."

As we worked our way up towards the entrance, Martín continued his mandatory, memorized preamble to set the scene for us. "Across the different ranges that make up the national park, these representations are mostly found in shelters and small caves. The fact we have found them in these places could be due to many reasons, but the most likely is these natural formations often offer more protection and thus the paintings are better conserved. Whatever the case, curiously enough, as you'll soon see, the paintings we have encountered aren't necessarily found in places where these populations made their homes. Most of them are located in difficult-to-access places that simply would not be practical to live in." I told Martín about my experience in the Maltravieso cave and the other sites around the province I had visited and then asked him how old the paintings we were about to see were. He replied, "The schematic art emerged around seven thousand years ago in the Neolithic period, when groups of people started to settle. Experts believe the abundance of schematic art in the area is due to the existence of the two large Copper and Bronze Age settlements that have been unearthed. One of which was discovered just up there on top of us," he pointed up towards the vultures and the hidden peak of the sierra, "in Peña Falcón beneath the remains of Monfragüe Castle and the other is in the vicinity of Puerto de la Serrana."

We stepped inside and turned around and looked out across the park. The fog down below had settled into some of the lower gullies and ravines, leaving the exposed hills with their crowns of oak trees. Folds that looked like polka-dotted, pajama-covered legs that were sticking out of blankets of white. From up here you could see just about everywhere. Martín said, "One of the main things to consider about prehistoric rock art is the essential connection between the art and the natural space that surrounds it. Here in Monfragüe that means the water that runs through it. In fact, in the geographical area of Monfragüe, more than 90 per cent of the rock art panels that have been discovered are visually oriented in some way towards one of these riverbeds. These clusters also tend to be concentrated around strategic transit areas. Like the narrow gateways that flank the park's riverbeds in the nearby Salto del Gitano, the Salto del Corzo, and the Portilla del Tiétar. If the vegetation looks dense now, you can only imagine how thick it would have been before centuries of grazing livestock thinned it out. The only possible way, or perhaps the path of least resistance through it, would have been along the riverbanks. From up here they created a watchtower that saw everything."

It took some time to adjust our eyes to the contrasts of light in the rock shelter. The sun was shining brightly on one side of the rock face, while the farther reaches were in semi-darkness. As Martín had stressed, this was not a place to make yourself comfortable. The metal structure of the stairs and various landings made the ascent easy, but without them you would have had to canyon your way up into the refuge. The interior continuously narrowed like a funnel as it continued upwards in staggered rises. "The existing cave paintings in the area begin at the end of the Epipaleolithic and continue until the Iron Age," said Martín matter-of-factly.

I had enough experience in Spain to know that tourist information often included very specialist words. Whether it was the language's close relationship with Latin or simply a refusal to dumb things down, I knew I would have to look "Epipaleolithic" up, along with several others, later on. "The size of the paintings range from the biggest at around thirty centimetres to the smallest being around two centimetres. The artists' colour palate was limited to the materials they had at hand and was made up of mainly red, black, and white. Red was the most commonly used colour, which was made with pigments of mineral origin. The cave artists produced these by grinding iron oxides like hematite or ochre and mixing them with water or with some sort of fat or resin." Here Martín pointed to the strands of oxide stains running down parts of the rock face. "Once they were painted on the rock, they were stuck there like some sort of prehistoric tattoo. They began by using their fingers, but as time progressed, they started to use brushes of some sort to produce finer lines. Here in front of you, you can see a fine example of the former technique."

I squinted and concentrated my gaze on the reddish-orange rock. Bands of parallel smooth rock cascaded down the face at about a fifty-degree angle, but I couldn't see anything in the bright light. Martín read the confusion on my face and pointed. "Focus your eyes here." And there they were. As my eyes adjusted, a stag with an impressive set of antlers materialized out of the rock in front of me. As I got used to the different shades of red, I saw the animal comprised part of what looked like a scene that could be read as a narrative. In front of the stag I could just barely make out the figure of a person, but they seemed to be upside down. "The figure you see upside down could mean they had been tossed by the animal, or it could mean they had died," remarked Martín. To the right of that person was another human figure, arms akimbo in a stance that could be interpreted as running towards the other. This latter figure was thicker, but not in a more simplistic way. It was as though it had been done on purpose. The hips were wider—perhaps suggesting it was a woman. Above all this was a blob of red that was impossible to interpret, and I wondered if this was their way of cancelling out part of a story.

Martín asked how many images we could see, and when we told him we were unsure, he then held up a white card under a slight fold in the rock below the image of the woman. "Can you see the other deer down here?" The white card reflected the light and another deer emerged, this time with less elaborate antlers. "Do you notice anything different between the two deer other than the size of their horns?" Martín was fond of rhetorical questions and after a short pause added, "This one down here has four legs, but what about the one next to the upside-down man?" He was right; when I looked closer, I saw the first stag had at least six legs and maybe a seventh if it wasn't meant to be its tail.

"There are many different theories regarding this," Martín said, "but one of the most interesting ideas is that these 'extra' appendages were meant to function like modern-day cartoons. If these images were used for storytelling, perhaps by the light of a fire, all of these legs could have been interpreted as movement." If this were true, these peoples would have had highly developed visual literacy skills. Most believe that, in our digital age, we are far more visually literate than those who lived in other epochs. But if this painting were indeed meant to tell a story or teach a lesson, these ochre rocks would have been the equivalent of today's GIFs and digital whiteboards. I looked over at Carlos and asked him what he thought. "It seems fairly certain the depiction of zoomorphic forms with many legs is genuine," he said. "You've travelled all over the Middle East and probably remember seeing those monumental Assyrian winged bulls and humans with five legs? Well, in schematic art these are sometimes so abstract we call them pectiniforms or comb-shaped, like with a simple horizontal line and then many vertical ones. It's possible this was intended to convey an idea of movement, of an animal on the run perhaps, or even in a herd."

Whatever the case, visual language must be learned. It's not necessarily easy to understand and it certainly isn't universal. We only need to see the different interpretations of various hand gestures around the world to highlight this. A simple "pinecone" hand gesture, with your fingers pursed together, in Italy might mean someone is looking for an explanation, whereas in the Middle East this same gesture would mean "slow down." The pictures in front of us were not self-explanatory. We lacked the verbal support and learning that would have been passed down through the generations that would have unlocked their meaning.

We climbed a little farther up the metal stairs to the next viewing platform and here Martín reminded us, "Remember I said the paintings span across thousands of years? In this next panel you will see something that brings us up to what we might call recorded history."

Once again, I scanned the rock, but here it was less uniform than before. I started imagining seeing things that in the end weren't there. Martín then raised his white card and there they appeared. Patterned scratches that looked like a series of M's descended down a smooth, elongated section of rock. These were the first black paintings I had seen. "What you see here might be the first instance of writing that we have here on the Iberian Peninsula. These are Tartessian letters, or what is known as the so-called Southwestern script, and are believed to be from around the fourth or fifth century BCE." The writing was interrupted on the extreme left side by the natural flaking of the stone. Somewhat lower down there were some very faded remains of more black strokes that perhaps made up the same text but were very washed out. Whatever the case, the message was untransmissible.

This was yet another example of the constant layering of civilizations in these lands. Sometime in the fourth century BCE, the Greek historian Ephorus of Cyme wrote of "a very prosperous market, the so-called Tartessos, an illustrious city, watered by a river that carries a great quantity of tin, gold and copper from Celtica." The historian of historians himself, Herodotus wrote in the fifth century BCE that Tartessos was an empire of great wealth beyond the Pillars of Hercules. It is true he might have exaggerated, as he also claimed their King Arganthonios ruled for eighty years and lived to be over 120 years old, but if there was one thing the godfather of travel writing always did, he always followed the money.

The Tartessian capital has never been found, but according to classical texts, it must have been located somewhere in the Spanish regions of Huelva or Cádiz, where the Guadiana and Guadalquivir rivers both flow into the sea. This pre-Grecian civilization's influence, however, extended far inland, and recent excavations, some just one hundred kilometres to the south of Monfragüe, in Guareña, have shown this. Along the navigable Guadiana River in the neighbouring province of Badajoz, researchers have recently unearthed an enormous Tartessian complex. A spectacular find where they have uncovered many items demonstrating the intense trade with the Greeks and Phoenicians that existed all along the entire Mediterranean at the time. Among the remains they found glass that had been shaped in far-off Macedonia and Carthage, along with a sculpture that was made of marble from the quarries of Mount Pentelicus, near Athens. Its pedestal is decorated with traces of Egyptian blue paint, Egypt being the only civilization that could synthesize and produce the colour blue at the time. But perhaps the most astonishingly unexpected find in the complex were the remains of more than fifty animals that had been sacrificed, mostly horses, mules, and donkeys, as an offering to their gods.

A friend of mine, Doctor Ana Isabel Mayoral, a professor of anatomy at the Faculty of Veterinary Medicine at the University of Extremadura, was involved in the dig. I later asked her about her impressions of the discovery and her experience working on it: "What struck me when I first arrived was the building itself. I mean, how could a building like that, with those walls, that courtyard, and those rooms have been buried for so long? There it lay for centuries, looking like just a simple mound in the middle of a field of crops, without any suspicion at all of everything that was hidden underneath." Ana has a way of making you live the stories she tells with her excitement and enthusiasm. She speaks with a friendly intensity that is also reflected in her hand gestures. She went on. "The first thing that caught my attention about the building itself was the stairs leading down to the courtyard. They were perfect. Their beauty shocked me. It was incredible to think that until only recently they had been underground. Many of them were still covered by slate slabs, but even those that were no longer covered were surprising due to their excellent state of preservation."

I asked her how she had become involved in the project in the first place. "Well, it was through someone you know, María Martín, a fellow veterinarian, as you know," she said. "Her specialization is horses and she was contacted by the archeologists and archeozoologists who were carrying out the excavation. They had discovered the skeletons of the animals in the courtyard of the building and wanted to form a multidisciplinary team, which would include veterinarians. They had found much, much more than they had expected at the beginning of the excavation. By forming this multidisciplinary team, things could be formalized more easily to obtain project funding and carry out a long-term study covering all the aspects related to the find. Naturally, we were all enthusiastic about the idea, even though archeological excavations were outside our normal scope of work."

I then asked her to describe what she had seen inside: "When we got there, the archeozoologists were working in the courtyard, extracting the skeletons with care, using the techniques they employ to avoid damaging the bones. It was very interesting to see them work. It was extraordinary to think that, in that courtyard, long ago, there had been no less than around fifty dead horses, in addition to a few other animals. We wondered what had happened to them...if they had been slaughtered. Why?

Especially when you consider they were one of the greatest riches in ancient times."

The whole thing sounded rather macabre, even if they were now just dried bones. I asked her what came to mind as she investigated it. She said, "Being there, you can be transported to that situation, but there are still many questions. How were the first horses sacrificed? We still don't know this yet, and then there were the rest. If you imagine the situation, these poor creatures would have been nervous in this enclosed space, smelling the blood, the death, perhaps sensing what was going to happen to them. Horses are extremely sensitive animals. How could the Tartessians handle them; how did they herd them into this closed space? After all, we are talking about almost fifty horses! Now we only see the skeletons, but it would have been impressive, certainly overwhelming to see that yard filled with all those bodies lying there." Here she stopped for a moment and shook her head. "Personally, and as a veterinarian, I can't help but feel sorry to imagine such a large number of these beautiful animals lying on the floor of the courtyard. On the other hand, I am very curious to hear about the new surprises that will surely be discovered in the still unopened rooms. The final part of the project will be very interesting, as it will allow the general public to get an idea of what the scene was like when they started excavating there. Some of the complete skeletons will be assembled and they will be exhibited as they were found, and then the site will eventually be opened up to visitors."

Back in the cave in Monfragüe, we pushed farther up inside and came to the next panel. Here the viewing platform sits somewhat above the paintings and Martín asked us to sit down to get a better view. He climbed down from the platform and edged along the wall of the cave so he could better point out where everything was. We were now in the shade, away from the bruising sun, and the paintings were better con-served. A jumble of figures of differing reds spread across the surface. High up on the right, a group of figures was presided over by a large, four-legged animal with horns. This animal differed from the others we had seen in that its body was longer with an elongated snout and horns more akin to a bull's. This animal was superimposed on a large human figure, with a further group of degraded anthropomorphic figures drawn with brushes above.

Then, among a series of dots, a pair of what looked to be eyes appeared. I asked Martín what he thought they were and he said, "Some theorize these represent the eye idols found across the Mediterranean, Mesopotamia, and Arabia. In the third and fourth millennia BCE, these types of 'eyes that never close' became a common motif across the Iberian Peninsula and have been found on idols carved in alabaster and bone." Here Martín showed a picture on his mobile phone. "This idol, which is currently found in the National Archaeological Museum in Madrid, dates from around the same time and was discovered while they were excavating a nearby dolmen." The statue's wide open, alarmed eyes, surrounded by tattoo-like lines rising up like a Dalí moustache, were indeed similar to the aghast eyes that stared out from the rock. These unclosing eyes raised the possibilities of some sort of shamanistic experience that would have surrounded the paintings. Sympathetic magic that could have meant the shaman was trying to access the spirits in the stones or perhaps to look beyond them to another world.

Martín then pointed to a place farther down the panel. "As you can see, this is one of the main reasons we have the gate below. Sometime after these paintings were discovered, treasure hunters or just plain vandals tried to chip the paintings away from the stone." Martín sounded rather discouraged as he pointed to the obvious chips that had been made in the rock. "They were probably trying to steal and sell this wonderful figure down to the left."

Shifting my focus, I encountered one of the biggest, clearest figures we had yet seen. Here was a male, clearly defined, that was surrounded by different anthropomorphic figures and varying angular motifs. Martín returned to his rhetorical questioning: "Look at his arms. The arm on the left is held straight out in front of him, while the other looks like it is flexed. This is probably the most naturalistic form in the cave. What does it remind you of?" Carlos remained silent as he had promised, and I had to ruin the suspense he was trying to create by admitting this time I had an advantage. I had seen similar paintings down in Almería and as far off as

Zimbabwe. Though it could no longer be seen, this was certainly a hunting scene and, judging from the man's stance, he looked to be holding a bow. Carlos turned to me and said under his breath, "I think that, in Monfragüe, this is easily the most naturalistic, anthropomorphic figure there is. They are usually more simplified, but this one clearly shows some sort of activity."

Martín continued, "Perhaps one of the most striking aspects of these panels is that even though they were painted many years after the well-known scenes in the south of France and those up in Atapuerca in the north of Spain, these paintings are seemingly much simpler and definitely less figurative. There is none of the hyperrealism you find in the bison painted sixteen thousand years ago in the north. The level of abstraction present here suggests the artists were moving beyond pictographs and towards attempts to communicate directly through the use of symbols. The design of new tools and brushes also helped in creating more abstract figures."

To the right, we saw a panel with a theme I would see repeated in several other sites around the park. On a small rocky outcrop the entire surface was covered with dark red dots. This one had some straight lines connecting the dots in the middle, but others we saw later were arranged as if they were counting something. To the left there was a clear, intentional zigzag, and then the rest of the forms were difficult to make out.

This abundance of dots continued on in the next panel we saw, but this one differed from the other in that it had human figures superimposed on it. Here we found several stickman-like figures, like those we had seen before but these were the first decorated human figures we would see. Looming large in the centre, the biggest and reddest of the figures had what looked like the spikes that adorn the Statue of Liberty's head. The comparison made me think back to the conflicting ideas I had heard about the Statue of Liberty. I had once heard the seven spikes on the statue's head represented the seven continents and the seven seas but had since read they are meant to be a halo or a nimbus to show that Liberty is divine. If a statue from 1886 had conflicting interpretations, it was clear this figure's real meaning was even more obscure. Whatever its meaning, it was meant to be differentiated from the rest. To its left are the funkiest paintings in the cave. Painted with a fine brush, a trio of headdress-wearing shamans looked like they were following the largest figure in a carnival parade. And if this wasn't the case, they were conferring in his shadow, getting ready to put a curse on him.

"The cave saves the best for last, or at least the most well preserved. If you look up, you'll see them just above your head," Martín said. And then I saw it, an entire panel of paintings that had gone unnoticed just centimeters above my head for the past twenty minutes. There, on the rough granite rock, was a prehistoric selfie reaching out across time. A group of extravagantly masculine men, some just out of the barber's, letting us know they, too, were once here under these same skies, caressing this same rock. A triangle of human forms, headed up by the largest alpha male, cascaded in a hierarchy down the rock. "You're obviously focused on the triangle of figures, but if you look behind them you will see the oldest painting of the cave," Martín told us. "Behind the largest male, if you look closely, you can make out the figure of a large deer. It is characterized by a technique that differentiates it from the rest of the figurative group. This is, above all, because of its semi-naturalistic style and then the flat ink that was used to fill in the body."

At times it took a minor leap of faith to believe the figures Martín commented on were actually there, but this time, after staring at the rock for a while, I saw the deer with its large antlers. "Similar paintings have been found in Las Villuercas, near Berzocana, and in the province of Badajoz," Martín said. "These can be dated to the Epipaleolithic period, a time when these groups of people were only beginning to settle. A greater importance was given to hunting animals, which really was the livelihood of these predatory societies. By comparing and contrasting these different figures, they have deemed this deer to be the oldest painting in the shelter. It constitutes the first phase of the entire graphic sequence that runs through the cave, a sequence, I remind you, that runs over the course of thousands of years." As a storyteller, I could understand why they had focused on game. A scene of people planting their crops wouldn't have held their listeners' interest in the same way.

Above this deer, the scene is hierarchical, with the most important figures dominating the centre. Added to this, the central figures also show small, almost imperceptible, complementary details. A line here or a stick down there at the waist suggest weapons like swords and daggers, making the storytelling potential all the more interesting. The lowest line of figures was painted with a finer brush and once again a spiked headdress appeared on the figure in the middle. To his right was the most puzzling figure, a person with both a penis and what looked to be breasts. Martín theorized the phallus could have either been a mistake or that the "breasts" had been added on later. I tittered at the idea of someone adding prehistoric graffiti to the painting, somewhat like all the graffiti I had seen at the entrance to the Maltravieso cave. But then I realized that, in an age where clothes would have been somewhat of a luxury, Neolithic peoples most certainly wouldn't have had the same puerile fear of female breasts that our nipple-free Instagram and Facebook world suffers from today. Martín mentioned that some speculate these add-ons could represent some sort of tattoo or even pectoral armour, but the figure to its right draws these conjectures even further into question. There, to the right, was a smaller male figure...a prehistoric boy standing next to his equally primeval Madonna.

These were easily the most impressive and visible paintings we had yet seen. The careful compositions and their privileged panel stood out from the schematic painting we had seen so far. Something inside me wanted to think it was a recreation of some concrete ceremony, like a depiction of a prehistoric Mardi Gras, complete with Dr. John-like shamans with headgear. The symbolic representation of some sort of social structure, or of a certain ritual order, was impossible to ignore. Try as I might, I had to accept this was no prehistoric gig poster. We thanked Martín for his detailed explanations and Carlos told him of the rest of our day's plans. We had only just begun and were now headed to see a few more of the panels over in nearby Serradilla. Martín told us he had never seen the other paintings. This reminded me of how fortunate Carlos had been to have volunteered on that project so many years ago.

Stepping out of the cave, the warming winter sun reflected off the wide ribbon of blue down below. There, the sleepy almost immobile Tagus River dawdled through a gap flanked by two towering palisades of quartzite rock. A chasm that must have been a ferocious spume of white water before the river was emasculated by the series of dams along its course. The five-hundred-metre-high Peña Falcón cliff rises up opposite the Salto del Gitano where we stood, which ascends another three hundred metres above the river. Both geological pylons help create the soaring thermals on which the vultures rode above us. The less-than-politically-correct name of the salto is derived from its shape. Somewhat imaginatively, some envisage the rock as the atypical tricorn hat that is part of the official uniform of the Spanish Guardia Civil.

During the Middle Ages, this densely wooded area was the ideal refuge for bandits that preyed upon itinerant traders. The Tagus had served as a natural boundary between north and south since the times of the reconquest, and the nearest populated crossing points are few and far between, making the park one of the only places possible to cross. The story goes that some merchants from Plasencia were bringing horses and mules to market down in Trujillo but were forced to stop for the night in the village of Villareal de San Carlos. A notorious gypsy bandit espied them setting up for the night. The fabled gypsy lay in wait in an ambush deeper in the woodlands. When the merchants passed through the next morning, he robbed them at knifepoint with some versions of the story saying that he brutally murdered them. The bandit collected their horses and mules and rode deeper into the woods. A short while later, he crossed paths with a team of the Guardia Civil, a police force that had originally been charged with putting an end to brigandage on the nation's highways. The thief quickly dismounted and tore off through the bush. The Guardia Civil laid chase through the Sierra de las Corchuelas until they finally reached Peña Falcón, the huge rocky outcrop over the Tagus River. The gypsy was trapped. He stopped at the very precipice of the rock, looked down, and saw the enormous empty expanse before him. He turned his head and understood the Guardia Civil had him cornered; there was nowhere left to run. He then did the unimaginable. He took a few steps back towards the guards as they ordered him to halt. He then pivoted around and raced towards the yawning divide and leapt from its highest point. Miraculously, he landed on the other side of the Tagus with nary a scratch. The guards watched in utter disbelief, and legend has it that, at that very moment, as a result of their amazement, the civil guards were petrified, thus forming the tricorn hat-shaped rock we see today.

Here were the fundamental pieces of the Monfragüe puzzle. Those that bring the heavens, earth, and water together. These inland Pillars of Hercules make up the heart of the park. It was a place where two once-mighty rivers converged and from which the entire area could be controlled, just as the scavengers soaring above us were doing. Looking out across to the opposite Herculean pillar, the wise words Paco Castañares had laid out to me before our visit came to mind: "The Tagus River is the backbone of the national park. Without it, the park simply would not exist. Monfragüe is a great valley, thirty kilometres long and six kilometres wide. It is formed by the Tagus River from its spectacular entrance at the Salto del Corzo to its no less spectacular exit at the Salto del Gitano. Whoever dismisses the role of the river in Monfragüe simply does not know the park."

On our way back to the car, Carlos reminded me, "You have to keep in mind the few paintings we have discovered are those that have managed to stand the passing of time." To highlight his point, we took a small detour off the road and approached the rock face. He paused and pointed to a little crevice in a rock surrounded by neon lichen. There, under the crags, was a red square next to another of the squid-like figures with numerous tentacles that can be found around the park. "Here in Monfragüe there is a clear predominance of red paintings, like these ones," Carlos said. "Reds that range from dark red, blood or brownish, to orange and even yellowish. All made with some sort of mix of iron oxide. Sometimes we even find veins of this mineral in the rocks themselves. There are also some white paintings made from mica or kaolin. But these are much less frequent. Then there are the black ones, made up mainly of manganese oxide. Like the one we saw with the Tartessian script, but again there aren't so many of these." We turned back around and clambered down the ashen stones. Carlos raised his eyebrows and said, "We can't rule out the possibility there was a more varied palette of pigments of organic origin, maybe from blood or vegetable pigments that have simply been lost over the passage of time. Thousands of years ago, this entire area must have been littered with paintings. Given the amount we have found, it must have been literally covered. I suppose we have to be thankful there are so many that still remain."

The Salto del Gitano and the Tagus River in Parque Nacional de Monfragüe.

MAKING
CONNECTIONS

17

ONLY ONE ROAD TRAVERSES THE PARK. Since it was declared a national park, these secondary country roads are often arbitrarily cut, sometimes for questionable reasons. Historically, the Spanish have zealously protected their right to roam over traditionally used routes, even if these easements fall on private property. This principle is enshrined in Article 139 of the Constitution, where it states that no authority may adopt measures that directly or indirectly hinder the freedom of movement and settlement of persons and the free movement of goods throughout Spanish territory. But this concept of *servidumbre* dates back long before the signing of the Constitution. It goes back at least to the beginnings of the Middle Ages with the transhumance, where flocks of sheep were herded between summer pastures in the north and winter pastures in Extremadura and Andalusia.

These laws have their interpretations, though. The dirt road that connects Serradilla with Villareal de San Carlos had recently been ordered closed by the director of the national park, apparently with the approval of the general director of sustainability and the minister of ecological transition of the regional government of Extremadura. The reason given was that a Bonelli's eagle had built a nest 205 metres away from the road. The nest can't be seen from the road, and it so happens the bird chose this specific place to build its nest a few years ago, meaning it did so all the while vehicles had been passing by. In other words, the road that has always been there, and that has never caused any disturbance to the protected species, was baselessly and despotically closed. A road, it should be added, that is used by only around fifty or sixty vehicles throughout the entire year.

The seemingly arbitrary nature of the decision had incensed the locals. They argued if the same logic were applied throughout the park, all of the major arteries would also have to be closed. At the time, around 150–210 metres away from the main highway through the park, across the river in the folds of the Peña Falcón from which the mythical gypsy made his leap, you could find four black stork nests, seventy-five griffon vulture nests, one peregrine falcon nest, and an eagle owl nest. Then there is the main highway on the very same side of the river as the cave with the paintings. Just 125 metres from where it runs, alongside the area where large crowds of people stand to observe and photograph the most emblematic bird species of the national park, there are twelve griffon vulture nests and one Egyptian vulture nest. A road that, according to statistics carried out by the very same national park, five hundred thousand people drive every year.

Our next destination, Serradilla, was only around seven kilometres away as the crow flies, but with the park and the Tagus between us, like the infuriated locals, we were forced to double back towards Torrejón and travel over thirty kilometres out of our way. Along the route, we decided to stop in Torrejón to pick up some picnic supplies and have a quick *tentempié*, a pick-me-up snack that literally means "keep you standing." The winter sun was warm and we installed ourselves on the plastic chairs that populate the sidewalks and corners of the country. Open-air terraces have always been an important part of Spanish life, but before the pandemic they were more seasonal. Now they have become a year-round phenomenon.

The park is very popular with foreign bird watchers, and I noticed the chalk menu board was written in Spanish with a passable English translation alongside it. Since the advent of Google Translate, more and more bars blindly trust the transnational's algorithms, lifeless churners of words that often conjure up the most delightful mistakes. My favourite is a translation for a cheese that comes from the village where my wife and I got married, Casar de Cáceres. It's a sublime, slightly bitter creamy cheese called la Torta del Casar. It is made from raw sheep's milk from the flocks that pasture on the plants and herbs out on the steppe, along with locally sourced vegetable rennet. The word "*torta*" refers to its cake-like shape and Casar denominates where it comes from. The problem is that both words have alternate meanings and I once saw the cheese listed on a menu as "Punch from Marry."

The waitress came out and was somewhat surprised to find us sitting there. Though still early, the breakfast crowd had long ago left and the midday *cañas* and *tapas* crew wouldn't arrive for another hour or so. She told us the keg was empty and the only cold beer she had were the small quarter-litre bottles you find all over Spain called *botellines*. These are my favourite bottles to drink from. They are the most refreshing, even if they don't last very long. We ordered a couple and sat back and took in the vitamin D-producing winter sunshine. The main street through the village rolled beside us, but there wasn't a car in sight. Instead, a shaggy black and grey mutt strolled down the middle of the street with less than a care in the world.

I kept turning Martín's words over and over and had to ask Carlos about something I couldn't quite get clear in my head. "I still don't get why these paintings, being so much younger than those up in the north of Spain, are so much more...simple." Carlos laughed and said, "It may seem paradoxical that the hyper-realistic bison paintings of Altamira are many thousands of years older than the pectiniforms of Monfragüe, yet somehow more advanced. But that is because we deduce, erroneously I might add, that artistic naturalism is somehow more evolved and that whatever is simple is primitive. And this is not so. You as a musician, and a blues musician at that, somehow know this instinctively." The waitress interrupted Carlos's thought and brought out our beers with a *tapa* that somehow proved his point. On the plate were four halves of simple boiled potatoes, but they had been sprinkled with *pimentón de la Vera* and rock salt, and then drizzled with a fruity, intense olive oil. Definitely not elaborate, but just the same, divine on that winter morning.

Carlos continued, "The more distant a representation is from reality, in artistic terms that is, the more capacity there is for symbolic representation, shared codes of communication. All of these come into play when we look at something like the paintings in Monfragüe. That is why it's a fairly widespread theory that writing is the last stage of abstraction of figuration. It's a form of communication that has been stripped of all naturalistic references. Things like hieroglyphic writings or ideograms would be the penultimate step before this."

We both pulled at our beers and dug into the still-hot potatoes. I had the idea a bit clearer, but still was not totally there. "Listen, I don't think anyone put it better than Picasso," Carlos said as he finished his potato. "He once said it had taken him four years to learn to paint like Raphael, one of the great Renaissance masters, yet it had taken him a lifetime to paint like a child."

We turned off the deserted main drag and walked a few streets into the village, looking for a store. We came across a woman crossing one of the empty streets who told us "the best shop in town is right over there and I'm not only saying that because the owner is my cousin." We stepped into the shop. It was packed to the rafters with just about everything someone might need. Supermarkets find it hard to make a go of it in such small towns. Thankfully, small shopkeepers who work hard to keep the villages alive have taken up the slack. "So what are you strangers after?" the shop-keeper playfully sang out to us from behind his overloaded counter. We told him we were looking for some picnic supplies, but he quickly answered, "I'm out of bread. You know, people tend to come in for that early in the morning. But if you head out to the restaurant on the edge of town, they should still have some." Carlos decided we should split up to save time. He would go for bread while I picked up the rest of our supplies.

We met back at the car and I saw the restaurant had indeed sold him some bread, but I had my suspicions. One of the things that has always perplexed me about my adopted life here in Extremadura is you invari-ably sit down to inviting foods dripping in celestial sauces that beg to be swept clean from your plate. But when you look around for the appropriate tool for the job, you almost always find the most insipid, characterless bread. Instead of finding something with taste, you encounter purport-edly wheat-based product boasting the visual appeal of a bleached sock that sits on your palate like a spoon full of dry breadcrumbs. Dress them up as Italian *chapatas*, dust them with a bit of flour and call them *rústicos*, or even claim they have been fired with loving care in a wood stove in a charming village, but the end result is always the same. The experience turns out to be the gastronomic equivalent of elevator music. Crack open most loaves of bread and instead of being greeted by the irregular beauty of odd shapes formed by escaping gasses, you simply get a pixelated vision of a stale brick with no mystery and certainly no art. It's like comparing aerial views of complex, convoluted medieval cities like Toledo, Trujillo, or Cáceres with the grid pattern of a no-name residential suburb of just about any North American city. Something without taste, without intrigue, without soul. With just a glance I knew this would be another of the imposter breads, but it would have to do.

The fog had long since lifted and we found ourselves back on the EX-390 until we turned off onto the CC-29.6 in the direction of Serradilla. The *dehesa* began to thicken, and once again the barrier of rock that ran through the park reared up in the distance, bringing the dip between the Salto del Gitano and Peña Falcón back into view. The scrub further thickened as we slowly descended, and then once again to our left the river returned. We crossed it over an uninspiring yet utilitarian bridge and came out into the sparcer *dehesas* on the opposite side. Approaching the village, tall eucalyptus, willow, and birch trees lined the road, looking completely out of place after kilometres of oaks. We found the sign that indicated the way to the Garganta del Fraile and turned off. "Here's where things get interesting. Like when we were in Guadalupe, depending on how the roads are, we may have to walk a ways...or not," Carlos said as we bumped off the paved road onto the dirt track. "Once we get there, we have to climb quite a bit, so rather than do the hike from here in the village, I'd rather save your strength for the climb up to the paintings."

It had rained a few weeks prior, but the winter had been abnormally dry. The road, while rutted and bumpy, was passable. Apart from some olive groves, the trees once again returned to their oak beginnings and the park opened up before us. We were forced to stop two or three times to test out the depth of some of the puddles along the way, but in the end the drought the region had been suffering from at least served to allow us to pass. With the windows open, I heard something that seemed out of place in these dry parts. It was the sound of rushing water. It's a quick-ening sound that rings out across these parched lands that patiently wait for the first drops to fall throughout the year. We came to a tight bend in the road and there was a waterfall gushing out of a break in the rock wall. "We're here," Carlos enthused. "Grab the picnic stuff and let's get a move on to the next set of paintings!"

Before us, the rock wall was rent in two where the water tumbled out. A sign warned that swimming was prohibited in the pool that formed below the falls because the stream was one of the main water sources for Serradilla. "I have never seen this waterfall dry, even during the hottest and driest summers," Carlos said as we began to make our way up the right bank of the stream. "If you look up to your right, you can see a sort of aqueduct they once used for diverting the stream's flow to power a mill farther down the valley." It was true; piled-up slate stone masonry hugged the wall of the canyon and ran off down towards the bottom of the valley. "I don't believe this water system is very old, but imagine the work that went into building that," Carlos said as he pointed upwards while plowing through the ferns and blackberry bushes that crowded the barely visible trail. He had come prepared and dressed for the occasion, as the Spanish often do. His hiking gear allowed him to slip through the barbs of the blackberry bushes while my sweater and jeans got caught at every step and left me further and further behind.

We crossed over to the left bank of the stream and then began to climb up through the scrub. Griffon vultures drew regular patterns in the sky high above us. The higher we climbed, the thinner the vegetation became. The cubist granite rock formations we had seen before, stained with red lines and fluorescent green lichen, appeared once again. Even though we had driven a long way, had we been able to simply follow the park's rocky backbone from Peña Falcón, we would have only had to travel about three and a half kilometres from the cave Martín had shown us. A distance that would have been a stroll for the prehistoric peoples that had certainly explored every nook and cranny of this area.

I was still turning things over in my head about what Martín had told us and at the same time was desperately trying to slow Carlos down as he sauntered up the scarped slope. "Carlos, what do you think about what

Martín told us about the timelines? Did it seem to you, too, that the dates he offered us were somewhat haphazard?" Luckily, this had the desired effect. Carlos slowed for a moment and said, "Just like I told you during the visit to Maltravieso, in rock art, and in archeology in general, there are two main types of dating. The first is the absolute method, with physical-chemical analysis. Only then can we give a more or less exact date to a specific painting. For example, when we use calcium carbonate layers, we test with a uranium-thorium method. And then there is the relative method. By using this method, the date is established, not individually but in relation or by comparison to some of the other previously dated remains. Remains that share common characteristics such as the technique used, the figurative style, the location, etc."

Carlos started off again and I had to struggle to keep up if only to catch what he was saying. "Personally, I believe that relative dating in schematic rock art is...shall we say, very complicated, and must be very well justified if it is to be scientifically sustained. The case of the superimpositions of figures in the same panel, which is not rare in Monfragüe, is interesting because it gives a diachronic vision of reuse and resignification of that place and their symbolic will." He practically dove through a dense stand of broom and came out the other side and continued, "We can determine which layer is the oldest and which were subsequently painted, but from there to actually certifying that because one is thicker than another, or slightly more or less naturalistic, there are 'x' thousands of years of difference? Well, that is a bit of a stretch to me. I don't think you can, as far as we know today, or at least in the cases I know of here in Monfragüe, be 100 per cent sure they are separated by thousands of years, or perhaps just by one."

He then disappeared behind one of the large blocks of granite that dotted the hillside while I was extricating myself from yet another blackberry bramble. Carlos called over his shoulder, "You also have to take into account the guide's job is to inform people. In general, he did a very good job and is used to simplifying matters so lay people can grasp what he is saying. But I think the most important factor is that, in general, the public loves dates and you have to give the public what it wants."

I fell further and further behind as the slope steepened. The way Carlos pounced from stone to stone reminded me of how he had galloped through the tunnel back in Maltravieso. I called out to him and asked where he had gone and he shouted, "You're just about there! Go round that big boulder and you'll see where I am, next to the big cut in the rock here in the shade." I edged around the rock and found Carlos prostrate, lying on the ground inspecting the rock. "These are the ones I was so excited to show you. They are meticulous, so delicately traced with a fine brush." There before him, below a ridge in the rock, I saw a circle with at least six "legs" and what seemed to be the figure of a human falling back from the circle. The painting was as delicate as a Persian miniature and no bigger than the palm of my hand. A crack in the rock rose to the left of the diaphanous miniature painting that was highlighted by a strand of green lichen. "These paintings were made to be observed closely," Carlos said, "and were obviously not meant to draw attention to themselves. I find this intimate character particularly moving. The artist didn't draw these to show off; that's for certain. There had to have been a more personal motive for these, if only because they aren't easy to see. Moreover, in all of the paintings I have seen, it is not at all common to represent a ground or surface on which a figure can be seen standing. In the case of this other figure, perhaps a little goat, it looks almost as if it is like a reflection on the water." The lower portion of this rock face was littered with paintings, mostly squid-like circles with lines like tentacles extending from them. I asked Carlos, "What about all of these squids? What do they make of these figures?"

"To be honest, I don't think I recall so many appearing in any other rock shelter, at least not the ones I know of, but they are everywhere in this one. For this reason we decided to call this panel the 'Jellyfish Rock.' I mean, it's clear they don't represent jellyfish, but their general shape reminded us of them. As I have said before, I don't think it is possible to know for sure what they represent. But if I had to say, they might represent clouds. Think of a storm letting loose its life-giving water. That would have definitely been something sacred. But then again, it could be a simple decorative effect achieved by spreading a bunch of pigment in these somewhat whimsical branches. Who knows, really? But I can say these are definitely some of the most delicate paintings in the park."

With the landscape being so distinct, I asked Carlos whether he had developed a sense for discovering these paintings over time. He replied, "Only in part. One of the most puzzling issues is it isn't possible to establish an unequivocal pattern regarding the location of the paintings. As Martín mentioned, it's true there is a very marked tendency to choose places with wide, panoramic views like this one, surely to visually control the territory. They are also found in places of natural passageways, like fords, streams, and the like...where they could stalk hunting prey or water their livestock, but this is not a 100 per cent rule. They are also more frequently found in the sunny parts, looking to the southwest, where from afar the yellow lichens and orange areas of the quartzite rock more readily catch your eye than in the shady areas looking to the north or northeast." He gestured towards the paintings in the shade we had been looking at and then assured me, "But, as I say, nothing can be ruled out. In Monfragüe there are countless places that would be ideal, due to their location, the size of the shelter, the good rock surface, etc., but they are clean. Meanwhile, there are countless others that contain paintings in the most implausibly small, almost hidden, crevices. Like the ones we saw in the cave, or the ones we have just seen, intimately buried under a fold of rock. On the other hand, we must always bear in mind the conclusions we draw are not absolute. Many, many paintings have been lost, and some may not have been discovered yet."

We edged around an enormous rock that looked like a Wile E. Coyote trap and then sat on a small platform of overhanging rock looking down into the gorge. The vultures were closer now. We were even higher than some of the nests on the opposite side of the canyon. They started at our appearance and then returned to their nests and scrutinized us from afar. "Now how is this for a picnic spot?" Carlos asked. The entire southern expanse of the park spread out before us. To the left we could see the cleft in the massif where the Tagus cut through at the Salto del Gitano, and the dappled *dehesa* fanned out before us. We could see the road we intended to take to circle back to the village looked dry and would be passable. I broke out the goat's cheese and spicy *patatera* I had bought back in Torrejón, and Carlos broke off chunks of the bread he had bought. The shopkeeper had promised me that the cheese from nearby Trujillo was unique, and he wasn't wrong. The *patatera*, the sort of blood sausage made up of equal parts potato and pork mixed with *pimentón de la Vera* that Alonso had told me about, was just spicy enough when it hit the back of your throat.

The view before us was that of Extremadura condensed into a microcosm. The jagged, wild sierra ran into dense brush and then thinned out as it became the patchwork *dehesa*. Just beyond the horizon lay Cáceres and the new life I had encountered there. The small stream fed by the waterfall slipped in and out of the woods and under the bridge farther off near the disused mill. It flowed as if it were somewhat self-conscious, meandering like a drunk and then disappearing once again in the undergrowth. Carlos, like my wife, was born in Cáceres and, like my wife, had returned after widespread travelling. I asked him where he felt his roots lie. He looked out at the view for a long time and then answered, "There's a Spanish proverb that says, '*uno es de donde pace, no de donde nace*,' which roughly translates as, it's not from where one is born, but where one grazes. In my case, there is some truth to this. That is, I should have it clear in my head about where I'm from. But no. Definitions, and perhaps above all self-definitions, that is, identity, require certainties...and I have less and less of those."

Thousands of years after they were painted, the figures that remain still convey with such penetrating immediacy the innate human need to tell stories and our desire to leave behind some sort of mark. We had only seen a handful of paintings, that is if you compare them with the more than one hundred panels across the park, but those we had seen shared these fundamental traits. In their apparent abstraction, they inspired the viewer to make an attempt to grasp the events the artists must have experienced and witnessed so long ago. If not to understand, then at least to somehow infer their purpose and gain access to their existence, their world. The "eyes" staring out from the rock kept coming back to my mind, so I asked Carlos to fill me in some more with what he knew about them. "These eye idols are representations in which the eyes are the main focus of attention of a figure. There are times, as in what we just saw, when only the eyes appear without anything more. They appear in schematic rock art but also in objects like the picture Martín showed us. The idols come in the form of plaques, cylinders, stela stones ceramic vessels, and bones. They are often found in funerary contexts such as dolmens, particularly in the southwest of the peninsula, and therefore here in Extremadura."

Carlos tore off another piece of bread and spread some *patatera* on it before saying, "We believe these types of representations arose sometime during the Neolithic period in the Near East, and then they spread quite rapidly throughout the Mediterranean basin. Although, as always, our interpretations remain uncertain, it seems clear they were not merely a decorative resource, but perhaps the expression of an idea, a symbol that was shared over a large area and over several millennia." He took another bite and once he had finished chewing, reflected, "In this process of figurative abstraction, of which you and I have spoken so much of when talking about cave painting, you have to ask yourself a question: What is the most essential or powerful attribute to represent a person or personification? It begins with the hands in Maltravieso, and then leads to the eyes, that penetrating gaze. Then, at the extreme end of this process, are the baetylus, the sacred stones that in Hebrew literally mean 'abode of the god' that are found throughout the Near East and the Arabian Peninsula. These often have eyes, but they end up being pure abstraction due to the aversion towards naturalistic representation of the divine inherited by Judaism, the pre-Islamic Arab peoples, and Islam itself. Bethel, in Genesis, is the first altar raised up by the father Abraham. The Black Stone of the Kaaba in Mecca is certainly a baetylus, as is the Omphalos of Delphi. Then there are those worshipped by the Nabataeans. Perhaps even the Lapis Niger of Rome, the Benben stone of Heliopolis, the lingam of Shiva..."

A line of sacred stones can be drawn from the temples of Shiva in the jungles of Cambodia and Malaysia to the banks of the Ganges, up through the Indus Valley and west through the houses of God in Arabia, the Holy Land, and into the Mediterranean basin. But these stones don't stop on the huge Eurasian land mass. There's the Aranda stone art in Australia, or the sacred idols and fetish stones in Africa, the healing stones in North America and the megalithic stone sculptures in South America. Even out in the middle of the Pacific, massive stone faces rise to greet you. I thought about this seemingly universal trend and asked Carlos if he saw any link between the eye idols and the Virgins adored all over the country. He exhaled sharply and shook his head, "The truth is, no. That said, there are many researchers who interpret the eye idols as being what could be called a prehistoric 'proto-religion' that would worship the 'goddess of the eyes.' I do believe a line could be drawn, not only starting from the belief itself but through the images and representations between the Mediterranean goddesses of life and fertility. This path, starting from the Innana-Astarte-Ishtar-Isis group, would lead us straight to the Catholic Immaculate Conceptions, the sun-moon-serpent, or a direct link from the sculpture of the Diana of Ephesus to the image of the Virgin of El Rocío."

Our immediate surroundings up on that stone ledge were consistent with the environment the prehistoric painters would have experienced. The cubist rocks piled on top of each other and the Mediterranean scrub that manages to cling to their parched sides all remain. This vantage point would have looked out upon a much more savage landscape, certainly less shaped by the hand of humans, but its expanse and its beauty would have been commensurate. The different waves of peoples that have flowed through the area would have had to either adapt to this somewhat extreme environment, altering their surroundings in some way in the process, or move on. Each successive wave has left behind some sort of statement that they had been there, that this had been where they had at least paused on their journey. Migrants, by nature, are flexible and learn to blend in with their new settings, hopefully reaching a place where they fit or a place fits them. Sometimes you choose a place and sometimes it chooses you, but some sort of flexibility is needed in order to adapt to your immediate surroundings. It is not always a two-way street.

I lay back on the warm stone. The sound of running water just barely reached our vantage point, where it blended with the gusts of the rising drafts on which the vultures continued to circle in their own particular symphony. I had spent so much time thinking about what the paintings meant and about what the artists were thinking I had forgotten to reflect on the reverse. I had been so focused on *them* that I had neglected *us*. I had ignored the viewer. What I saw now was how we were experiencing this art and its intractable bond with place. If indeed these were shamanistic attempts to communicate with another world, they had succeeded. We may not ever know their precise meaning or what the artists' intentions were, but through their art, we were now connected.

And that is the first step in any conversation.

ACKNOWLEDGEMENTS

This tale began deep in the Maltravieso cave just days before the COVID-19 lockdowns in Spain. They were some of the harshest, most draconian confinements in the world. Measures so restrictive my kids weren't permitted to leave the house for over three months. And, of course, there was no going out and meeting people for that ever so civilized Spanish tradition of a *caña* and *tapas*. The PPE gear we had to wear in the cave foreshadowed the collective psychosis that was about to take place.

The book started from a need to reach out and connect with others. To remember I was connected with a community that had welcomed me, even though we were confined to our homes. Even if we couldn't make contact, we still had stories to share.

Many of the stories in the book began as email conversations with my neighbours who were also feeling the need to connect and tell their stories. I want to thank everyone in the book that took the time in those dark hours to bring about some much-needed light to remind us all we were still connected. Friends, neighbours, and people who I had never even met face to face responded selflessly to the call. Without their commitment and participation, this book could never have happened.

Some of these tales also saw their first embryonic imaginings in my column in *Hoy* in Extremadura. Many thanks to the newspaper for giving me a free hand to write about whatever comes to mind for all these years.

It also would have never looked as good as it does if two people didn't take up the challenges I presented them with.

To my sister-in-law, Anka Nahumko, for answering the call when we realized some illustrative maps would help readers navigate the province as the book moved around. I asked her if she could create them and she didn't hesitate.

Then there was the mind reading of Fátima Gibello. She was uncannily able to transmit the images I had in my mind so clearly onto paper, making the book truly stories behind the images. Stories behind the stones.

Books don't just happen. They need to be nurtured and cared for, and I want to thank all of those who were my first readers. This book couldn't have happened without your suggestions and your gentle editing.

And, of course, to my two homes. To Michelle and everyone at University of Alberta Press who in a way welcomed me back home, back to Alberta, and, of course, to where I have now made my new home in the province of Cáceres.

It's to the people who have moved through here over the generations whose stories I have been fortunate enough to tell. Now it's my daughters' turn to leave their trace on these precious stones.

FURTHER READING

Just days after we entered the Maltravieso cave, COVID-19 pressed pause on the world. This story began in the darkest days of the lockdown in Spain. Nonessential workers were only allowed to leave the house individually to get supplies and take out the garbage. Dog walkers could only stray one hundred metres from their front door, and children were meant to stay indoors. Overnight, the exuberantly social streets of Spain became a desert. Conversations in the street were silenced and neighbours cautiously communicated with each other from their balconies.

Talks with the protagonists in the book began by email, each from our own pandemic bubble. Later, when conditions permitted, these were expanded upon in person via recorded conversations. Much of the commentary and information found in the book comes directly from these first-hand accounts. From these conversations, my research grew both online and in print. For those interested in learning more about some of the subjects mentioned in the book, these are a good place to start.

"The Abdication of Emperor Charles V (1555/56)." German History in Documents and Images. https://ghdi.ghi-dc.org/sub_document. cfm?document_id=4388#:~:text=The%20campaigns%20I%20 undertook%2C%20some,the%20years%20to%20my%20individual.

Allen, Jay. "Slaughter of 4,000 at Badajoz, 'City of Horrors' Is Told by Tribune Man." *The Grand Archive*. https://thegrandarchive.wordpress.com/slaughter-of-4000-at-badajoz-city-of-horrors-is-told-by-tribune-man/.

'Arabī, Ibn. *Sufis of Andalusia: The Rūh al-quds and al-Durrat al-fākhirah*. Translated by R.W.J. Austin. Oxfordshire, UK: Routledge, 2007.

Benitez Floriano, Santos. "Puerta de Coria." Real Asociación Española de Cronistas Oficiales. https://www.cronistasoficiales.com/?p=152520.

"Brief History of the National Parks." Library of Congress. https://www.loc.gov/collections/national-parks-maps/articles-and-essays/brief-history-of-the-national-parks/#:~:text=Yellowstone%20became%20the%20first%20national,%2C%20Agriculture%2C%20and%20the%20Interior.

Carr, Raymond. *Spain: A History*. Oxford: Oxford University Press, 2000.

Darby, T.L., and B.W. Ife. "The Travels of Persiles and Sigismunda: A Northern History, Miguel de Cervantes, Early Modern Spain." King's College London. http://www.ems.kcl.ac.uk/content/etext/e006.html.

de Unamuno, Miguel. *Extremadura*. Madrid, Spain: Casimiro Libros, 2020.

Domínguez, Íñigo. "El Gobierno contabiliza 20.014 templos y 14.947 fincas inscritos por la Iglesia de forma legal gracias a la reforma de Aznar." *El País*, February 16, 2021. https://elpais.com/sociedad/2021-02-16/el-gobierno-contabiliza-20055-templos-y-14906-fincas-de-la-iglesia-catolica-en-espana.html.

Domínguez Moreno, José María. "El Mito de la Serrana de la Vera." Biblioteca Virtual Miguel de Cervantes. https://www.cervantesvirtual.com/obra-visor/el-mito-de-la-serrana-de-la-vera/html/.

Goytisolo, Juan. *Cinema Eden: Essays from the Mediterranean*. London: Eland, 2003.

"Las 25 propiedades de la Iglesia en Las Hurdes." Alma Hurdes. https://www.almahurdes.com/las-25-propiedades-de-la-iglesia-en-las-hurdes/.

Lorenzo, Sergio. "La 'eterna' polémica de la Cruz." *Hoy*, July 18, 2009. https://www.hoy.es/20090718/caceres/eterna-polemica-cruz-20090718.html.

Neves, Mario. *La Matanza de Badajoz: Crónica de un Testigo de uno de los Episodios más Trágicos de la Guerra Civil.* Editora Regional de Extremadura, 1986.

"No queremos una España de proletarios sino de propietarios." Biblioteca Fundación Juan March. https://www.march.es/es/coleccion/archivo-linz-transicion-espanola/ficha/--linz:R-73814.

Pérez de Urbel, Justo. "Orígenes del culto de Santiago en España." *Hispania Sacra* 5 (1952): 1–34.

Rina Simón, César. "Las 'guerras de la memoria' entre militares y falangistas en Cáceres, 1936–1942." https://ifc.dpz.es/recursos/publicaciones/31/24/303rina.pdf.

Ruoff, Jeffrey. "An Ethnographic Surrealist Film: Luis Buñuel's *Land without Bread.*" *Visual Anthropology Review* 14, no. 1 (1998): 45–57.

"Una empresa peruana transformará el Palacio de Godoy de Cáceres en un hotel y restaurante de lujo." *El Diario*, December 19, 2018. https://www.eldiario.es/extremadura/caceres/transformara-palacio-godoy-caceres-restaurante_1_1778607.html.

Vaca and Others. "Original Narratives of Early American History Spanish Explorers in the Southern United States 1528–1543. The Narrative of Alvar Nunez Cabeca de Vaca." The Project Gutenberg. https://www.gutenberg.org/files/42841/42841-h/42841-h.htm#Page_160.

Vidal Castro, Francisco. "Abu I-Hasan 'Ali, Real Academia de la Historia." *Diccionario biográfico electrónico.* https://dbe.rah.es/biografias/4817/abu-l-hasan-ali.

"Yuste imperial Historia de su restauración." *ABC.* https://www.abc.es/viajar/noticias/abci-yuste-imperial-historia-restauracion-200810120300-91542021908_noticia.html.